PRAISE FOR *NURTURING RESILIENCE*

"In this well-written and researched book, the authors have condensed and made accessible many of the important philosophies that underlie modern psychotherapy practice. [*Nurturing Resilience*] integrates current relational, developmental, and somatic knowledge to help within the growing populations of emotionally, physiologically, and behaviorally dysregulated individuals presenting in all levels of our society."

—TONY RICHARDSON, somatic psychiatrist

"This book synthesizes the simplicity of our human quest for safety and connection with the complexities of our biological design. As vanguards in somatic therapies, Kathy and Stephen have trained thousands of therapists all over the world and are now graciously imparting their strategies for resilience through this gift of their combined wisdom."

—CHRISTOPHER WALLING, PsyD, president of the
United States Association of Body Psychotherapy

"*Nurturing Resilience* explains how early childhood trauma not only affects us psychologically but has a profound effect on our physiology. Stephen J. Terrell and Kathy L. Kain are leading experts in the physiology of trauma and how to untangle the mystery of modern disease."

—SHIRLEY IMPELLIZZERI, PhD, SEP, author of *Why
Can't I Change?: How to Conquer Your Self-Destructive
Patterns* and coauthor of *Scared Speechless: 9 Ways to
Overcome Your Fears and Captivate Your Audience*

"*Nurturing Resilience* is a tour de force contribution to the growing field of neuroscience-informed, somatic approaches. Its argument foregrounds a central problem: a disconnect between medical approaches to complex, physiological symptoms and psychological support, the impact of which has compromised understanding of what constitutes and builds resilience. *Nurturing Resilience* stands apart in its ability to bridge, in accessible ways, medical and somatic psychological conversations."

—KESHA FIKES, PhD, RSMT, anthropologist, somatic
therapist, and core somatic studies faculty member at
the Pacifica Graduate Institute

"At last! A book written by two of the master teachers in somatic touch and trauma! *Nurturing Resilience* blends theory, stories, and clinical examples beautifully and skillfully into a reader-friendly volume. This will be a valued resource on my bookshelf for years to come and is a 'must-read' for anyone who works with early and developmental trauma."

—ELLEN KEATING, PsyD

"This is a go-to book for any practitioner working with clients dealing with trauma. Terrell and Kain beautifully outline the origins of developmental trauma, how our nervous system adapts and supports the complexity of symptoms later in life, and how to respond/intervene in service of greater health. To understand developmental trauma as beautifully explained here is to understand and appreciate our most challenging clients. If you read only one book, this is it."

—BERNS GALLOWAY, MEd, Somatic Experiencing®
instructor at the Somatic Experiencing Trauma Institute

"Kathy Kain and Steve Terrell have produced a scholarly, comprehensive and coherent exploration of the complex terrain of developmental trauma. *Nurturing Resilience* promises to inspire clinicians to cultivate new, somatically based approaches that engage the physiological foundations of healthy attachment and inner regulation."

—ALAINE D. DUNCAN, MAc, LAc, Dipl.Ac

"This is the book we've been waiting for. Kathy Kain and Steve Terrell, two exceptional clinicians and trauma trainers, share with us their joint expertise in the therapeutic healing of early, developmental trauma. With insight and clarity, they lay out a conceptual framework that elegantly integrates theories of attachment, neuro-development, the autonomic nervous system, and mind-body psychology in order to illuminate the complex underpinnings of early trauma."

—JACALYN BRECHER, health and wellness advocate

"Terrell and Kain have found an intersection between our earliest physiological development and attachment patterns and developed a method that helps increase regulation in even the most symptomatic clients. Their deep understanding of stress and attachment physiology, combined with the psychological and emotional components, opens a path to healing that is often much easier for clients to undertake than traditional talk therapies. This work has absolutely transformed my practice and given me a whole new lens to see the root cause of deep hurt in my clients."

—BRANDY VANDERHEIDEN MA, MFT

"Brilliant! Kathy and Stephen have produced a groundbreaking work that provides a deeper understanding of the interface between developmental trauma and mental and physical disorders and most importantly the pathways to their healing. "

—MICHAEL OCANA, MD, medical director of Kelowna Adolescent Psychiatric Unit and clinical assistant professor at the University of British Columbia

"Kathy Kain is one of the world's leading experts on working through the body to resolve trauma and expand resilience. She brings breadth and depth into her approach, yet teaches in a way that is practical and clear. She is masterful at interweaving the principles and strategies of Somatic Experiencing®, attachment therapy, and polyvagal theory to create a powerful foundation for finding and working with the challenges of early preverbal and nonverbal elements of traumatic experience to promote the permanent reintegration of self. I strongly recommend her work."

—MAGGIE PHILLIPS, PhD, coauthor of *Freedom from Pain: Reversing Chronic Pain* and *Healing the Divided Self*

"[Steve provides] an experiential space wherein learning and growth can happen. It is a difference between the 'top down' teacher approach, and the 'we are all on the same plane and open to the possibility of experience' facilitator approach. We each change in relation to the experience and what we are ready to take in at that moment."

—SAMANTHA PERSOFF, LMFT, trauma therapist

"The work of Kathy Kain and Stephen Terrell has provided a missing piece in working with developmental trauma, complex PTSD, and attachment trauma. Their understanding of the physiology of trauma and the complexities of attachment bring well-grounded hope to clinician and client alike. With their work, you will learn to use compassion with practical, hands on techniques that support change, growth, and healing. Their work has transformed my understanding and work as a therapist."

—TERRY D. TROTTER, MFT

"[Kathy Kain and Steve Terrell] have worked as a team towards the development of an integrative treatment philosophy that combines heart and the best of known science. Their unique practice domains approach the spectrum of dysregulation from its earliest inception all the way to the other end of the spectrum. The music underneath their lyrics hums with resilience and optimism."

—KATHLEEN ADAMS, PhD

NURTURING RESILIENCE

HELPING CLIENTS MOVE FORWARD FROM DEVELOPMENTAL TRAUMA

KATHY L. KAIN AND STEPHEN J. TERRELL

North Atlantic Books
Berkeley, California

Published by
North Atlantic Books
Berkeley, California

Cover art © Shutterstock.com/KindheartedStock
Cover design by Rob Johnson
Book design by Happenstance Type-O-Rama

Printed in the United States of America

Nurturing Resilience: Helping Clients Move Forward from Developmental Trauma is sponsored and published by the Society for the Study of Native Arts and Sciences (dba North Atlantic Books), an educational nonprofit based in Berkeley, California, that collaborates with partners to develop cross-cultural perspectives, nurture holistic views of art, science, the humanities, and healing, and seed personal and global transformation by publishing work on the relationship of body, spirit, and nature.

MEDICAL DISCLAIMER: The following information is intended for general information purposes only. Individuals should always see their health care provider before administering any suggestions made in this book. Any application of the material set forth in the following pages is at the reader's discretion and is his or her sole responsibility.

North Atlantic Books' publications are available through most bookstores. For further information, visit our website at www.northatlanticbooks.com or call 800-733-3000.

Library of Congress Cataloguing-in-Publication data
is available from the publisher upon request.

1 2 3 4 5 6 7 8 9 KPC 22 21 20 19 18

Printed on recycled paper

North Atlantic Books is committed to the protection of our environment. We partner with FSC-certified printers using soy-based inks and print on recycled paper whenever possible.

CONTENTS

FOREWORD

THE THERAPEUTIC WORK with clients who have experienced early and chronic stress and trauma is one of the demanding challenges facing the depth therapist and body psychotherapist. Particularly, as these experiences are often preverbal, and before autobiographical memories are formed, there is a great need for specialized approaches that help these clients process their traumas, integrate them, and regain a cohesive sense of self.

These authors focus on the developmental unfolding of the fetus, infant, toddler, and child so that we can map precisely where our clients have become stuck or thwarted in this intrinsic growth process. This provides a way for therapists to find access points to reach their clients where they have become stuck and gently bring forth the healthy developmental processes. The material in this book spans the fields of neuroscience, attachment theory, child development, Somatic Experiencing®, Stephen Porges's polyvagal theory, and the appropriate use of touch. Using these powerful tools, Kathy L. Kain and Stephen J. Terrell show therapists practical ways to help these clients regulate, feel safe, and resolve their early, preverbal (procedural) engrams. By understanding not only how the body stores trauma, but how, through interoception, it can restore the sense of balance and goodness, the body becomes a powerful vehicle for restoring resilience, while nurturing growth into selfhood and wholeness.

In this inclusive book, Kathy and Stephen have contributed vastly to this great need through their understanding of how to work directly with the living, sensing body. Kathy has established herself as one of the preeminent international teachers of Somatic Experiencing and other somatically based hands-on work, and Stephen has worked extensively within the adoption community and knows directly the wounds that can be carried by these children into adulthood. Together they have contributed greatly to the field of somatically based therapies and to the informing of clear interventions for developmental arrest and trauma.

This comprehensive and rich volume goes to the deep roots of attachment and developmental stressors. It is a must, not only for body-oriented therapists, but all therapists, and also all of those who guide children, professionally as educators or as caring parents.

PETER A. LEVINE, PHD

Author of *Waking the Tiger, In an Unspoken Voice,* and *Trauma and Memory*

ACKNOWLEDGMENTS

ONE EVENING A FEW YEARS AGO, after teaching in New York City, we sat down together in a tiny, short-term rental apartment and began the discussion of what would first become a training series, and later this book. We were excited about bringing together in one place our knowledge about the somatic effects of early developmental trauma. Our training backgrounds and practice experience are very different, and yet we deeply recognized the other's understanding and skills.

It was a daunting task to transform our course material into a book, but we had so much support for taking on this project that we decided to jump in. Our close friendship and tremendous respect for each other's knowledge had already proved to be a powerful mixture for bringing this material alive in the classroom. Now it was time to see if we could translate all we had learned onto the written page.

It is such a challenge to try to thank all of those who helped bring this project to fruition, simply because there are so many who contributed to our learning, and everyone we encountered along the way has been so helpful.

We are deeply grateful to all the clients who have sought us out over the years for care and treatment. They have been our greatest teachers. Each has had the willingness to persevere in their search for change and growth, in spite of sometimes overwhelming challenges. We are grateful for the trust they placed in us, and the learning we accomplished together, which in turn allows us to share that knowledge in ways that will help many more people.

Thanks also to the many class participants who have taken part in this adventure by attending our newly developed trainings, providing valuable input and feedback about what has gone well—and what hasn't. The material in this book is much better as a result of the willingness of our class participants to share their own knowledge and to challenge us to organize our material in an understandable way. It has been an honor to learn from these many talented clinicians, educators, and fellow professionals. We have learned much, and we feel fortunate to be part of such a vibrant learning community. Special thanks to Rouel, who provided us with the title of the book during a training in Los Angeles.

We believe in the old adage "When the student is ready, the teacher will appear." We have been fortunate enough to have the best teachers appear. Thank you to Peter Levine for developing Somatic Experiencing as a modality for the treatment of trauma, which has very deservedly been accepted by professionals around the world.

From Kathy, a generous thank you to Arthur Pauls, Julie Henderson, and Tony Richardson, who were unwavering in their support of my learning; and to Daniel Weber for providing the opportunity for me to begin sharing my knowledge with the somatic psychotherapy community.

From Steve, much gratitude to Dan Hughes, father of Dyadic Developmental Psychotherapy, who was the first person who seemed to understand attachment and attachment ruptures at the raw level that was so powerful for me.

From both of us, we want to express our respect and gratitude to Allan Schore, Stephen Porges, and Bruce Perry for their work on affect regulation and on polyvagal theory, and for bringing an understanding of the impact of childhood trauma more into the forefront.

It's impossible to name all of those who have contributed to our understanding of the impact of trauma, but the rich and varied community of researchers, clinicians, and educators who had the courage to explore their own learning has helped us do the same.

We also had a great team in developing the content and structure of this book. Leslie Eliel, Cecily Sailer, and Katy Adams were a tremendous help in refining the structure and organization to make it more understandable, making preliminary edits and helping with finding all of our citations. Our editors at North Atlantic Books, Erin Wiegand and Ebonie Ledbetter, supported us through from start to finish.

And finally, a huge, heartfelt, warm thank you to our dear friends and family for being there when we needed them most, giving up time with us so we could write, cheering us on when our energy was flagging, and keeping hearth and home together for us. For Steve's two sons, Luke and John Michael, who stood by and supported me while I was traveling to teach, or spending late nights at my desk writing—without your love and support, I would not be the person I am today. For Kathy's husband, Gordon, a fellow writer who fully understands the demands that writing places not only on the author but on the author's loved ones, thank you not only for supporting me in my efforts, but also for miraculously wrangling a move to another state in the midst of it all. To my stepson, Benjamin, who makes me proud every day to be one of the "parental units."

With great gratitude and appreciation, we hope this book does justice to all of the support we have received in bringing it to fruition.

KATHY AND STEVE

INTRODUCTION

THERE IS A QUIET REVOLUTION taking place in how we provide help to those who have experienced trauma in their earliest years. Theories relating to developmental trauma have been slowly moving to the forefront within psychotherapy communities, trauma therapists, neuroscientists, and perhaps most of all, clients who are seeking help for their lifelong challenges. In this book, we explore that body of knowledge, and propose a body-oriented, somatic approach to reaching and healing the core of developmental trauma.

We now know from a growing body of research that early trauma takes a staggering toll on our physical, psychological, emotional, and social health. Those who have experienced developmental trauma struggle to receive treatment that adequately addresses their complex symptoms, which often cross boundaries between symptoms that require medical attention and those that require psychological treatment.

This book's primary purpose is to educate those who work with developmental trauma, and enumerate the dynamics that cause deep somatic changes for those who have experienced early challenges in life. Although trauma plays out in very different ways for different people, the feeling of overwhelming helplessness lies at its core. Understanding developmental trauma helps us educate our clients so they might better understand how that helplessness translated into the symptoms they experience. That understanding also helps us better support our clients to become more empowered, to gain the agency lost to trauma, and to develop resilience and access to greater vitality.

In our respective practices and collective teaching, we—the authors—work with this underserved population of clients, and the dedicated clinicians who serve them. Steve sees children and adults who have lived through developmental trauma, while Kathy works with the adult population with the most serious somatic symptoms of early trauma. We aim to improve lives by providing care that works with the somatic effects, as well as the psychological and emotional effects, of developmental trauma.

We have been assembling the pieces of this clinical puzzle for decades through achievements and failures with tens of thousands of clients. This book provides information from different disciplines that each hold distinct parts of the puzzle that helps us better understand how developmental trauma impacts clients. Those areas of thought include:

- Attachment theory
- Porges's polyvagal theory and other neuroscience research
- Traumatic stress research
- Somatic interventions for developmental trauma
- Child development theory

Utilizing our fifty years of combined clinical and teaching experience, *Nurturing Resilience* offers an introduction and foundational framework for mental health therapists and other care providers seeking more effective means for responding to people whose bodies or spirits have been altered by developmental trauma and attachment difficulties.

This book is an introduction to a rich, compassionate approach that combines the best of today's research on the physiology of trauma and attachment in a new and profoundly effective way, one that takes a positive approach to the potential for the development of resilience even for those with severe early challenges. The somatic approach we have developed synthesizes models, theories, and treatments in such a way that clients struggling with the effects of their earliest challenges are nurtured in all aspects of their healing.

Developmental trauma is often understood in the mental health community to be a result of chronic maltreatment by a caregiver. But that is too simplistic an interpretation. Trauma's complex influence on development is sometimes, but not always, tied to faulty parenting. It can also be caused by medical procedures, birth difficulties, frightening events, and caregiving failures that have nothing to do with maltreatment.

Just as more current research is giving us a better understanding of developmental trauma, likewise we are revising the framework of what constitutes resilience as we learn more about it. The previous understanding of resilience has now been expanded by the more recent research that shows it is not just about an individual's traits, but includes many factors—such as family, community, and larger cultural contexts—that influence how resilience is developed or restored. The field of resiliency research is expanding rapidly, providing helpful new information, but also bringing into question how to define the concept of resilience itself, and how to know which factors directly influence it. For our purposes in this book, we can define "resilience" as the ability to achieve positive outcomes— mentally, emotionally, socially, spiritually—despite adversity.

Although current research is still developing our understanding of resilience, we do already know that there are some identifiable protective factors that support the development of resilience in children, even in spite of significant adversity (Shonkoff et al. 2012; Walsh 2015):

- Supportive adult-child relationships

- A sense of self-efficacy and perceived control

- Adaptive skills and self-regulatory capacities

- Sources of faith, hope, and cultural traditions

Some people seem to be born with a fortunate predisposition toward resilience, but that is not the most potent influence on its development. Harvard University's Center on the Developing Child suggests that "the single most common factor for children who develop resilience is at least one stable and committed relationship with a supportive parent, caregiver, or other adult" (Center on the Developing Child 2017).

It would be accurate to say that each of the protective factors that support resilience is nurtured in the context of relationship. As will be discussed in the first few chapters of this book, healthy adult-child relationships include within their dynamics the healthy development of self-regulatory capacities, as well as a sense of agency and perceived control. Part of the educational focus of this book is to help clinicians understand more specifically what the elements are that contribute to resilience—how those all-important supportive relationships lead to more positive outcomes.

Of equal importance for clinicians is an understanding of how developmental trauma interferes with those protective factors and negatively impacts resilience. The causes of developmental trauma are less important than how trauma manifests in a client's life. We see that people in this demographic are often trapped in survival physiology. They develop management techniques to override their anxiety or perceived negative social behaviors. A chronic feeling of disconnect or "not belonging" gradually leads to a masking of their symptoms out of a very human desire to fit in. However, no matter what skills individuals may develop, the underlying symptoms of their early history still exist. As a result, many of the adults and children we work with struggle with activities of daily living.

> *I listened as the parents, Natalie and Gregg, continued to cry. They were distraught and unsure which direction to move next. Their six-year-old adopted son, Mark, had been admitted into a psychiatric hospital in a nearby city, where he'd been given large doses of medication to keep him from acting out.*
>
> *The parents were overwhelmed by their distress. They were hurting. They blamed themselves. They were angry and sad and grieving all at the same time. They explained that the hospital's psychiatrist believed their son would never survive as an independent adult—he either would require help at home or would need to spend his adult years in a group home where he could be supervised. The hospital staff told them to take their child home and save whatever money they could for the psychiatric care he would need as a teenager and an adult.*
>
> *Mark had been abandoned at birth and placed in an eastern European orphanage until he was adopted. His adoptive parents were witnessing signs of Mark's developmental trauma. He had become the victim of his own survival physiology, which evolved as an override system to compel him (and all of us) to act, disregarding higher levels of cognition. For a child like Mark, who had not yet received the needed social connection and co-regulation (a concept discussed in part I), healthy regulation was an impossibility.*
>
> *He had experienced a pervasive rupture in the neurodevelopmental system that would affect him in all aspects of life: spiritual, emotional, mental, and physical. In order for the family to maximize their collective well-being, corrections were needed to help Mark's brain and neural networks learn to manage activation and make use of his new, loving, supportive environment. In parallel, Natalie and Gregg needed to take on new learning of their own, and embrace good practices for supporting their own stability and regulation to provide better support for Mark's.*

This combination of psychological and somatic symptoms is, unfortunately, a common one for those who have experienced developmental trauma. Many people with similarly challenging beginnings go on to lead productive lives, but often with very complex symptoms that sometimes require heroic efforts to manage.

Working with adults with severe early trauma histories almost always includes a process of sorting through complex and interrelated symptoms. This category of client often experiences what initially appear to be straightforward and separate physical issues: high blood pressure, autoimmune disorders, or diabetes, for example. But we now know that developmental trauma can trigger these somatic symptoms and conditions. Indeed, early trauma can activate genetic predispositions toward certain diseases, apparently "turning on" that genetic predisposition; it can alter the size of the developing brain; it can cause the immune system to create chronic inflammation; it can contribute to a wide range of physical, as well as psychological, disorders (Ellason, Ross, and Fuchs 1996; Felitti et al. 1998; Perry 2004a, 2006).

In our experience, treatment that addresses all levels of the wounds from early trauma is most effective. It is our belief that the somatic responses must be included as part of treatment in order to effectively address and resolve developmental trauma. The clinical realities we have experienced over decades have been illuminated, contextualized, and more deeply understood thanks to the trailblazing efforts of John Bowlby, Mary (Salter) Ainsworth, Bruce Perry, Peter Levine, Bessel van der Kolk, and others, particularly the theoretical contributions of Stephen Porges surrounding the polyvagal system, discussed in chapter 4, and the vast public health research based on the Adverse Childhood Experiences (ACE) Study, which informs the whole of our work and is described in chapter 6. The ACE Study, which has correlated early childhood trauma with later development of various types of diseases and disorders, along with the abundance of research that continues to spring from its conclusions, confirm how devastating trauma can be when it occurs at an early age. This study also underscores the importance of not separating a client's physiological and somatic symptoms from their psychological struggles.

This book's synthesis of diverse areas of study and research occurred in part through simple trial and error in our work with thousands of clients whose symptoms demanded creative interventions that went beyond what we already understood. Our willingness to learn, and our clients' willingness to experiment with us, have facilitated a rich journey of exploration and discovery that has yielded more effective ways for working with developmental trauma.

The result is a rich, still-evolving synthesis that has shown powerful results. We have seen hopeful and sometimes dramatic improvements for our clients thanks to somatic intervention informed by attachment wisdom and cutting-edge knowledge of survival physiology and traumatic stress physiology. This blend of knowledge and approaches has drastically improved lives, one nervous system and one family system at a time.

STRUCTURE OF THE BOOK

The chapters of this book are organized roughly in the basic structure that is often used in the treatment of developmental trauma. As you continue through the book, you'll move through two parts designed to provide the foundational knowledge necessary to work effectively with developmental trauma from a somatic perspective.

In part I, Understanding Developmental Trauma, you will be oriented to how the foundation of healthy function and regulation will develop when all is going well, and given information about how and why function gets disrupted under the stress of developmental trauma.

In part II, Regulation and Resilience, we present information that supports the clinician in understanding the myriad signs and symptoms that can indicate that unresolved developmental trauma is influencing their clients' ability to recover and change. We also provide an overview to help clinicians understand how working with developmental trauma is different from working with other forms of trauma, and articulate what clinicians need to understand and take into account in their interventions with clients.

PART I

Understanding Developmental Trauma:

A Healthy Beginning and How It Can Go Wrong

SAFETY AND SECURITY are the underpinnings of resilience and are key in supporting the capacity for self-regulation. The material in part I is designed to broaden the clinician's understanding of healthy development and how it supports healthy attachment patterns; how healthy development provides the foundation for the physiological capacities needed to accurately perceive safety and connectedness; and how healthy development also builds the capacity for productive self-communication. We will also present information on the ways in which developmental trauma may disrupt and impact that early development.

1

The Cornerstones of
Relational Development

SOMEWHERE IN THE WORLD, every 4.3 seconds, a child is born. Many factors then emerge to determine how the child will grow and create her own individual self with a sense of autonomy. Humans are born completely dependent on their caretakers. Present "launch" times have pushed out to eighteen to twenty-five years, meaning that children are now commonly reaching those ages before leaving their caretakers' homes and living independently. In this chapter, we will explore the cornerstones of relational development at play in the early weeks, months, and years of life. We will examine how safety, co-regulation, bonding, and connectedness contribute to healthy and secure development. We'll first look at the work of several of the early pioneers in the formulation of attachment theory and child development theory—John Bowlby, Mary Ainsworth, and Mary Main.

SAFETY AND ATTACHMENT

Attachment, according to Bowlby (1969) and Ainsworth (1973), is a deep, enduring emotional bond that connects one person to another across time and space. Attachment is not always mutual, however, and can easily travel in only one direction, when a child attaches to a parent, for example, but the parent doesn't attach fully to the child, or vice versa.

Before John Bowlby came along, behavioral theory (Dollard and Miller 1950) was the accepted line of thinking for understanding how humans become who they are as they mature. John Dollard and Neal Miller believed that an infant or young child would develop a strong bond with the adult who fed him. This essentially identified the mother as the primary caretaker, especially if the mother breastfed her infant. The mother-child relationship was seen as the most intense and bonded over time as the mother consistently nurtured the child. Looking back at this theory today, we can see the inherent limitations of the behavioral theory framework. A disconnected and unavailable caretaker can feed an infant and attend to a child's biological needs without ever tuning in to the child's need for emotional nurturing. Bowlby, and the others who came later in the exploration of attachment theory, began a paradigm shift in this first understanding of caregiver-child bonding.

Looking through the eyes of his own personal experiences of having been sent to boarding school when young, Bowlby began to theorize that the proximity of the parent to the child was important, and in fact foundational, to the attachment/bonding relationship. Bowlby's early insights led to the development of modern-day attachment theory; and he is now considered, along with Mary Ainsworth, to be the founder of this psychological framework for understanding relationships and human development.

John Bowlby was born in 1907 in London, one of six children. Bowlby's father worked as a medical doctor caring for England's royal family. As was common at that time for upper-class families, his mother enlisted the services of a nanny to care for the children.

It's unlikely Bowlby experienced a strong, nurturing relationship with his mother, given his own account of his childhood. The family's nanny became Bowlby's primary caretaker and the adult in whom John put his early trust. Unfortunately for Bowlby and his siblings, the nanny left her position when Bowlby was just four years old. This devastated young Bowlby, and he experienced an overwhelming sense of sadness.

Like many children of the era, Bowlby was sent away to attend boarding school at age seven, just three years after the loss of his nanny. He resented being sent to school, and would later declare boarding schools to have a detrimental effect on the well-being of children. Bowlby's early feelings of isolation and abandonment would lay the foundation for his later work examining and outlining attachment dynamics.

Bowlby went on to attend the prestigious Cambridge University, where he studied behavioral science with an emphasis in psychology. He excelled at Cambridge and later studied medicine at the University College Hospital in London, specializing in child psychology. Sigmund Freud's work in psychoanalysis had a significant influence on Bowlby's studies, and Bowlby became a psychoanalyst after graduation. Working under the supervision of Melanie Klein and studying the works of Anna Freud, René Spitz, and Dorothy Burlingham, Bowlby ventured beyond the accepted theories of the time and pursued his own research in attachment dynamics and child development. Alongside his professional work, he began volunteering at a home for distressed boys, and this would come to greatly influence his research and findings.

Bowlby began his career working at the Child Guidance Clinic of London, where he developed a strong interest in the question of distress, particularly the distress of children caused by separation from the mother/caretaker. One group of boys in the center had been placed there because of their criminal behavior—they had been arrested for theft—and Bowlby became interested in how their early development may have influenced their later behavior.

Bowlby's interest deepened as he examined the boys' histories, which revealed a common theme of separation from their mothers. Simultaneously, two boys in the center seemed to develop an attachment to Bowlby. These two boys had a profound impact on Bowlby's research as he began to understand the deep need for attachment that was underlying their behavior (Bowlby 1947). In little time, the boys in the center opened his eyes and heart to the study of relational bonding and its disruption.

By 1958, Bowlby realized that part of an infant's dependency on his caregiver for survival included the need for a strong relational bond. This idea of bonding as an active survival effort was a new addition to the prevailing theories of the time. It is impossible for infants to survive on their own, and we all need someone to provide safety and security for us to grow and develop throughout our lives. Survival becomes the common need we all share, and is the basic building block in development. The idea that the infant and small child would be active in their survival efforts by how they bonded with their care providers had not been considered before. Prior to this, infants were considered passive in their role as dependents, and it was thought that bonding would happen as a natural side effect of their physical needs being met by the caregiver.

Because of the mother's biological role in child-rearing—including carrying the child, giving birth to the child, and often breastfeeding the child—Bowlby identified the mother, or the caregiver, as the one responsible for meeting the infant's emotional need for survival, not just the infant's physical needs. The mother's proximity to the child became increasingly more relevant to Bowlby's research, in terms of not only her physical presence, but her ability to meet the child's emotional and spiritual needs as well. He also observed that the proximity of the caregiver was even more vital to the child's sense of safety in moments when the child felt distressed.

Bowlby designed a study (Bowlby 1944) centered around a group of forty-four boys at the center whose rule-breaking behaviors—mostly theft—had led to their assignment at the center. This study would become the seminal set of research in attachment theory, and would provide the first collection of empirical evidence that early maternal relationships affect a child's personality well into the teen years and adulthood.

As he began his project, which he called "Forty-Four Juvenile Thieves: Their Characters and Home-Life," Bowlby noticed that the boys in the study showed little to no empathy toward others. They seemed noticeably disconnected from the world and people around them, and operated with little to no respect toward life or property. His results indicated a direct correlation between the boys who committed theft and a separation event from their mothers or primary caregivers. Bowlby viewed maternal separation and deprivation as a direct cause of the boys' altered view of their environment (Bowlby 1944), which more than likely gave Bowlby insight into his feelings about his childhood and separation from his mother.

This initial research at the boys' home propelled Bowlby to continue his research into attachment dynamics, and it ultimately led to his articulation of attachment theory. As part of this framework, Bowlby identified four distinct elements that must be present in order for an infant to form a healthy attachment with a parent or caregiver (Bowlby 1969). We now term these the four components of attachment:

- **Safe haven:** Bowlby argued that infants need a relational space in which the child's need for attachment is satisfied by the caregiver, who provides protection, nurturing, and care. The child feels he can return to and rely on this space during high levels of stress in order to be soothed by the caregiver. At this stage of development, the child is not able to soothe himself on his own and therefore must rely on an adult to recognize and respond to his emotional needs. Within this space, the child begins to learn a sense of safety and connection.

- **Secure base:** Bowlby felt the mother, or primary caregiver, should remain with and available to the child through age five. He believed it required a minimum of two full years in order to build a fully secure attachment between child and caregiver. The additional three years would strengthen the child-caregiver relationship and form a secure base with the caregiver. This relationship would repeat itself in the child's life, including in adult relationships, and the child could return again and again to a secure base (even with his contemporaries and peers) during times of overwhelm or stress.

- **Proximity maintenance:** A child maintains a certain level of proximity to his caregiver and begins to expand his range of exploration, but maintains a sphere of connection so he can develop greater autonomy and explore the world around him while still feeling securely connected to (and able to locate) the caregiver if the need should arise. Proximity maintenance provides the child with the relational support needed to safely experience new aspects of life. Through this process of moving away from and back into connection with the caregiver, the child develops confidence that the caregiver will provide him with a sense of safety at a moment's notice.

- **Separation distress:** In this phase, the child begins to develop an independent sense of self, separate from his caregiver, but feels secure in the knowledge that the caregiver's absence is temporary and reunion can be restored. When this secure knowledge is not established, Bowlby argued, the child develops a sense of disconnection. The child might become unable to bond, or would form unhealthy bonds with others and become unable to develop a normal empathic response. Bowlby viewed this element as crucial to the child's healthy development, and he saw this as the phase in which emotional maturity became stunted in the forty-four boys he counseled (Bowlby 1947).

Bowlby was already identifying the critical elements of safety, stability, and security in the adult-child relationship that we now know are so important for the development of resilience.

Bowlby also categorized the development of attachment into four distinct time periods, or phases, providing insight into how each stage paved the way for the next and identifying opportunities where healthy development might be disrupted (Bowlby 1969):

- **Pre-attachment period / birth to six weeks:** This is the phase when connection begins to develop between the caretaker and infant. The infant seeks proximity to the caregiver by crying or cooing. She recognizes her caretaker's voice and smell and begins to respond when the caretaker holds her and interacts with smiles and whispers.

- **Attachment-in-the-making / six weeks to eight months:** The infant begins to seek out and prefer her primary caregiver over other adults. Her verbal skills with the preferred caregiver begin to increase, and the infant responds differently to her caregiver, compared to the occasional visitor.

- **Clear-cut attachment / eight months to eighteen months:** It becomes quite obvious from whom the toddler seeks comfort and to whom she feels most attached. Toddlers at this stage will perform for the primary caregiver in order to gain her attention. They climb and jump on the caretaker in order to remain the center of her focus. During this phase, toddlers will exhibit stress when separated from their primary caretakers, but they are also receptive to other caring adults who attempt to meet their needs and form attachments.

- **Formation of reciprocal attachment / eighteen months to two years:** Words become more important to the child as she expands her capabilities and learns new techniques in terms of movement, communication, and play. Language helps facilitate this stage of learning. Though the child is aware that her caretaker will return from an absence, she may still show distress when left behind. The child will purposely speak, act out, or express frustration to prevent the caregiver from leaving. This is an important phase when the caregiver should slow down, listen to the child, and engage her so she can trust that her needs will be met consistently.

As Bowlby's work continued after World War II, he became director of the children's ward at Tavistock Clinic in London. He later renamed the ward the Department of Children and Parents. This new name demonstrated Bowlby's commitment to children and the importance of the entire family, as he saw it, in the development of young personalities.

In 1949, prior to having more fully developed his model, Bowlby authored a paper detailing his successes in family therapy, focusing primarily on the process of having parents describe directly to their children their own experiences of growing up (Bowlby 1949). This early use of narrative in therapy became a key element in his treatment of children, and we continue to see the power of narrative today in the treatment of developmental trauma. Daniel Hughes later developed the theory of Dyadic Developmental Psychotherapy (DDP) (Beck-Weidman and Hughes 2008), in which the therapist focuses on meeting the child developmentally, and meeting the adult at his emotional age, in order to hear the narrative and accept it without judgment. Hughes's work is also integrated into the approach articulated in this book.

Bowlby was not a one-man show, however. In 1950, Mary Ainsworth—who had already been doing research under her maiden name, Salter (1940)—moved with her husband, Leonard Ainsworth, from Canada to London, where he intended to complete his graduate degree. Although born in the United States, Ainsworth had moved to Toronto with her family as a small child, and began her studies in the honors psychology program at the University of Toronto at age sixteen. During her graduate studies, she had worked with a mentor, William E. Blatz, on what he referred to as "security theory," or the types of healthy or unhealthy dependency that children developed on their parents. This paralleled parts of Bowlby's work.

Ainsworth wanted to continue her work in the area of child development when she and her husband moved to London. When she found a posting by John Bowlby seeking a research assistant, she saw an opportunity to continue her earlier work in the same field of interest. Neither Bowlby nor Ainsworth could have anticipated how their fortuitous match would profoundly influence their future work. Bowlby's son later argued that neither Bowlby's nor Ainsworth's research would have been nearly as powerful without the other's. If John Bowlby is considered the father of attachment theory, Mary Ainsworth is considered its mother.

She remained at the Tavistock Clinic as a research assistant to John Bowlby through 1954, when she left to conduct her own research in Uganda, which focused on a common weaning practice of sending the child away from the mother for a few days to "forget the breast." Ainsworth learned to speak the native language, and this provided great insight for understanding cross-cultural ideas of child-rearing and attachment. As a result of that research, she later authored *Infancy in Uganda* (Ainsworth 1967), in which she outlines how the attachment process has universal characteristics that are consistent across cultural, language, and geographic lines.

In 1958, she moved with her husband to Baltimore, where she secured a position as associate professor of developmental psychology at Johns Hopkins University. As Ainsworth's skills and knowledge grew, she and Bowlby transitioned into an equal partnership in their research work, exchanging weekly letters for many years, because he remained in London. Their work began to merge and overlap further, though they were rarely able to work in the same city at the same time.

Early in 1960, while giving her first public presentation on her Uganda research, Ainsworth was challenged by developmental psychologists in the audience to more clearly define what she meant by "attachment." This motivated her to more specifically articulate the elements that influenced the attachment process, and to identify the behaviors that would differentiate healthy attachment from unhealthy attachment.

By 1965, Ainsworth and her assistant Barbara Wittig had designed the Strange Situation procedure. The goal was to study the individual attachment differences among children experiencing small moments of attachment distress. Each child in the study was presented with eight three-minute situations in a laboratory outfitted with toys and children's furniture to make children feel comfortable.

For this study, a mother and her child of twelve to twenty-four months of age would enter the lab, and the child would be allowed to explore. After one minute, a person the child didn't know would enter, speak with the mother, and then attempt to establish a relationship with the child. The mother would then "conspicuously" leave the room, leaving the child with the stranger. During this first separation, the stranger tries to interact with the child. The mother is gone for three minutes and then returns. She greets and comforts the child, only to leave again—with the stranger—for another three minutes. During the initial part of the second separation, the child is alone briefly before the stranger returns. During the mother's second absence, the stranger attempts to care for and comfort the child. After her brief time away, the mother reenters the room, she greets and picks up the child, and the stranger conspicuously leaves.

Throughout these interactions, researchers observed the child's reaction to the stranger, as well as to the mother's return. Based on these behaviors, researchers could draw conclusions about the nature of the child's attachment relationship with his mother.

By examining the types of communication and interactions between child and mother, the child's ability to regulate his emotions, and how the child responded to perceived threats, the original twenty-six children in the study were divided into three categories, which later became known as attachment styles.

- **Secure attachment:** During the study (Ainsworth and Wittig 1969), children in this category felt comfortable looking around the room and exploring their new environment with their mothers present. This echoed Bowlby's idea of the secure base. The mother functioned as the secure base for the child, allowing her to safely explore and engage with the stranger while the mother was present. The infant began to cry when the mother left the room, but was excited to see her when she returned. This category of attachment is the one most strongly affiliated with the protective factors that foster resilience (Shonkoff, Boyce, Cameron, et al. 2004).

- **Anxious-avoidant insecure attachment:** Children in this category seemed to avoid the mother or ignore her departure from and return to the lab. The children seemed uninterested in the room itself and typically chose not to explore the space. Their emotions were more limited and constricted, regardless of who was present in the room or any attempts made to comfort the children. As research continued, this group was later divided into two subsets: one group completely ignored the mother upon her return, and the other group attempted to approach the mother but tended to then turn away from or ignore her. At the time (in the 1970s), Ainsworth and Silvia Bell, with whom Ainsworth conducted some of her research, believed this avoidant behavior functioned as a form of emotional self-protection for the child. Later, using heart-rate monitors with the children, the researchers discovered this group was equally activated emotionally compared with the other groups in the study. This indicated that the anxious-avoidant children still had rich emotional responses to their mothers, but had, for some reason, learned to hide or withhold their emotions.

- **Anxious-resistant insecure attachment:** These children showed distress even before the mother left the room. They became clingy and difficult to comfort upon the mother's return. This group was later divided into two subsets: one showed signs of resentment toward the mother for leaving, and the second showed signs of helpless passivity. The level of stress among this group was so great in the original trial that Ainsworth had to end the study prematurely. There was also a group in this category with an even higher level of distress noted, which was not categorized until Mary Main, with Judith Solomon, added another category, noted below.

- **Disorganized/disoriented attachment:** This fourth category was noted by Mary Main and Judith Solomon (Main and Solomon 1986), who developed the Adult Attachment Interview. They noticed a group of children who didn't meet the criteria of the original three categories of attachment behavior. The children in this group appeared not to possess coping skills. Some moved toward their mothers when they returned to the room, whereas others moved away. Their reunions seemed disoriented and inconsistent. This category is the one most strongly affiliated with the risk factors impairing resilience (Shonkoff, Boyce, Cameron, et al. 2004; Shonkoff, Levitt, Boyce, et al. 2004).

In studies of the three initial attachment classifications (secure, avoidant-insecure, and resistant-insecure), about 70 percent of American infants have been classified as secure, 20 percent as avoidant-insecure, and 10 percent as resistant-insecure (Ainsworth et al. 1978).

Van IJzendoorn and Kroonenberg's meta-analysis (1988) supports these earlier findings. More recent studies show worrying declines in secure attachment, with percentages in the general population now closer to 60 percent (Andreassen, Fletcher, and Park 2007). Percentages related to the disorganized attachment category depend on the particular sample studied (Greenberg, Cicchetti, and Cummings 1990; Andreassen, Fletcher, and Park 2007). The prevalence of disorganized attachment among middle-class, white American children is 12–15 percent in the Mary Main studies (Main and Solomon 1990). Infants of adolescent mothers have a rate around 30 percent (Broussard 1995). And infants of abused mothers and psychiatrically ill or substance abusing mothers can be as high as 70–80 percent (Carlson et al. 1989). We again see a correlation within these different population samples in relation to resilience. Children of mothers with psychiatric illnesses or substance abuse issues have more risk factors that are correlated with poor resilience (Shonkoff and Eisels 2000; Shonkoff and Phillips 2000).

The early research conducted by Bowlby, Ainsworth, and others at this stage of understanding attachment focused on the mother-baby dyad. One of the criticisms of this early research is that it places too much emphasis on the mother and her sensitivity to her child, and that there are other factors influencing the child's attachment behaviors (such as the child's own temperament). More current research has also considered additional types of relational bonds and attachment, such as bonds with grandparents, between siblings, or between a child and unrelated caregivers. The term used for these nonparental sources of care and attention is "alloparent." In Bowlby's later work, he did include the role of the alloparent; when a mother was not available, the father or another caring adult could meet the infant's need for survival. Bowlby also included the belief that the caregiver was responsible for the external regulation of the infant/child's nervous system, what we would now refer to as co-regulation.

Bowlby opened the door to considering that regulation of the infant/child's physiology is one of the key elements that occurs within the attachment process, and we now understand more fully how critical this element of the co-regulatory function of care providers is. In chapter 4, we will discuss the more modern framework of this neurophysiological process of development, which has now provided a deeper understanding of how complex and multidimensional the attachment process is, with many variables. One of those variables is exposure to early trauma.

Regardless of the influences on the child's attachment style, the four components of attachment that Bowlby articulated (safe haven, secure base, proximity maintenance, and separation distress) provide a helpful structure for understanding which elements of connectedness and safety provide the foundation for attachment. Likewise, the attachment styles themselves can provide therapists with useful information about what may have gone awry in the early attachment and bonding process, and how best to structure their interventions.

In the approach articulated in this book, we look at Bowlby's four components of attachment and apply them to the relationship between therapist and client. Understanding how early attachment ruptures caused by trauma can affect the capacity of the client to interact relationally is critical when working with developmental trauma. In later chapters of this book, we will provide simple methods to support the therapist in understanding how to work with this type of client with the least amount of sympathetic arousal, while at the same time creating a greater felt sense of safety.

REGULATION

Regulation is the term used to describe our ability to manage our emotional state, to calm ourselves during times of heightened emotion—when we become fearful, deeply sad, angry, or frustrated. Regulation is a learned process, one we integrate into our own lives by observing others and, importantly, through the attachment phases with our early caregivers.

Infants, of course, are unable to regulate their emotions independently. They feel, and feel strongly, and they express those emotions in the moment without regard for what may be socially appropriate or convenient. Their emotional responses are instinctual and unregulated.

Physiologically speaking, moments of intense emotion activate the reptilian part of the brain, the first part of the brain to develop in utero. This is the root of our autonomic nervous system—the origin of our fight-or-flight response, which affects blood pressure, heart rate, breathing rate, body temperature, digestion, metabolism, and multiple other bodily functions. This neurological response is powerful and easily triggered when threats are perceived, which is why it's so important for parents to step in and help children literally "calm their nerves" during times of distress.

For example, an infant may hear a loud noise or become spooked by the sudden movement of a pet that wants to play. The infant perceives these small disruptions as potential threats to his survival. Unable to "fight back" (or do anything to stop the pet), the infant cries out for a caregiver to intervene and rescue him from the situation. If the parent is attuned to the infant, she will pick up the baby, provide a physical embrace, and use soothing language to help calm the child's neurological fight-or-flight response.

In this way, parents and caregivers play a crucial role in helping young children soothe their intense emotions, and these interactions between parent and child will shape the child's ability—or inability—to regulate his own emotions later in life. This process is called co-regulation because the parent steps in as a mentor and external source of soothing when the child feels distressed.

This process of co-regulation creates a foundation for neurosequential development for the child (Schore 1994). In other words, once this co-regulation pattern is formed, the child can grow in productive, healthy, and predictable ways toward emotional maturity. This isn't purely about feeling a "better" emotion, but about regulating our level of arousal when the autonomic nervous system is activated, and about regulating our affect in the company of others.

Dr. Allan Schore (2001) sees the transfer of regulation from external (relying on others) to internal (developing the capacity to self-regulate) as the primary task of early development. This ability to move toward internal regulation is critical to our ability as humans to process our environment and distinguish between real and perceived threats, allowing us to develop impulse control and self-control. As noted in the introduction, self-regulatory capacity is one of the protective factors affiliated with the development of resilience. Self-regulation also enables us to form relationships aligned with the social norms of our group.

One of the critical elements that parents/caregivers offer to a child is co-regulation. Without a rupture in attachment, this system comes on board without complications, happening automatically as parents naturally respond to their child's needs. This co-regulation also lays the foundational blocks of neurosequential development for the child, meaning that her neurological development progresses along healthy and predictable lines. Regulation is not only about regulating the physiology of the autonomic nervous system. It's also about regulating levels of arousal, and eventually being able to regulate our affect.

It's important to emphasize the fact that co-regulation involves mutual interaction between the caregiver and the child. The child's alarm signals the parent, who may also become alarmed, but who steps in to perform a nurturing function. The child's transition to a more settled state will in turn influence the caregiver's state. Therefore, the co-regulation process is about the ability of the caretaker to understand the infant's needs, and the caregiver's willingness to provide comfort and to allow back-and-forth interaction—the attachment dance between parent and child. This process of co-regulation sets the stage for critical physiological processes, including the maintenance of homeostasis (or physiological equilibrium).

We use co-regulation and self-regulation constantly, and both support the development of higher-level thinking. In relationships, co-regulation helps us maintain more effective self-regulation. David Sbarra and Cindy Hazan note that "The ability to quickly use the resources of a close other may represent a so-called fast route to emotional regulation" (Sbarra and Hazan 2008, 157). Because there is little to no thinking involved, co-regulation can more quickly bring down arousal because we don't have to think it through on our own. Access to the reliable capacity for both self- and co-regulation is important when responding to stressors, including potentially traumatic stressors. As will be discussed more fully in chapter 4, our ability to regulate during times of stress is one of the key elements for responding in healthy ways to challenges, and in building and maintaining both resilience and a sense of safety. Being in co-regulation is a bottom-up process because it bypasses the thinking brain, giving us access to regulation even when we are so stressed that our thinking isn't as clear as it could be.

The loss of regulatory capacity is one of the consequences of traumatic stress. With the loss of regulation comes loss of healthy functioning in many physiological, behavioral, and social processes. In the next three chapters, we will discuss these disruptions in more detail.

CONNECTEDNESS

Healthy bonding, access to co-regulation, and the eventual development of self-regulation inoculate us against traumatic stress (Stroufe 1995). Social engagement supports and builds early developmental neurological "programs" that help us feel a foundational sense of safety. Healthy bonding and attachment allow us to develop the early ability to self-regulate our systems and trust the shared experience of co-regulation and connectedness. Resilience research indicates that the interplay between caregiver and child promotes healthy brain development (Schore 2001; Shonkoff, Boyce, Cameron, et al. 2004) as well as resilience. Experiences of safety and connectedness impact us deeply, supporting important physiological benefits, such as strengthening our immune system and increasing our chances for better health overall by promoting homeostasis. It would not be an exaggeration to say that a strong sense of connectedness is one of the best ways to prevent developmental trauma, and one of the remedies that should be brought into play for repair of early trauma (Felitti et al. 1998).

It is perhaps uncommon to consider connectedness as the key to trauma prevention, but when high stress threatens our existence, our sense of belonging and connectedness helps us respond in healthier ways, including reaching out for support. Through our sense of connectedness, we grow and we heal, which is exactly what helps develop resilience.

2

Knowing When We Are Safe

AS OUR SENSE OF CONNECTION develops with our care providers, so too does our ability to recognize cues that indicate safety. As clinicians, we can sometimes forget there are physiological and physical mechanisms that must develop in healthy ways in order to support a felt sense of safety and security. In this chapter, we will discuss some of those mechanisms, because their disruption can have such a profound impact on the issues that arise as a result of developmental trauma.

Understanding first what can happen during healthy development will provide a better understanding of what happens when this development is disrupted or altered by trauma, which we'll discuss in more detail in the following chapter.

One key area in which our care providers help us develop involves the differentiation between threat and excitation—understanding when something is exciting but enjoyable versus when something causes excitation because a real threat is present. Although it may seem that in some experiences the inherent differentiation is obvious, such as excitation about an upcoming trip to the toy store, versus something like an injury, our care providers' behavior in relation to these experiences and stimuli has a very strong impact on how we interpret them ourselves.

We may experience certain stimulating experiences as unsafe, for example, if our care providers respond to those experiences as if they are frightening or anxiety-producing. Worried parents tend to produce children who are more prone to anxiety and worry themselves (Eley et al. 2015). By contrast, if our care providers play with us in a sensitive and safe way, show alarm only when something is truly alarming, and soothe us when we have been frightened, we slowly learn how to calibrate our perception system and develop more nuanced responses to stimulation. We learn that play (excitation with safety) can be enjoyable and enhance our bonds with our social group. We learn that some things are interesting but dangerous, and we should move away from them, such as the mesmerizing flame that can burn us. We perhaps even learn some of the social cues that might tell us if a person isn't safe to be around.

> *Charlie is the first child of his parents, Martin and Raul, who are connected and loving toward Charlie but somewhat inexperienced at being around small children. At ten months old, Charlie is playful and exuberant but tends to startle easily, which then incites long bouts of crying followed by difficulty settling. Charlie's dads have received some coaching to help them support Charlie in widening his range of responses to stimulating play.*
>
> *Martin and Raul have been using gentle play, like peekaboo, to increase Charlie's capacity for engagement in exciting play without becoming overstimulated. Today, Martin starts a game by hiding behind his hands, but—encouraged by Charlie's laughter—he adds a little growl into the next round when he moves his hands away from his face. And . . . Ooops! . . . that was too much for Charlie, who dissolves into tears. Martin takes Charlie into his arms and soothes him, cooing gently that everything is fine, and apologizing for startling him. "I'm sorry, Peanut. I was just playing. I didn't mean to scare you."*
>
> *After Charlie settles, even as the tears are still drying on his face, he begins a first, tiny invitation to play by peeking at his dad through his fingers. Martin, having been coached to be on the lookout for these small signs of recovery, gently responds with a smile and a little peek back.*
>
> *Now the game of peekaboo has begun again, this time with Charlie leading the way and Martin carefully trying to keep his responses within Charlie's range of comfort. In the final round, Charlie's laughter erupts into something similar to the growl his dad originally offered, and Charlie responds with even more laughter when Dad playfully growls back and gives him a little tickle.*
>
> *Through interactive play behaviors, Charlie's parents help him differentiate between excitation in the context of safety, versus excitation resulting from an actual threat. This type of parent-child interaction is termed the "serve and return" interaction (Shonkoff, Boyce, Cameron, et al. 2004) with caregivers that is essential for developing healthy brain architecture, and is one of the factors of healthy child-parent interactions that supports the development of resilience. This interplay also*

supports the social engagement system as well as the development of a nuanced somatic "vocabulary" that allows Charlie to better regulate his responses to both social interactions and other sources of excitation.

As infants and small children, we are exposed to so many new experiences that we need an attentive parent or adult to help us understand how to sort through those experiences and respond to them. Play can be a valuable form of support to help children differentiate between excitation and threat or alarm. In play experiences, such as peekaboo, care providers bring a gentle stimulus into the play. Then, through their responses, care providers let children know they are not under threat and can enjoy the experience of excitation without feeling endangered. Excitation without fear helps us understand how we can experience play, pleasure, and connection through shared experience (Porges 2004, 2011a).

To build the healthy ability to differentiate between threat and excitation, we need the foundational capacities—the foundational architecture—to activate this ability to perceive accurately, to understand what we are perceiving, to make meaning of it, if necessary, and to respond in nuanced ways. These foundational capacities are developed contextually, strongly influenced by our social interactions (or lack of interactions), by our external environment, and by our own physiology.

Developmental trauma can have a profound impact on all aspects of the development of this neurological, psychological, and social "safety system." Bowlby, in his later work, came to believe that a child's experience of connection and safety was not only about the child's appraisal of the caregiver's ability, but how the child felt internally about his security (Bowlby 1998). When our social environment is chaotic and lacks consistent feedback about safety versus threat, our differentiation between these two possibilities can become confused or even absent, tuning us more acutely toward assessment of danger and perhaps limiting our ability to recognize safety.

As clinicians, we've all had the experience of hearing a client describe feeling a lack of safety. To support our clients in developing a better "safety system," it can be helpful to understand the various contributing physiological and sensory mechanisms that inform their sense of safety and security.

In the previous chapter, we discussed the relational components of healthy attachment. Here we focus more on the perception systems and systems of meaning-making that also contribute to our safety system.

INTEROCEPTION

Interoception is the process by which we notice our internal state. We evaluate a combination of sensations and perceptions of physical processes to assess our interior milieu and decipher what it's telling us about what we are feeling, how we are, and even who we are.

This includes our perception of physiological processes, such as heart rate, the digestive process, sensations of the skin, and any other internally experienced sensations of our own bodies. Using our evaluations of these sources of bodily information, we take action, make meaning, make predictions (like predicting our own illness by feeling the initial sensations associated with the onset of a cold), and make judgments about who we are and how we are—are we hungry, are we safe, are we loved?

Stephen Porges refers to interoception as the "infant's sixth sense" (Porges 1993). If an infant cannot accurately perceive whether or not he is hungry or thirsty, if he needs sleep, if he is too warm or too cold, then he cannot accurately communicate his needs (or distress) to care providers. That, in turn, can prevent care providers from responding properly to the infant's needs, which may then increase the infant's distress and instill a feeling that safety and connection are lacking.

In this way, it is critical that the infant and small child develop an accurate interoceptive language for communicating her most basic needs to care providers—it's an essential component of the healthy attachment and bonding process. As the care provider meets the need of the infant, attachment is strengthened.

As we mature, our need for a nuanced, interoceptive vocabulary becomes even more critical. We need a reference system for understanding how we feel about different people, different circumstances, and different types of needs. It's easy to assume that this system of reference develops of its own accord, but in fact it develops contextually, requiring regular feedback from our social system in order to calibrate points of reference and rely on them with confidence (Bermúdez, Marcel, and Eilan 1995).

For clinicians working in any somatic form, it's helpful to understand how interoception informs our clients' experiences of self and environment, both internal and external:

- Interoception provides a significant portion of the information we use to form our experience of self and our view of the self in relation to others.

It provides a large portion of the self-communication we use to assess whether or not we are safe or unsafe and whether an external event or person is pleasurable, exciting, or threatening (Ceunen, Vlaeyen, and Van Diest 2016; Bermúdez, Marcel, and Eilan 1995; Cameron 2001; Craig 2015).

- Interoception develops in context; our day-to-day experiences inform our perceptions and evaluation of various internal sources of information. This includes our social context—our social group provides a significant amount of feedback, which we use to "calibrate" our interoceptive perception and interpretation.

- Interoception can be easily influenced, including by something as simple as our mood when we are asked to rate our pain levels: positive emotion increases our tolerance for pain, and negative emotion decreases our tolerance for pain (Carter et al. 2002; Zweyer, Velker, and Ruch 2004). Although it may seem there could be "objective" measures for physical sensations like pain, our interoceptive experience will shift based on many factors that have nothing to do with physical qualities, so it may seem there is not a stable "baseline" for any given interoceptive response (Craig 2015).

- The interoceptive system is meant to inform us in a predictive assessment of our internal and external environments, but it can mislead us if this system developed without congruent context and feedback, in which case, our markers for perception and meaning-making may be overly sensitive or tuned to signals that don't provide the most reliable information. In other words, our points of reference for making a judgment may be off-base and therefore lead to false conclusions (Bechara, Damasio, and Damasio 2000).

- Information gathered via interoception tends to be experienced as factual, not evaluative, because it comes from what many of us call "inner knowing," or gut feeling. Part of our job as clinicians is to support our clients in changing and revising their interoceptive "conversations" with themselves.

- Because interoception remains plastic, it's possible to help our clients change their interoceptive vocabulary and conduct more nuanced assessments of their inner world, resulting in more helpful self-conversations.

The study of interoception is an expanding field of scientific study, which means there is not yet full agreement on vocabulary, or even how to categorize what's considered interoceptive and what isn't. The basic definition of "interoception" is the perception of internal (endogenous) sensations that contribute to our subjective experience of body state, although even that foundational definition is up for debate. Interoception is often contrasted with exteroception, or the perception of the outside (exogenous) environment. On the surface, this may seem rather straightforward, but it quickly becomes more complex when we begin to define what is meant by "state" and what constitutes "internal" versus "external."

There are many bodily sensations whose origins could be internal or external: the perception of heat, for example. If we are in a warm environment, we will perceive heat. If we have a fever, we may feel just as we would if the room were hot. In addition, some biological systems, such as the skin, interface with the outside world and therefore allow us to feel something that is clearly outside the body—a soothing touch, for example—while also providing sensations that most of us attribute to the internal body, such as pain.

Because this inside/outside categorization isn't always clear-cut, some researchers use different types of categorizations, such as perceptions from internal organs, compared with perceptions from other body systems, like the skin. Although there is still quite a lot of debate about definitions, mechanisms of perception, and the ways in which we process interoceptive information, researchers tend to agree that interoception is a flexible and responsive system of awareness—one that clinicians can attend to in therapy with positive results.

The interoceptive system's flexibility also helps us hone our learning and survival skills, and keeps us responsive to changing circumstances and environments. But this malleability also leaves the system vulnerable to alteration by environmental factors, such as early trauma, which can have a profound and lasting impact on how the system responds to ordinary and extraordinary circumstances.

The importance of gaining a better understanding of interoception is reflected in the amount of research being conducted on this topic. There are now many areas of research exploring various aspects of interoception: pain, emotions, anxiety and affective disorders, addiction, sexual functioning, food and water intake—the list goes on and on. Certainly, in the coming years we will have a much better understanding of the role interoception plays in our experiences of many things, including safety, connectedness, and resilience.

The subject of interoception is more nuanced and complex than we're able to cover in this book. But, for our purposes, it offers a useful framework for better understanding our clients' experiences, particularly their concept of safety, which can impact so many other areas of life and health. In this chapter, we are most interested in how our clients use their interoceptive experiences to inform their behavior and make meaning about themselves and their relationships with others. For this purpose, we can adopt the newly emerging definition that "the only thing determining whether something is interoceptive is whether it contributes to the subjective perception of body state" (Ceunen, Vlaeyen, and Van Diest 2016).

EXTEROCEPTION

Whereas interoception provides us with information about our internal environment, helping us pay attention to our internal experience of self, our exteroceptive systems help us pay attention to our external environments. There are many similarities between interoception and exteroception, but both systems:

- Develop in the context of environmental and social factors

- Contribute to our perception of safety and lack of safety

- Are influenced by day-to-day experiences

- Contribute to our predictive assessments of experience

- Contribute to meaning-making about our experiences

Like interoception, exteroception aggregates information from a combination of sources. But, in this case, the information helps us perceive and make sense of the outside world, rather than the interior world of the body and the psyche. The traditionally recognized exteroceptive sensory systems are sight (vision), hearing (auditory), taste (gustatory), smell (olfactory), and touch (tactile)—what we might informally call the "paying-attention systems."

When healthy development occurs, our sensory systems support accurate perceptions of our environments and are coordinated with other systems—physiological, social, and emotional—allowing us to function with an integrated perception system that works congruently with our developmental needs. To develop in a healthy way, our exteroceptive systems need appropriate stimuli and feedback, and we need our care providers to help us make sense of what we perceive. We again rely on our social group to help us place our different perceptions in context to arrive at understanding.

However, as is the case with interoception, the processing of information about the external environment does not derive entirely from our obvious paying-attention systems. There are additional sources of information that contribute to our overall assessment of our internal and external environments: the vestibular (balance) system; the proprioceptive system, which tells us where different parts of our body are in relation to each other and how fast they are moving; temperature perception; vibration perception; and pain perception.

Once again, it's often difficult to clearly differentiate between information that originates outside the self and information that originates within. Some information we perceive as external can instead originate inside the body. One example is the change in vision that occurs with the onset of a migraine, or when fainting. The external environment seems to blur and fade away, but it's our own vision that has been altered. We also see this impact when cross-modal influence is present, such as occurs with the visual system and the perception of satiety. When research subjects are exposed to foods that look more appealing, the regions of their brains related to satiety become more active. In other words, external visual cues influence our experience of anticipating how satisfying and filling a meal will be (Cornier et al. 2007). As with interoception, we sometimes take for granted that our sensory systems simply develop to produce accurate perceptions of our environment, when in fact, these systems are strongly influenced by environmental factors, including trauma.

It's important to remember that we cannot exclusively use cognitive processes when assessing our safety. Rather, our body's holistic response tells us whether or not we are safe. We can certainly evaluate our external environment with conscious thought, but, as noted in the previous section, our inner responses to that information will provide the bulk of the information we'll use to determine whether we are in fact safe.

In the simple act of walking through a garden, for example, we use a wonderfully complex feedback system to coordinate our movements, to maintain our balance, and—if we generally find gardens pleasant—to enjoy the sights and smells of the flowers, sense our pleasure in the environment, and make connections to past experiences of pleasure. By contrast, if we have been raised in an environment where being outdoors felt unsafe, our experience of the garden will be dramatically different. We will instead listen for predators or signs of danger, visually scan our surroundings for potential threats, and constantly assess the environment rather than enjoy a sense of pleasure or connection to positive memories. In this way, one environment can produce very different experiences depending on an individual's perceptive interpretation of that environment, and the various influences that inform that individual's interoceptive system. Our experiences over time, as well as the interactions between our interoceptive and exteroceptive systems, also influence how our perceptions of the outside world are processed.

As is true with interoception, our methods and processes for attending to the outside world are altered by stress physiology. Even a completely healthy perceptive system, when operating under stress, can provide distorted information about the surrounding environment. One of the key influences during stress physiology is the sympathetic nervous system, which prepares us for activity, including threat response. The sympathetic nervous system increases our heart rate and breathing rate, and sends messages to our muscles to prepare for action. It also makes subtle adjustments that are more difficult to notice, such as changing our hearing and vision and bringing an overall heightened focus to perception of the external environment. For example, Porges's research suggests that our hearing changes when our sympathetic, or arousal, system becomes physiologically dominant. When under the influence of stress physiology, we literally hear differently. Specifically, our middle-ear muscles change so that our hearing is tuned toward lower frequency, vibratory sounds—sometimes referred to as "predator" sounds—and we are less able to extract the sound of the human voice from other noises in our surroundings. Beyond our actual sense of hearing, the ability to perceive content is also altered during times of stress. We are less able to make sense of what we hear when we switch into a constant state of vigilance (Porges 2004, 2011a, 2011b).

As clinicians, we should be aware that our clients may be better able to hear the air conditioning unit outside our window than hear our voices when we are trying to calm them. In later chapters, we will discuss the ways in which traumatic stress physiology, particularly when it arises very early in development, can profoundly alter perception systems, response systems, and the ability to connect socially. All of these, in turn, will necessarily alter the clinical interventions we select and pursue.

For our purposes in this chapter, what's most important for clinicians to understand is that all our sensory systems are influenced in the same way our developmental systems are shaped and constructed. Ideally, those sensory systems had the opportunity to develop in a healthy and integrated way, but we cannot presume all of our clients gained the healthy foundational perceptual architecture to accurately process information from the environment. We may need to attend carefully to our clients' signals and cues about possible "miscalibration" of their perception systems, and find ways to subtly and safely investigate our clients' perceptive experiences. We may need to alter our clinical interventions to accommodate these differences, which are very commonly associated with developmental trauma, as will be discussed in the following chapter.

NEUROCEPTION

"Neuroception" is a term coined by Stephen Porges, who summarizes the term this way: "Neuroception describes how neural circuits distinguish whether situations or people are safe, dangerous, or life threatening" (Porges 2004, 19). He also describes neuroception as a "dynamic and interactive process" whereby we respond to cues about safety and threat, while simultaneously transmitting similar cues in our social interactions. Interoception and exteroception both inform neuroception. If we have a healthy, well-developed safety system, our interoceptive and exteroceptive systems will work in an integrated fashion to help us differentiate information and determine when we are safe and when we are not. Likewise, our social systems will have helped us experience a sense of safety and security in our relationships, which reinforces our ability to perceive safety and experience a sense of belonging and security.

Neuroception refers specifically to the neurophysiological processes involved in the perception of safety and threat, what Porges refers to as the neural platforms that support certain categories of behavior (Porges 2007). Porges differentiates the physiological processes from the behaviors themselves. This is important to understand as we work with clients whose perception systems may be inaccurately signaling them of false threats. That perceived lack of safety may in turn trigger the behaviors of threat response, even if there is no legitimate threat to respond to. This can then create a self-fulfilling process whereby others in the social interactions react to those threat behaviors with their own, and the client's felt sense of lack of safety becomes reality, further justifying his initial reaction. For example, the client may respond to a perceived sense of threat by behaving aggressively toward the other person in the interaction. That person in turn responds with their own aggression, because they now feel attacked, confirming the client's experience of threat. If, as clinicians, we respond only as though the behaviors need to be addressed, we will miss a very important source of support for our clients: to help them develop a more accurate neuroceptive system and better calibrate their experience of their environment and social interactions.

In the attachment and bonding process, we learn on many different levels—socially, behaviorally, and physiologically. Because so much of our behavior is based on underlying neurophysiological processes, Porges has for a long time argued for a better understanding of the physiological drivers for behavior, even when working primarily from the psychological perspective.

The development of neuroception can be influenced by trauma, and altered profoundly by developmental trauma. Clients who lack a "safety map" are primarily tuned to danger. They have well-developed filters and somatic narratives about what danger is and what it means—because danger has been an imperative in their lives—but they often have a somewhat limited ability to recognize safety, either within their interoceptive self-communication, or in the perception of their external environments. Once the scales are tipped, the frame of reference can become radically altered—if we are tuned toward danger, we will certainly find it. If we discard or otherwise ignore information that indicates we are safe, or we don't know how to perceive safety in the first place, we will certainly have a difficult time recognizing it. In the following chapter, we will discuss this type of faulty neuroception in more detail.

To experience healthy neuroception, we must first be able to *differentiate* between safety and threat. Neuroception is about the detection of *both*, but to properly make the distinction between the two, we need: (1) reliable access to a sense of safety; (2) care providers who help us regulate our responses and understand environmental cues contextually; and (3) coherent feedback from our social group about how we ought to categorize our experiences. Together, these three elements support the development of necessary and healthy neural platforms that neurophysiologically help us differentiate between safety and threat.

Kate was on vacation in Hawaii, staying in a large hotel near the beach. During the night, a strong windstorm rattled the windows in the hotel and caused it to sway slightly. As a native of California, Kate's neuroception had developed "knowing" that buildings move when earthquakes hit. What she'd learned throughout her childhood—both in school and from her family—was to take action immediately in response to the first tremors of movement, and to move to the safest place she could find. As the gusts of wind rattled the building, Kate repeatedly woke in the night with great alarm, then had to take a few minutes to settle, reassuring herself that the movements of the building were simply responses to the wind, nothing dangerous or life-threatening. But even after waking to the swaying building a fourth or fifth time, her physiology continued to respond to the all-too-familiar movements of the building as if they were coming from an earthquake.

Kate was experiencing the contextual learning that is part of the development of the neuroceptive system. The training of her early years was so ingrained that it continued to override her intellectual response. But she was at least able to invoke logical thinking as a way of calming the neuroceptive process that caused her to react with alarm. Had she never experienced an earthquake, her response to the windstorm would have been very different, even though the external cues would have been the same. In this case, her previous experiences about potential threat activated a partly unconscious response that was both misleading and unnecessary given the circumstances.

One of the brain structures involved in this kind of contextual learning is the amygdala. Although each hemisphere of the brain contains an amygdala—and there are slightly different functions in the left and right amygdalae—we often talk about them as a single, functional pair. The amygdala performs many different functions, but two of these are important to our discussion here. The amygdala plays a role in emotional learning and memory, and in fear conditioning, and is therefore involved in both our behavioral and physiological responses to threat (LeDoux 2015; Levine 2015).

We learn and store information about emotional experiences with the aid of the amygdala. This type of learning and memory is often implicit, meaning we aren't consciously aware of what we're learning. (Explicit learning and memory—which, as the name implies, means we are aware of the process of learning and the source of the memory—is mediated by the hippocampus.) Although we know the most about the amygdala's role in fear and threat response, it is also involved in reward learning and motivation, and in the modulation of attention and perception. It is thought that these processes are the result of the amygdala's assessment of the emotional significance of external stimuli (LeDoux 2015).

Interestingly, the strong emotions felt during a certain experience seem to prompt the amygdala to signal the hippocampus to place a stronger "value" on that experience, so that it makes a greater imprint in our memory (LeDoux 2015). Our past experiences, particularly if they include strong emotional responses, accumulate as memories that inform our current responses to similar types of experiences. In what's called fear, or operant, conditioning, we learn to predict aversive events such as feeling afraid in an earthquake, and which types of stimuli are likely to indicate threat or unpleasant experiences. In this way, the contextual learning supported by our amygdalae helps us assign valence, or relevance/value, to various types of environmental information based on learning and the cues our social group has provided us. This allows us to more quickly sort and assess familiar environmental information into categories: safe/not safe, food/not food, friend/not friend.

If the environmental information is either unfamiliar or misunderstood, we then must turn to other evaluative and sensory systems to formulate a proper response. A classic example of this is the snake-or-stick proposition. We've encountered an object that could be a snake (dangerous!) or could be a stick (harmless), but we need more information from our sensory systems in order to make a final determination about whether it is or isn't a threat. Is it moving? Does it have a head? Are we in an environment where there are usually snakes?

With neuroception, we will simultaneously make a contingent assessment based on previous experience—while the additional sorting of information unfolds—and quickly marshal a response to that preliminary assessment. If we have previously encountered dangerous snakes, we will respond physiologically with more immediacy and greater arousal, and perhaps back away without consciously deciding to do so. From a survival perspective, we can't risk not responding *just in case* it's a snake. Our neuroception is signaling us that there is indeed the possibility of threat, and we must respond accordingly.

If our physiology has developed in a healthy way, and if our further assessment confirms that it is a stick and not a snake, then we will deactivate our survival response and return to a more neutral awareness of our environment. If, on the other hand, we grew up in a city, we've never seen a live snake, and we're walking through a shopping mall, we will be less inclined to respond with that same threat response and may be more curious about how a stick ended up in the mall. Our neuroceptive system has indicated that the likelihood of threat is small, and so we don't marshal a survival effort in response to that stimulus. As shown by this example, the interpretation of signals and the resulting reaction are heavily influenced by memories of similar encounters, or lack thereof.

Healthy neuroception develops in the context of healthy social engagement. Our social group provides a great deal of information about what is safe and not safe. The people in our social group—family, friends, and peers—help us learn by modeling various responses and ways of sorting the information we receive. If that social support and instruction have been missing, or if our social system was the source of danger or did not protect us from threat, we can assume our neuroception will not have developed in a healthy way. For many of our clients, as we will discuss in more detail in the following chapter, neuroception is tuned almost entirely to perception of threat—there are always snakes. Part of our role as clinicians is to help clients develop a more well-rounded neuroceptive system, one that also provides information about the felt sense of safety.

FORMING A NARRATIVE

The somatic, body-oriented narrative of safety, lack of safety, connection, awareness of self, and meaning-making of our experiences is informed by our early development. In our infant and childhood years, our brains are not fully developed, and are unable to acquire and assimilate memories in a narrative fashion, the way we can as adults. We are little somatic beings, responding to our experiences in a noncognitive way. We may later overlay our early experiences with narratives that express our more mature understanding, or simply make our best attempt to explain our experiences by formulating or reconstructing a story that matches, but our earliest experiences will inform that narrative in a way that is largely invisible to us. In our early developmental years, we form what could be termed "somatic narratives." We respond to simplified information from our internal and external environment: *Am I hungry? Am I cold? Do I see the person who comforts me?* As we grow and mature, we can derive meaning from our sensations and perceptions and make more predictive assessments: *I'm hungry. Mommy is coming, and she's holding a bottle and smiling, so she's going to feed me and I don't need to worry.*

In effect, we begin to calibrate our meaning-making and narrative formation within the attachment and bonding systems of our relationships, and this begins to shape the interoceptive, exteroceptive, and neuroceptive systems that will inform so many of our future reactions and decisions. We create our earliest foundations for narrative by developing a somatic vocabulary for understanding our experiences, often in relation to other people, namely our caretakers. If our development has been healthy, we will form narratives that are fairly congruent with the actual situation, and that include different categories of information, much like those within our neuroception: safe/not safe, fun/not fun, scary/exciting.

Through this process, we develop a frame of reference for the felt sense of safety, fun, threat, shared excitement, and so on. We come to know the nature and contours of each feeling, the cues within ourselves and within our social group, and the environmental cues that inform our understanding of more and more complex experiences. We absorb the knowledge that safety can equal any of the following: feeling warm and fed, experiencing comforting touch, engaging in gentle play that isn't frightening, or being in a quiet, softly lit space.

Each of us will have a different narrative for how we understand our experiences—even the same types of experiences—but the foundation for those narratives is built on early experiences that hopefully enabled us to develop a nuanced and wide-ranging somatic language. As we continue to mature, our somatic narrative supports more complex and mature cognitive narratives of our experience.

Unhealthy formative experiences, by contrast, will stand in the way of developing a fully formed somatic language. They skew our vocabulary and interpretative skills, causing us to view most situations as suspect or potentially threatening. This greatly limits our opportunities for connection and accomplishment, and creates a cycle that becomes difficult to break. It's important for therapeutic interventions to take into account the need for repair in our deepest somatic and physiological selves, as well as our social, emotional, and behavioral selves. The role of narrative is such a critical aspect in supporting our clients' recovery from developmental trauma that chapter 8 is devoted to this topic.

3

How Things Go Awry

IN THIS CHAPTER we will discuss some of the unfortunate ways in which things can go awry—beginning with the more historical and moving to the more current—to orient clinicians to some of what happens when the foundations for healthy development are not in place. Fortunately, most people experience a healthy childhood that provides the foundation needed for healthy functioning to support them during adulthood. A majority of children experience "good enough" care from their care providers, feel a consistent sense of safety, form secure attachments, and do not experience the types of trauma that interrupt normal development.

This will not necessarily mean they will automatically develop resilience, as will be discussed further in this and later chapters, but it does provide the foundational elements in the attachment system that encourage resiliency-related factors such as healthy brain development, support for dealing with manageable stressors, and a sense of belonging (Shonkoff et al. 2015).

While some sources of research indicate that 7–12 percent of the population experience developmental trauma, more than 60 percent of adults report having experienced some form of abuse during childhood (Felitti et al. 1998), which indicates that there will be a range of experiences that might fit into a somewhat gray area in terms of the lasting impact on any given individual, who might not meet the threshold to be clearly defined as having experienced developmental trauma, but resiliency may have been compromised and other impacts felt.

This also indicates that there are many people who need good help, who are often underserved by the care delivery system, in part because their symptoms can be complex and nuanced, and include psychological, emotional, and physical difficulties. Because developmental trauma occurs prior to, and during, the times of our most rapid development, its effects impact every area of our developing selves and imprint us in sometimes unique ways. This means those with developmental trauma, particularly severe developmental trauma, will experience symptoms that don't fit easily into a single category, such as addiction, obsessive-compulsive disorder, or anxiety. The effects often seem so deeply rooted that they have become habituated and therefore masked. The individual living with the effects comes to accept his difficulties as "the way life goes" or "the way I am."

We often think of trauma as a singular event in which something extraordinary and painful unfolds—a car accident, a crime or assault, a tragic event. But experiences that may seem rather common—such as divorce, a death in the family, or a surgical procedure—can also produce a traumatic stress response. The medical term "shock trauma" is used to describe the physical events related to traumatic injury. In the context of psychological trauma, shock trauma is often used to differentiate trauma related to specific traumatically stressing events—specific events that can be identified as discrete incidents—from those of a more chronic nature, such as ongoing abuse. Shock trauma would be considered a subset of the overall term "psychological trauma." In recent years, the vocabulary has evolved even further to include another form of trauma: developmental trauma (D'Andrea et al. 2012).

The most commonly used criteria for differentiating developmental trauma from shock trauma, or the more widely used term of psychological trauma, is that developmental trauma occurs in the first three years of life. However, some researchers and clinicians extend that timeframe to include the first four to five years of life (Perry 2006). The same experiences that would be categorized as traumatic are those that may also disrupt development overall. For example, research shows us that a child who has experienced severe abuse within her home situation will likely have a smaller brain, slowed motor development, and lower IQ than a child who benefited from a healthy home environment (Perry 2004a). A five-year-old child who has experienced significant trauma will often experience sufficient developmental delays that he will effectively function like a much younger child. The most common source of developmental trauma is fairly straightforward: When we were young, bad things happened, and those who should have been there to help and care for us did not come to our rescue or help us to navigate the situation.

The Adverse Childhood Experiences (ACE) Study, which will be discussed in more detail in chapter 6, has demonstrated the tremendous impact of developmental trauma, proving that children exposed to certain environments, experiences, and family dynamics face increased risk of physical diseases as adults. The ACE Study has specifically correlated childhood neglect and abuse with the later development of diseases, such as diabetes, heart disease, and asthma, in adulthood. This study has been critical to our understanding of developmental trauma—and there's still more to discover beyond this landmark study.

In this chapter, we note some of the earliest impacts of developmental trauma—including those of epigenetics, in which the traumatic experiences of previous generations may impact the health and well-being of subsequent generations. It's important for clinicians to understand that trauma may not be expressed primarily through the client's own narrative or his apparent trauma history. Not only may there be transgenerational impacts the client is unaware of, but the client may also simply be unaware that his experiences, which he sees as normal, may actually constitute trauma.

In the same way that healthy development builds over time in various aspects of our physical, psychological, emotional, and spiritual selves, unhealthy development also impacts multiple elements and layers of the self, some of which establish a foundational architecture that may result in greater sensitivity and diminished resilience in the face of challenge. In this and the next few chapters, we will discuss not only the impact of developmental trauma, but also how clinicians can begin to understand the complex dynamics and guises in which this form of trauma appears.

EPIGENETICS

Some clients arrive at our office doors presenting all the obvious signs and symptoms of developmental trauma but no known history of a troubled childhood. They report nothing out of the ordinary having occurred during their mother's pregnancy or after their birth. Then why do they show signs and symptoms of early trauma?

Epigenetics may provide one possible explanation. *Epi* means "above"—so *epi*genetic changes occur "above" the gene, not actually altering the underlying DNA sequence itself but rather the *expression* of those genes. Epigenetic influences are like a control panel that determines which genes are on and which are off. The term "epigenetics" refers to the study of trait variations caused by external or environmental factors that do this switching on and off—such as DNA methylation—and affect how cells read our DNA sequence, and it also refers to the impacts of these types of changes. Epigenetic research studies the process by which our genetic tendencies can be influenced or altered in their expression due to outside stimuli or exposures. These epigenetic changes may last through multiple cell divisions for the duration of the cell's life, and may also survive through multiple generations within a family line. The term "epigenetics" also refers to the changes themselves.

A new body of research is developing to help us better understand the environmental, cellular, and biological mechanisms that make these alterations possible. Although we don't fully understand these mechanisms yet, we do know that early trauma is one of the factors that can cause epigenetic changes. Furthermore, those epigenetic changes can then influence the genetic makeup and development of the next generation and beyond (Elsevier 2016; Kellermann 2013; Yehuda and Bierer 2007; Yehuda et al. 2016).

Children of Holocaust survivors, for example, are more likely to develop PTSD and other mood and anxiety disorders, whether or not they're exposed to traumatic events in their own lives (Yehuda et al. 1998). In this way, epigenetics can provide a "hidden" source of developmental disruption that may affect clients who don't have a matching trauma history to explain their symptoms. This is one of the possible manifestations of transgenerational trauma.

The ACE Study mentioned above proves that exposure to neglect and abuse in childhood can dramatically increase one's vulnerability to disease, and creates an increased risk of early death. Children of abuse survivors, Holocaust survivors, refugees, or others who survived traumatic experiences are more vulnerable to PTSD or anxiety. Children who "inherit" parental trauma and also experience trauma themselves experience a double-whammy of sorts, and may face symptoms that arise out of two sources of trauma and either commingle with, complicate, or contradict one another. As a result, some clients have more trauma to sort through, separate, and address than they might have ever expected.

Ongoing research suggests that greater vulnerability toward epigenetic impact exists for children of those with PTSD, of war veterans or survivors of war trauma, of refugees or torture victims, and of those who experienced childhood sexual abuse (Zerach 2016). This transmission of epigenetic changes did not appear to stop with the first subsequent generation, but also affected grand-children and great-grandchildren.

Animal studies have already pointed out that the HPA axis (hypothalamic–pituitary–adrenal axis), which is often referred to as the stress axis, is affected by prenatal stress—the mother's stress during pregnancy directly impacts stress responses in her offspring. (The interplay between the hypothalamic region of the brain and two of the endocrine glands—the pituitary and adrenal—creates the major neuroendocrine system that not only controls response to stress, but also regulates many body processes, such as digestion, immune response, sexuality, mood and emotions, and energy storage/usage.) Haley Peckham noted in 2013 that early prenatal stress in mice can be traced epigenetically to enduring changes in the HPA axis. Male adult mice whose mothers were subjected to mild stress early in the pregnancy had higher levels of chemicals, such as corticotropin-releasing hormone (CRH), that activate the HPA axis, and fewer receptors in the brain region that helps regulate the HPA axis. These mice also exhibited behaviors affiliated with depression, and, when subjected to stress, had higher levels of stress chemicals than did mice whose mothers had not been exposed to early prenatal stress. Early postnatal stress has also been linked to enduring epigenetic changes that alter the reactivity of the HPA axis. Also, in human studies a correlation has been found between experiences of trauma and neglect and changes in gene expression (Peckham 2013). Maternal stress in humans is also affiliated with low infant birth weight and pre-term birth (Duncan, Mansour, and Rees 2015; Wadhwa et al. 2011).

Human children have a long period of dependence on care providers, with a concurrent, extended period of brain development. The most rapid period of brain development takes place during the first three years of life. During this period, the brain creates an excess of synapses (Huttenlocher 1979; Huttenlocher et al. 1982), which allows for greater awareness of the environment and an increased response to external input. This "capture" of experience and learning is accelerated during these initial years, after which the brain begins to prune unnecessary synapses, consolidate necessary neural pathways, and further shape the brain structure and function (Huttenlocher et al. 1982; Huttenlocher and de Courten 1987; Huttenlocher and Dabholkar 1997). This ability to self-shape is referred to as plasticity.

Plasticity accelerates our ability to adapt to our environments more rapidly than if genes alone determined our wiring. In the case of healthy development, this is good news, because we can grow and change in direct response to the environmental inputs and demands we encounter as we mature. However, this also leaves us more susceptible to severe stress and its impact, which may then alter our genetic expression to the point that we may develop diseases, such as heart disease, that we might have otherwise avoided. We will discuss this effect more fully in chapter 6. Plasticity has another upside—we can heal from the effects of trauma by altering neural pathways in new directions. For example, baby rats bred with a tendency toward anxiety did not end up expressing this anxiety when they were paired with especially competent mother rats (Weaver et al. 2004).

Peckham's 2013 research also showed that reciprocally enriched positive environments—environments with varied but nonthreatening physical and mental challenges, like toys, running wheels, and peer play—can elicit different and positive genetic expressions. In the authors' clinical experience, we've gathered significant anecdotal information to indicate that even older adults can dramatically change health outcomes when the effects of traumatic stress are addressed. Resiliency research supports this view (Ong, Bergeman, and Boker 2009).

Epigenetics underline the importance of conducting a thorough history with our clients, and may provide the missing link for clients who report no trauma history but exhibit traumatic symptoms. For this reason, it's important that we venture beyond standard questions and inventories with our clients. Both client and therapist will benefit from an examination of not only recent or lifetime events but also the trauma history of the client's genetic past. What happened to parents and grandparents that could have significantly influenced the client's current symptoms or behaviors? Attending to these more historical questions can open a window to more beneficial and lasting treatment.

PRENATAL AND PERINATAL TRAUMA

We know the experiences of previous generations can impact us via epigenetics, but we sometimes forget that events for the fetus during pregnancy, as well as the mother's experiences during pregnancy, can have a similarly powerful impact, as noted above in the research related to the mother's stress during pregnancy.

In order to better understand the potential impacts of prenatal and perinatal trauma, it helps to understand these formative moments in the development of the fetus. During the first few weeks of a fetus's development, the survival brain (or reptilian brain) begins to form. Immediately after birth, this survival brain will oversee breathing, the heartbeat, and other survival functions within the body.

Fetal brain development begins with the growth of the neural tube. At approximately fourteen days, the embryo creates a layer of specialized cells known as the neural plate. This structure begins to fold onto itself with the flexibility we might ascribe to a tortilla. This folding process forms tube-like structures similar to pipes. As development of the neural plate continues, the edges of the folds fuse together completely sometime around the twenty-eighth day of growth. Through continued change, these tube-like structures form the brain and spinal cord.

Our first neurons and synapses begin to develop in the spinal cord. This development is believed to begin in the seventh week after conception, and the developing neurons and synapses allow for the first physical movements of the growing fetus. At this point, the fetus and its movements are so small and subtle that the mother rarely feels the changes in her system; but considerable, remarkable change and growth are taking place. The small movements of the fetus at this stage activate sensory input and encourage further development of the brain. These early, random movements gradually become more organized and intentional in the weeks that follow.

As the fetus grows into the second trimester, the gyri and sulci, the ridges and valleys of the brain, appear on the surface of the brain. Myelination, the formation of the electrically insulating fatty layer around nerve cells and nerves that speeds up the processing of information, begins to develop and continues all the way through adolescence. Reflexes that affect fetal breathing and reactions to external stimuli become more apparent. This is also a significant period for the beginning of learning. The brain will generate excess synapses through age three in order to increase the ability of the brain to receive and absorb knowledge and facilitate the learning process.

Because the brain and neurological system are in such a fragile and formative state at this point, disruptions during pregnancy can radically shift the trajectory of development. As Dr. Bruce Perry of the ChildTrauma Academy in Houston points out, injury during brainstem development during gestation and the first three years of life can disrupt the development of the brain as a whole, the neurons around the viscera, and much of the body (Perry 2009). This window of development to which Perry refers stretches from early fetal development through the third year of life, when the cognitive, thinking brain comes online. Perry identifies three potential threats to the developing brain during this phase that can inhibit an infant's normal neurological development: trauma in utero (intra-uterine insult); attachment trauma after birth; and other post-natal trauma (Perry 2009).

One of the most common forms of intra-uterine insult is maternal stress and anxiety during pregnancy. This is associated with an increased risk of miscarriage, shorter gestation, lower birth rate, and lower birth weight. Infants who experienced intra-uterine trauma tend to have greater difficulty being soothed or settled after a small emotional disturbance, and generally appear more fussy or temperamental, with increased reactivity. This directly interferes with the child's mental development. For boys, this exhibits as increased hyperactivity; for girls, it may exhibit as conduct problems; and for boys and girls, it exhibits as increased emotional problems more broadly (Perry et al. 1995).

There appear to be direct links, depending on the severity of the trauma, to later severe mental health diagnoses, such as schizophrenia and severe depression. Some research indicates that mild to moderate stress during pregnancy can have a more positive effect on the infant in the form of better motor development and a healthier immune system, whereas more severe stress has a more negative impact (DiPietro 2004). Of course, there's a fine line between moderate and severe, so the general definitions used from the perspective of science research may not hold for any given individual pregnancy.

However, during times of high stress, we secrete stress chemicals, such as cortisol, adrenaline, and noradrenaline, which prepare us for a threat response. These stress hormones are shared with the fetus during pregnancy, so if the mother experiences constant stress during gestation, these usually helpful hormones can instead have a negative impact on the development of the fetus.

The relationship between maternal stress and long-term impacts on later development of the child is well established. The greatest impact is seen in the development of the brain, but there are other wide-ranging impacts. Among these, maternal stress is affiliated with higher levels of allergies and asthma in offspring; it reduces blood flow to the fetus, reducing the flow of oxygen and other healthy nutrients that help the fetus develop normally; and it increases the secretion of CRH (corticotropin-releasing hormone) in the placenta, in turn activating higher stress responses in the fetus. "Early-life adversity shapes stress neurobiology, resulting in disturbed regulation of endocrine and autonomic processes (e.g., the hypothalamic–pituitary–adrenal [HPA] axis and the sympathetic–adrenal–medullary system).... Infants of mothers who have prenatally programmed biobehavioral sequelae from stress may, thus, inherit biological vulnerabilities that alter reactivity to subsequent challenges" (Wright and Bosquet Enlow 2008, 535).

There is also a significant body of research indicating that high levels of stress impede our ability to reason and utilize logical decision-making processes (Porges 1995). As a result, a mother may make poor choices about her diet and perhaps engage in higher-risk behaviors, such as smoking, that impact the fetus negatively. Stress usually disrupts sleeping patterns, as well, making it easier to feel overwhelmed by the needs and demands of pregnancy, including hormonal changes, physical changes, and even logistical demands, like scheduling and managing prenatal care. This can create an unfortunate spiral, whereby stress creates further stress for the mother and fetus, while also getting in the way of health care interventions that could potentially assist mother and child through the gestation period. These recent discoveries about fetal development have dramatically altered our understanding of the process and its complexities. As Dr. Allan Schore states, "One of the great fallacies that many scientists have is that everything that is before birth is genetic and that everything that is after birth is learned. This is not the case" (Schore 2013). Schore goes on to note that the infant brain at ten months contains more genetic material than at the time of birth.

Perry and Schore agree that the brain stem—the primitive brain responsible for autoregulation—is the only section of the brain that's well developed at the time of birth. The brain continues to grow and develop extremely rapidly over the next two to three years as myelinated neurons form elaborate connections with one another. There is no fixed recipe for ideal brain development, but environmental factors absolutely play a significant role, the primary influence of course coming from the primary caretaker.

Neurobiological development is most directly influenced by what occurs to the infant/toddler emotionally and psychologically within the first two postpartum years. The first nine months will have the most powerful impact on growth in the brain. As Schore points out, "Certain experiences are needed. Those experiences are embedded in the relationship between the caretaker and the infant" (Schore 2013). These experiences directly affect the part of the brain that involves the "emotional and social functioning of the child." Schore continues, "There's something necessary . . . that the human brain needs in terms of other human contact, for it to grow. It's a 'use it or lose it' situation. Cells that fire together, wire together. Cells that do not, die together." Without necessary stimuli during critical periods of growth, certain developmental functions may never be achieved. Schore and Perry both argue that without appropriate interaction and attunement with the fetus, and later with the infant, the brain will not develop to its full potential.

UNHEALTHY ATTACHMENTS

In conjunction with the formation of neural pathways in these early phases of development, attachment patterns become interwoven and extremely important in the continuation of that development. When attachment is disrupted or distorted, such as by extended separation from the caregiver, or by abuse, it will trigger a survival effort on the part of the infant or child. In such cases, the child's behavior is driven by this unresolved survival effort (fear with no remedy), which further contributes to unhealthy attachment patterns, such as anxious clinging and unremitting distress even when in contact with the caregiver. We can consider the different attachment styles summarized in chapter 1 as different types of survival strategies on the part of the infant and child.

As noted earlier, as infants and small children, we need our caregivers to provide us a sense of safety, as well as the necessary feedback to help us differentiate between positive excitation and will threat. Attachment problems make it difficult to differentiate between threatening arousal and positive arousal, resulting in a danger-oriented system with little to no integration of safety experiences, and thus mistrust of others and a sense that security is forever out of reach.

As an infant struggles to manage her arousal, she may be forced into attachment behaviors that help her limit and manage what feels like overwhelming levels of response. As we see in the Strange Situation study, for example, the infant or small child may ignore the mother or actively avoid contact with her when she returns to the room, as a way for the infant to manage her distress over her mother's absence. This way of reacting carries into adulthood and affects interpersonal relationships. As can be seen in figure 1, the caregiver's capacity for connection will impact the child's attachment behaviors.

There is a wealth of information available on attachment styles and their impact on relationships. It's beyond the scope of this book to provide an in-depth articulation of attachment dynamics. However, there is one category of attachment style that is particularly relevant here—disorganized attachment.

Caregiver behavior	Child's developmental attachment style
Available and able to use "coo" language ⟶	Secure attachment
Unavailable and rejecting language ⟶	Insecure attachment (avoidant)
Angry and confused about relationship ⟶	Insecure attachment (ambivalent)
Presents as frightening ⟶	Disorganized attachment

Figure 1: How a caregiver's capacity to interconnect with the child affects developmental attachment style.

Infants are born completely dependent on their caregivers; their survival is threatened without their caregivers' awareness of their needs. They cry when they need food, water, comfort, or rest, and look for their caregivers to meet those needs. When the caregiver is consistently unable or unavailable to meet the infant's needs, the infant constructs a new survival system to account for and accommodate the caregiver's absence. A lack of ability on the part of the caregiver to show constancy in her response may move the infant into an ongoing state of fright and terror that she must begin to manage. The infant will no longer be able to perceive safety and will therefore treat most situations as though they're riddled with possible threats. We also know from more current resiliency research that the lack of responsive care disrupts the development of the brain (Shonkoff et al. 2012), and has a limiting effect on the development of resilience.

Early research by Bowlby and Ainsworth did not include a classification for the fourth type of attachment—the disorganized/disoriented attachment style—although they had noted that some children did not fall into the other three categories. In her later research, Mary Main, with Judith Solomon, also noted that some infants had a much more difficult time utilizing coping skills and regulating their behavior. This fourth group was eventually categorized into a new attachment style (Main and Solomon 1986), and Main's research ultimately concluded that unresolved trauma and loss in a parent's life is the best predictor of disorganized attachment between parent and child. Main was specifically referring to developmental trauma in the parent's life. Via the Adult Attachment Interview, she observed that parents who had not resolved their painful pasts and created new narratives to explain their histories were more likely to exhibit overall and prolonged disconnection with and disinterest toward their infants (Main and Hesse 1990, 163).

These parents may have experienced early medical treatments that separated them from their parents, or experienced neglect, abuse, or unresolved trauma as young children. These early experiences reduced the parents' ability to regulate their own responses when aroused, often resulting in a complete lack of impulse control. This escalation into behavior that frightened the child or created circumstances in which the caregiver was noticeably frightened appeared to be the primary risk factor for disorganized attachment. We could say that these parents' lack of resilience was passed on to their offspring, at least in part via the attachment dynamics from their own unresolved trauma.

Although studies show that disorganized attachment is the rarest of the four attachment styles, as much as 80 percent of children with abusive parents are at risk of developing disorganized attachment. Epigenetically, disorganized attachment can be passed on for generations. The parents' limited capacity to regulate their responses can look like anger toward the infant/child—and may in fact manifest as anger toward the child—while the child has no coping skills to help him tolerate the scary parent. He is instead constantly on the lookout or preparing for another outburst, attack, or scary moment, and is rarely able to let his guard down.

Untreated disorganized attachment children tend to become disorganized attachment adults. Oftentimes their parenting toward their own children is confusing and unpredictable, which is one of the categories of behavior that contributes to disorganized attachment patterns. What are referred to as "affective communication errors"—contradictory behaviors by caregivers such as using soothing language while simultaneously moving away from the child's attempt to connect—are strongly correlated with disorganized attachment (Lyons-Ruth and Spielman 2004).

When a disorganized parent is unable to provide a safe haven for the child's development or provide co-regulation and help the child integrate self-regulation, the child is more likely to grow into an adult who is incapable of calming himself, and who will likely find relationships challenging.

Mary Main understood that any given attachment style, including disorganized attachment, is not a life sentence. Her research showed—and subsequent research has confirmed—that an adult with disorganized attachment could in fact move toward what is often called *earned secure attachment style* regardless of her history, given the right circumstances. The key factors in this transformation are a capacity to make sense of our past, and to create a new narrative that helps us understand our lives now. It is also often the case that those who move into an earned secure attachment have been able to establish a closer emotional relationship with someone who helps them develop more secure attachment patterns (Siegel 1999).

UNRELIABLE NEUROCEPTION

Children who experience limited safety and unreliable caring and connection also receive limited access to support that can help them differentiate between threat and safety. Their ability to accurately perceive safety and lack of safety may be distorted; the "filters" for determining whether something or someone is safe or unsafe don't function properly. As discussed in the previous chapter, children need consistent access to safety in order to support reliable differentiation between what is safe and what is not. Children also need access to a social group that provides congruent and consistent feedback about the environment so they can learn the cues and signals that indicate threat versus safety. Without that access, neuroceptive systems develop in ways that cause children (and later adults) to misunderstand or misinterpret internal and external environmental information. In other words, our interoceptive and exteroceptive processing provides misleading and inaccurate information.

As is true with many types of disruptions in functioning, we may have both exaggerated and inadequate versions of distorted responses. Both might exist in a single classroom, where two children respond very differently to the environment. One child might appear agitated, constantly scanning for potential threats, unable to settle and attend to the learning task. He is more likely to be engaged in boisterous and uncontained distraction behaviors. As noted in the previous chapter, we can expect that his agitated state has altered his hearing, making it difficult for him to distinguish the sound of his teacher's voice from the background sounds of the classroom, creating the appearance that he is willfully resistant to any corrections to his agitated behavior. He may be feeling anxious about what will happen during the lunch period, where he will be confined in a loud and chaotic environment that consistently overwhelms him, causing him to act out aggressively. He is now at risk for becoming the problem child in the group, disrupting the classroom and acting aggressively toward other children. Others around him will explicitly or implicitly label him as such and he will continue to behave according to those expectations, while also occasionally rebelling against those expectations through additional disruptive behaviors. He will continue to feel misunderstood and uncared for, participating in his own self-fulfilling prophecy.

Another child might be sitting quietly at her desk, apparently attending to the learning task but in fact numbed to any of the environmental cues around her, out of touch with her own experience of the room, and unavailable for any real social connection or learning. She sits by herself at lunch, keeping her distance from the other children. She is less likely to be flagged as having behavioral issues, but will likely perform below her actual skill level in the classroom. She is not exhibiting the same outward signs of stress, but underneath her physiology is putting the lie to that and impairing the functioning of her brain via release of stress chemicals. Both children are expressing their perceived lack of safety, but in very different ways.

In this example, there may be many children in that same classroom who are comfortable enough with the other children and the classroom environment that they feel sufficiently safe to engage both socially and in the learning tasks. There is congruence for them between the environment itself and their experience of that environment. Probably without being aware of it, they are responding to information both in their internal somatic dialogue, as well as in the external environment, evaluating it for safety or threat, and responding to that evaluation with physiological states that regulate their behaviors such that they are congruent with the setting.

Rebecca is an eight-year-old elementary school student. She was adopted by a single mom, Diana, when she was five years old. The details of Rebecca's first five years of life are sketchy, at best. Her mother relinquished parental rights after multiple arrests for prostitution and drugs. Rebecca still remembers her mother and can recall incidences of her mother having strange men in their motel room and her mother locking her under the bathroom sink so that she wouldn't be seen by the men. Rebecca has been diagnosed by the school psychologist as having oppositional defiant disorder. It is noted in Rebecca's records that she has been aggressive toward adults, teachers, and other children. She also exhibits impulsivity issues and oftentimes finds it difficult to follow directions or pay attention to her mother or teachers.

Diana has been referred for therapy for her daughter because of Rebecca's severe trauma history and the problems they're having with attachment dynamics. In the home, Rebecca screams in terror at random times and attacks her mother. Rebecca has a history of bedwetting and breaking items in the home. She has no close friends and is unable to express her true feelings.

Her teachers report that Rebecca is constantly moving around the room and talking. When asked to sit, she sits for short periods and then gets up and starts moving around again. She also seems to be looking toward the door and searching for other adults. At home, she is triggered when someone knocks at the door, or by other loud noises. Her mother reports that it seems like Rebecca is always on guard and ready to fight anyone at any time.

This high level of anxiety initially seems to increase when she begins therapy, but later begins to reduce. As the therapist focuses on regulation and safety with Rebecca, Rebecca is able to tell more stories from her early childhood and describe the lack of safety she experienced in her life. She reports that she still wants to be with her birth mother and that she is constantly expecting her new mother to abandon her like her birth mother had. She states repeatedly in sessions that she is planning on running away someday and finding her "old" family.

The therapist requests a meeting with the school psychologist, teacher, and Diana. During the meeting, after gaining more information about Rebecca's behavior in the classroom, the therapist realizes that Rebecca may have been misdiagnosed by the school psychologist. The therapist discusses and explains how neuroception provides the internal radar for safety, and that Rebecca's ability to sense safety or lack of safety in her immediate environment is currently limited. Diana's observation that Rebecca is always on guard and ready to fight at any time is probably an accurate description of Rebecca's internal state given her inability to notice when she is safe. Her aggression, her inability to pay attention, and her wandering may all be symptoms of both dysregulation and perceived lack of safety. Rebecca has never felt a sense of safety, and her early life provided little in the way of healthy development for the perception of safety to develop. As in Rebecca's case, faulty neuroception is frequently misdiagnosed as oppositional defiant disorder and other mental health diagnoses.

Because of the chronic lack of predictability and safety in Rebecca's early life, the therapist suggests emphasizing both of these as much as possible. The school district provides a teacher's aide who will be available for Rebecca in the classroom. Because Rebecca still finds men somewhat concerning, the aide is female and she is there each day (rather than trading shifts with other aides)—this provides the predictability and consistency Rebecca needs.

When Rebecca gets up to walk around the classroom, the aide goes with her, and they explore the room together, talking quietly about what Rebecca sees.

"Are there people in those cupboards?"

"I don't think so, but let's check just to be sure."

Now that the therapist has brought Rebecca's perceived lack of safety to the teacher's awareness, it's now understood that Rebecca's agitation in the classroom should be addressed differently than just insisting she sit back down. Part of the focus now is helping Rebecca feel safe in the classroom, and to provide predictability that will help her regulate. Slowly, Rebecca's "wanderings" around the room evolve into more focused exploration, eventually ending with her sitting together with the aide on the floor, with the aide quietly reading to Rebecca. Often, Rebecca ends up taking a short nap during story time.

While this work is happening at school, Rebecca's mother focuses on regulation, predictability, and safety. She warns Rebecca if she is expecting someone at the door, and that person is introduced to Rebecca with an explanation about why they are there. To strengthen their attachment, Diana and Rebecca are given some choices of repetitive rhythmic exercises to do at home so they can share activities that help build a sense of co-regulation. They choose a walking exercise in which they walk at the same pace, putting the same foot forward at the same time. Rebecca, in particular, likes this exercise, which she calls "marching with Mom." Rebecca is also paying more attention to moments when Rebecca seems to feel agitated or unsafe and responds by soothing and offering connection.

At home, at school, and in therapy, both Diana and Rebecca are encouraged to notice their internal selves and to use this interoception to notice how they are feeling, and what they anticipate might happen. Through regulation at home and at school, Rebecca's world begins to change. She's able to have a friend, and her grades begin to improve. Her mom reports that Rebecca no longer wets the bed and that her responses to triggers are reduced.

For someone whose neuroceptive system is poorly calibrated, her experience of the environment may not match the objective level of danger or safety around her. She may experience a sense of danger even when the environment is relatively safe, or she may miss the cues in her environment that indicate threat. What makes this even more challenging is that this perception doesn't arise from a cognitive process. A majority of this response system operates beneath the level of conscious awareness, driven by neurophysiological processes that developed over time in the context of the safety or lack of safety in which she was steeped during her early years.

The amygdala and hippocampus work together to provide an implicit and explicit referencing system that we use to evaluate new experiences. As noted previously, strong emotions give greater weight to certain experiences in our memory system, effectively creating a filter for our evaluation of safety and threat. If our early history contained many experiences lacking perceived safety, then we are likely to have mapped that experience more heavily and attuned ourselves to the perception of danger. We may be functioning primarily from a "danger map," rather than having access to experiential and memory mapping of *both* safety and danger.

From a neuroception perspective, this means we are more likely to interpret any new stimuli, any change in our environment (internal or external), or anything that gives unpleasant sensations as possibly dangerous, which is why healthy interoceptive development is critical.

INTEROCEPTIVE DYSFUNCTION

Interoception develops contextually. When this self-communication system is not tuned within the context of safety or when it develops without reliable feedback from our social group, it may produce unreliable conversations with ourselves, especially somatically. We may misinterpret healthy sensations and responses, and assign exaggerated or lopsided meanings that are incongruent with our outside environment, but we will be unaware of our errors. There can be a severe mismatch between our internal experience and that of those around us. We do use cognition in this process, but often to our own detriment. We are likely to construct a narrative that explains or dismisses that mismatch, such as believing those around us are naive and unaware of how much danger there really is in the world.

One of the "loudest" sources of interoceptive information is our visceral (organ) system, particularly the digestive tract. The autonomic nervous system is the primary supplier of information from our organs to our brain. Eighty percent of the fibers in its main nerve—the vagus—are sensory in nature, meaning it sends a tremendous amount of information about organ sensations back to the brain, making interoception a primarily bottom-up process (Porges 2011a). Understanding the functions of the vagus system is critical when working with developmental trauma, so we have devoted chapter 4 to a full discussion of this system.

For the moment, it's important to note that the interoceptive sensations arising from the viscera are more diffuse than the sensations delivered to the brain via the spinal cord, such as information from the skin. This makes it difficult to accurately label visceral sensations, or locate a specific source of information that's contributing to our inner experience. Visceral information is often sensed more as a general quality that imbues our perceptions with a felt sense that may take on important meaning, but for which we have little in the way of specific indicators, which makes the signaling process more prone to misinterpretation and misattribution. Difficulty with interoception has been linked to many of the same disorders that correlate with developmental trauma: anxiety disorders, trauma spectrum disorders, eating disorders, and drug and alcohol addiction (Garfinkel and Critchley 2013).

Interoceptive sensitivity (a heightened awareness of even the smallest interoceptive information) (Paulus and Stein 2010) has long been implicated in anxiety disorders. Those with anxiety tend to be extremely sensitive to their own interoceptive signals, tend to amplify those signals, and then tend to associate them with negative outcomes (Garfinkel and Critchley 2013). Research suggests that the more our interoceptive systems give us unclear information, or the more they create "noise" due to amplification of our bodily information (which, ironically, tends to make our perception less accurate), the more we tend to rely on our brains to more actively and more cognitively make sense of our bodily experiences, thereby imposing a top-down evaluation of interoception. This produces a self-referential looping of bodily sensation and meaning-making, which creates an unreliable witness to our own experiences (Ceunen, Vlaeyen, and Van Diest 2016).

Quinn, who identifies as gender queer and uses the pronouns they/them, had a history of multiple health issues, and of severe anxiety. It was rare for them to go more than a week or two without a panic attack. They also had a history of early neglect, having been sent to their grandmother's home as an infant after their single mother was killed in a car accident. Quinn's grandmother was resentful over the burden of having to assume full care of a young child, and attended only to Quinn's physical needs, while otherwise essentially ignoring Quinn. Some of Quinn's earliest memories are of sitting alone outside their grandmother's house, playing with rocks and sticks because they had no friends, no toys or books, and they weren't allowed to watch television.

Quinn's physical symptoms included dizziness, fatigue, digestive pain after eating, migraines, sensitivity to light and strong odors, and lower back pain that was persistent even after a back surgery to fuse their lower vertebrae. They had undergone a number of medical tests to try to determine the source of their dizziness, and had undergone a colonoscopy and endoscopy in an attempt to find the source of their digestive pain.

To try to manage their anxiety, they turned to mindfulness exercises they found on the internet. Unfortunately, that caused their anxiety to mushroom to the point that they were having almost daily panic attacks. Rather than being able to notice the sensations and then refocus attention elsewhere, their attention was now riveted by each and every new sensation that came into awareness. Each small twinge caused a cascade of panic that a new symptom might be emerging, and that each symptom would inevitably become yet another debilitating disorder.

Quinn was now locked in a terrible paradox of wanting to seek medical attention to be sure they were not ignoring an important symptom, but then the medical visits themselves triggered severe panic.

Quinn and their therapist embarked on many months of methodical work to increase Quinn's capacity for regulation and a sense of safety. This was coupled with work to find and track positive sensations, which started by tracking less alarming sensations and progressed to tracking what could then be identified as "positive" sensations. Quinn began to finally feel some relief from their symptoms. As Quinn's sense of safety increased, the need to carefully track every sensation decreased. "I'm less inclined to keep scaring myself with my own physiology now," Quinn said. As their access to self-regulation increased, panic attacks decreased in frequency and severity. Other symptoms, such as digestive pain, were also slowly changing, although stress still produced flare-ups of symptoms.

Our interoceptive systems enable us to make predictive assessments of our internal states. An example of this is knowing that we will soon need to use the toilet once we feel the first indicators of pressure in the bladder. This apparently routine process of information-gathering and responding to that information is part of a dynamic interplay between our physiology, behavior, and emotional state, which shapes our overall experience of self, and self in relation to other. Internal states, particularly visceral states, may provide motivational fuel for many behaviors, such as eating, drinking, and sexual activity, both implicitly and via cognitive awareness (Critchley and Harrison 2013).

The ability to notice our internal state, and make choices about what to do with that information, is an important part of our overall ability to regulate our physiology, affect, and social interactions in healthy ways. As Porges notes, "An important feature of autism, which is shared with other clinical disorders, is the inability to regulate visceral state in the presence of others" (Porges 2011b, 4).

With greater research being conducted on interoception, links with panic, anxiety, and other symptoms related to trauma are more firmly being established. Interoceptive sensitivity is correlated with social fear (Garfinkel and Critchley 2013), and the misattribution of bodily sensations is often implicated in panic and anxiety disorders—those with clinical anxiety disorders have a tendency toward interoceptive sensitivity, and even those whose anxiety has improved can still experience heightened interoceptive sensitivity (Ehlers and Breuer 1992; Garfinkel and Critchley 2013; Pollatos, Matthias, and Keller 2015). Those with anxiety disorders also tend to track their interoceptive experiences with a greater intensity of awareness, as well as amplify those sensations and attribute more negative meaning to them (Paulus and Stein 2010).

As might be apparent at this stage, the factors discussed in earlier sections of this chapter can create circumstances that make it quite difficult for a child to achieve healthy development as he matures. Even one of these factors on its own can be challenging, but they often occur in conjunction with each other. Making matters worse, these same factors—described in more detail below—can contribute to an inability to engage socially in appropriate and accurate ways. If we don't have an accurate framework to determine whether or not we are safe, and we can't accurately tell how we feel about something, we are more likely to be misattuned in our interactions with another.

SOCIAL MISENGAGEMENT OR MISATTUNEMENT

Without reliable feedback from caregivers, our ability to interpret social cues and engage with others in healthy ways is unlikely to develop fully. We may engage socially in ways that are inappropriate, unhealthy, or damaging, particularly if our neuroceptive and interoceptive systems are imbalanced and inaccurate, causing us to misinterpret the behaviors and facial expressions of others. Exposure to conditions that contribute to disorganized attachment can be particularly damaging to healthy social engagement practices. We may have received chaotic cues from our caregivers—angry faces, frozen expressions, aggressive body postures—but also received more attentive and inviting social cues at other times. We may have received inadequate social tuning to help us accurately interpret the facial expressions and other social cues of those around us. Damage to the amygdala, for example, renders us incapable of identifying fear in others (Adolphs 2008). Porges found that a functional neural platform that regulates the visceral state is necessary to support social behavior (Porges 2011a), and the neural platforms for social engagement and regulation are often compromised by developmental trauma.

In our earliest interactions with our caregivers, we are tuning our ability to interpret and respond to social cues, and cues about safety. In the healthy attachment cycle, the infant is asleep, the infant wakes up because of a need (either a diaper change or feeding), the need is met by the caregiver, and the infant returns to sleep. If the infant does not develop a sense that his needs are being met, his cry will intensify and his facial expressions will become grimaced to express his negative response to the caretaker's actions. His distress will grow at not having an attuned response. Even a newborn infant expects a level of face-to-face interactions with animated facial expressions and vocalizations. Studies by Olga Bazhenova (Bazhenova, Plonskaia, and Porges 2001; Bazhenova et al. 2007) and others demonstrate that when the face of the caregiver is not responsive to the infant, the infant will initially attempt to socially engage the caretaker with displays of animated sounds and facial movements (essentially turning up the volume on nonverbal communication). If this attempt is unsuccessful, the infant will become increasingly agitated, but will eventually move toward a collapsed and exhausted emotional state.

As we mature, there are more and more complex demands on our social capacity. If we have difficulty differentiating a friendly face from an angry face, or difficulty interpreting body posture and subtle facial expressions, we will likely be misattuned in our social interactions—perhaps even to the point of behaving in ways that are completely inappropriate to the social setting. This, in turn, will of course reduce our experience of belonging and connectedness, contributing to a feeling that we don't belong within the social circle. This can provide ongoing challenges when trying to create healthy and intimate relationships, and may interfere with our ability to maintain employment if we are unable to navigate the demands of social interactions in the work environment.

As will be discussed more fully in the next chapter, the development of our full social engagement system is dependent on healthy interactions with caregivers, accurate interoception and neuroception, and the capacity for self-regulation.

4

The Neural Platforms for Regulation and Connectedness

IN THIS CHAPTER, we focus on the autonomic nervous system (ANS), one of the physiological systems most profoundly impacted by early trauma. As has been discussed in previous chapters, there is a strong relationship between the development of our attachment styles and social systems, and the development of our physical, or somatic, systems. In particular, our early experiences—or lack of experiences—with social connection, which provide a sense of safety and security, help tune our physiological responses and provide the underlying architecture for healthy—or unhealthy—function later in life.

Here, we introduce the specific processes within the ANS that are influenced by developmental trauma. Before we can articulate the problems that arise when these critical physiological systems are disrupted, we need to first provide an overview of how these systems function.

POLYVAGAL THEORY AND ITS IMPLICATIONS IN DEVELOPMENTAL TRAUMA

The ANS regulates the function of our organs, such as the lungs, heart, and digestive system, as well as various processes that are essential for life, such as maintaining blood pressure and regulating sexual arousal. Dr. Stephen Porges developed a theory—the polyvagal theory—that hypothesizes greater differentiation within the ANS than has traditionally been understood in relation to ANS function.

Prior to Porges's articulation of the polyvagal theory, the standard framework for understanding the ANS described a two-branch system that worked reciprocally to regulate itself. The *sympathetic* branch of the ANS is the portion that prepares us physiologically for activity—exercise, active play, and threat responses that include active survival efforts, such as fighting or fleeing. We can think of the sympathetic branch as the "on" branch of the ANS.

Acting as a brake to the sympathetic system, the *parasympathetic* branch of the ANS prepares us physiologically for rest and relaxation, as well as other behaviors that require only low-energy or limited movements, such as nursing a baby. We can think of the parasympathetic system as the "slow," or "pause," branch of the ANS.

In this traditional model of the ANS, the sympathetic and parasympathetic systems work together in a reciprocal fashion to provide a balanced mix of activation and relaxation response to support the behavior or task at hand—greater activation of the sympathetic system for things like fighting or fleeing, and lesser activation for resting and socializing. Porges's model expands on this traditional model by proposing that there are actually two sub-branches within the parasympathetic system.

Porges has made tremendous contributions in helping us better understand the "neurophysiological foundations of emotions, attachment, communication, and self-regulation," as he describes it in the subtitle of his book *The Polyvagal Theory* (2011a). His theory outlines a map that helps us understand the complex dynamics of the development of the underlying physiological architecture for social engagement, the perception of safety, and self-regulation. When things go awry in the building of these neurophysiological foundations, the side effects reverberate in multiple areas of function.

Along with Dr. Peter Levine, who developed the Somatic Experiencing® approach to healing trauma, Porges articulated how important it is to understand ANS responses to threat when working with traumatic stress of any kind. For those with developmental trauma, it becomes even more imperative to understand how the neurobiology of trauma functions.

There is a tremendous amount of information available about the ANS, the impact of traumatic stress physiology on the ANS, and Porges's polyvagal theory, so we will not provide an exhaustive explanation here. In addition, the ANS is not the only system engaged in these responses—there are complex signaling responses within the brain and endocrine system that launch a cascade of physiological responses more complex than what is summarized here. For our purposes, we present a simplified version of the material to orient the reader to basic information on this topic.

The ANS is critical in supporting our co- and self-regulation capacities, because it helps regulate the physiological systems that support both activity and rest. These neurophysiological underpinnings are termed by Porges as the "neural platforms" that support different categories of behavior. Key to Porges's model is the understanding that healthy attachment and its related sense of safety support the development of healthy functioning of the ANS. That healthy development then supports meaningful connectedness and our ability to benefit from that connectedness. In Porges's model, we find an explanation for the crucial role early attachment and social engagement play in our healthy development. When our early attachment is disrupted, so are those important neural platforms.

The major nerve that mediates the parasympathetic branch of the ANS is the vagus nerve, the tenth cranial nerve. Porges's model is called the polyvagal theory (*poly* meaning "many," and *vagal* referring to the vagus nerve) because it further divides the parasympathetic functions of the vagus nerve into two sub-branches—the ventral vagus and the dorsal vagus, both discussed in more detail below. ("Ventral" refers to forward facing, and "dorsal" refers to backward facing, with regard to the areas within which these portions of the nerve arise in the brain stem.) According to this theory, we have two different but related pathways for slowing our physiology, or two different forms of the parasympathetic brake to apply to the sympathetic system.

The polyvagal model theorizes that the development of this system follows the phylogeny (evolutionary history) of vertebrates. The details of phylogenetics are not necessary for our purposes, but key components of that puzzle help us understand what occurs physiologically in response to threat. The first is that, under threat, we will try to mediate the threat using a reverse phylogenetic journey through our evolutionary development, beginning with the most socially and physiologically complex responses and descending to the most ancient and primitive responses.

We will first try to mediate the threat via social engagement or social behaviors, such as friendly connection, appeasement behaviors, submission, or negotiation. This utilizes the ventral vagus system. If that doesn't work, or if social engagement isn't appropriate because the threat is purely physical, we will then mobilize our active threat response, such as fight-or-flight behaviors like kicking, screaming, or running. This utilizes the sympathetic system. If our more active efforts to ward off the threat response are unsuccessful, we will then cascade into a physiologically induced freeze state, numbing ourselves to pain and causing physical immobilization (controlled by the dorsal vagus nerve). Although this process may sound the same as dissociation, Porges notes the difference this way: the freeze response is a physiological state; dissociation is a psychological construct.

Figure 2 summarizes the actions of each of the three branches of the ANS in accordance with the polyvagal model.

In the next chapter, we will discuss in more detail how the hierarchy of threat response just described is directly involved in the dynamics of developmental trauma.

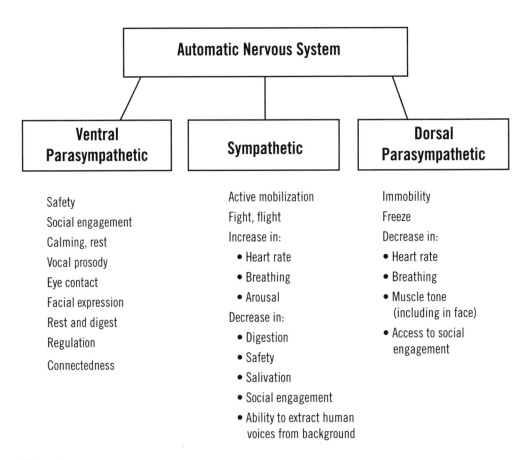

Figure 2

It's important to acknowledge (and these theories do) that individual humans are significantly complex and distinct from one another, so the same "threat" will not produce the same threat response in two individuals. In other words, the sequence outlined above will not necessarily be followed by every individual, even if the "input" or initiating event is equal. Nevertheless, this knowledge of the physiological process helps us understand Porges's perspective on traumatic stress, which can be termed the "polyvagal perspective"—the dominant perspective among biophysiological models of traumatic stress, such as the Somatic Experiencing® model.

This perspective, and the biophysiological model of traumatic stress in general, is foundational in our approach to working with developmental trauma (Porges 2007). To more fully understand developmental trauma and the symptoms it produces, it's necessary to understand how these two pathways for slowing our physiology (the ventral and dorsal vagus) function differently in relation to the sympathetic system.

THE VENTRAL VAGUS

This portion of the vagus nerve arises within the nucleus ambiguus in the brain stem. It is myelinated, meaning it's protected by a fatty covering that acts as electrical insulation for the nerve. Importantly, myelination allows the nerve to function quickly and accurately. We'll point to the importance of this again later in this section. The ventral vagus nerve is found only in mammals, and it supports the activities of social engagement. In fact, Porges's model is sometimes referred to as the polyvagal theory of social engagement.

The ventral vagus provides nerve supply for structures and organs above the diaphragm, such as the esophagus and bronchi of the lungs, as well as the structures of speech—the larynx and pharynx. It also communicates with the nerve that supplies the muscles of the face. This supports what we call "vocal prosody," or the ability to vary our vocal intonation and rhythm according to our situation and audience.

The ventral vagus also partly governs and influences regulation of the heart. It acts as a brake on the sympathetic system, slowing the heartbeat and lowering blood pressure. Because this portion of the vagus is myelinated, it can perform that function with accuracy and nuance. Porges refers to this process as the "vagal brake."

The vagal brake can also be lifted with equal accuracy and delicacy, allowing the heart's own pacemaker to increase the heart rate without needing to secrete the stress chemicals that would perform the same job neurochemically. This process is critical in the support of social engagement. The heart has its own built-in pacemaker, the sinoatrial node, which is a group of cells that spontaneously produce electrical signals that cause the heart to contract. When the vagal brake is lifted within a gentle enough range, the heart's pacemaker increases our heart rate, without our having to secrete stress chemicals that would signal the sympathetic system to activate more fully. In other words, the vagal brake allows us to react with greater discernment and less overall physical disruption. Although we might feel our heart rate increase, we would not feel the rush of adrenaline that would accompany a sympathetically induced activation response. This finely tuned interplay between the vagal brake and the heart creates a nuanced dance in our physiology that supports our ability to engage with others (Porges 2009).

When we are able to access this part of our physiological "platform," we have the physiological support for productive and helpful social behaviors—the ability to interact with others in ways that preserve our relationships and connections. Additionally, as will be discussed later in this chapter, lifting the vagal brake in this way conserves body resources that would otherwise be "spent" on the activation process.

Because the vagal brake is quick and accurate, we can slow and speed up our heart rate at a moment's notice, nicely supporting behaviors like social gesturing, storytelling, and laughter. We can change our vocal prosody and facial expressions in a lively and engaging way, and we can do all of this without secreting stress chemicals that disrupt other bodily systems. When this system develops properly, in a healthy, supportive environment, we benefit from a neural platform that brings us greater safety and more satisfying survival by letting us interact and bond with our social group with relative ease and responsivity.

Porges sometimes refers to the ventral vagus system as the portion of the nervous system that supports the perception of safety (Porges 2011a). If we have full access to this physiology, we likely had sufficient experiences of safety and connectedness in our childhood to lay down the architecture for those neural platforms. As we will discuss more fully in the following chapter, when we don't have reliable access to this aspect of our physiological function, we will inevitably develop compensation strategies to bridge the gaps in our neural platforms.

Although these strategies may "get the job done," they may do so in ways that are effortful or counterproductive.

One of the most important things to understand about the ventral vagus in relation to developmental trauma is that it takes time for its myelination process to occur. Myelination begins in the third trimester of pregnancy, and continues through adolescence, with the most rapid phase of myelination taking place during the first six months after birth (Porges 2011a). This means that during the first few months of life, and to a certain degree the first few years of life, we are dependent on our caregivers for many of the more nuanced functions of the ventral vagus system. Some of the methods for soothing via caregivers are built into normal parent-child behaviors. For example, the muscles used for suckling and mastication are "wired" via the vagus system to downregulate our heart rate when they're in use, which is partly why the infant will seek out the soothing activity of suckling and skin-to-skin contact to calm himself (Porges 2011a). Later in life, we may share meals and hugs with friends and family as a way of building and reinforcing these same soothing social connections.

Beyond these "built-in" mechanisms, the infant or small child relies on its caregivers to provide active soothing and comfort behaviorally, providing a sense of safety and belonging within the relational bond. It is through this ongoing interaction within the social engagement system that the neurophysiological "platforms" are consolidated and strengthened, providing the foundational requirements for resilience and access to healthy regulation.

THE DORSAL VAGUS

The dorsal vagus is the second sub-branch of the parasympathetic system, also slowing our physiology, but in a less nuanced way than the ventral vagus. It arises within the dorsal motor nucleus of the brain stem and primarily controls the organs below the diaphragm, although it also interacts with the lungs and heart, as discussed below. Unlike the ventral vagus, the dorsal vagus remains unmyelinated during our entire lifetime. This causes the dorsal vagus to act more slowly and with less accuracy than the ventral vagus; Porges refers to the dorsal vagus as the "sloppy" branch of the pair.

The dorsal system is considered a holdover from a phylogenetically more primitive system that was later adapted for other purposes in the human physiology. It developed within the group of diving mammals, the marine mammals that can remain underwater for more than a few minutes at a time. The dorsal vagus system is the aspect of the ANS that we associate with the freeze response, but it's more helpful for our purposes to recognize this system as having been adapted to enable us to conserve bodily resources. This is the part of our ANS, for example, that is dominant during the sleep phase, when we don't need to respond to environmental stimuli, move, or otherwise support activity.

Diving mammals can help us better understand the functions of the dorsal system and how it operates to conserve bodily energy. In these mammals, the system works in this way: Once underwater, without access to additional oxygen, a diving mammal must slow its use of oxygen, or make the limited oxygen it gathered at the surface last as long as possible. To do this, the mammal must shut down nonessential functions and limit the use of large muscles that require the greatest consumption of bodily resources. All air-breathing vertebrates, including humans, still retain the "dive reflex," whereby dunking the face into cold water will precipitously slow the heart rate and redirect the circulation preferentially to vital organs, particularly the heart and brain, rather than larger, active muscle groups.

In times of elevated survival stress, we may require an extreme version of this conservation physiology, provoking a rapid slowing of our heart and breathing rates, immobilizing our muscles, and increasing our pain tolerance. Under the influence of this physiology, we secrete analgesics that numb us to pain, increasing the probability of survival by allowing us to ignore or be less slowed by injury. Many predators are triggered in their predatory behaviors by movement, so inhibiting our movement via immobility responses—"death feigning," as this process is often called—will also increase the probability of our survival. This is the classic tonic immobility, or freeze, that is most typically associated with the dorsal system. However, as many studies point out, this is a high-risk survival strategy, with an increased risk of death when the heart is stopped rather than slowed (Porges 2007). Considering that the dorsal system is less nuanced and accurate than the ventral vagus system, any survival strategy relying on the dorsal system inherently brings greater risk, due to its more "ham-handed" approach to regulation. It simply lacks the speed and precision of the ventral vagus system, and therefore leaves greater room for error.

The dorsal vagus system performs two other critical, but sometimes overlooked, functions for our survival: it supports prosocial bonding behaviors and maintains health by regulating bodily functions, such as digestion.

The dorsal system's support of prosocial behaviors occurs using a process or approach that Porges refers to as "immobilization without fear" (Porges 2011a, 172). Behaviors such as cuddling or nursing require a certain level of immobility. When a mother is nursing an infant, for example, the mother must be still enough to allow the infant to nurse unimpeded. These functions are supported by the dorsal vagus system at the lower-tone end of its range of function. That is, rather than acting within the survival range of extreme conservation physiology that's precipitated by fear, it instead supports a more moderate level of immobility and conserves bodily resources only partly while we engage in behaviors that don't demand activity, or that relate to nourishment and satisfaction within the context of quiet social connection. This immobility "setting" allows us to engage in those behaviors without secreting stress chemicals or otherwise using too many bodily resources, increasing our sense of safety and interconnection.

Research by Sue Carter (2014) and others has shown that oxytocin, a neurochemical affiliated with bonding behaviors, appears to support social behaviors that promote experiences of safety—that quality of immobility without fear. Oxytocin is released not only during birth and nursing, but also when we engage in activities that increase social bonds and a sense of safety (Porges 2011a).

By contrast, immobilization *with* fear induces the dorsal vagus system to alter the physiology in potentially dangerous ways, such as the precipitous reduction in heart rate, as noted above, which of course is not compatible with the behaviors we associate with safety and bonding.

As with the ventral vagus system, we need a reliable experience of safety in social interactions in order to create the neural platforms needed for these social experiences of immobility without fear. In the absence of that safety, immobility will feel too risky, even dangerous, in which case our physiology will help us avoid that "vulnerable but cradled" feeling—because we don't trust it—and this will further disrupt future opportunities for connection (Carter 2014; Kozlowska et al. 2015).

In addition to supporting these types of prosocial behaviors, the dorsal vagus system helps regulate important functions that contribute to healthy homeostasis. It aids in the regulation of food intake, and the digestive process more broadly, by stimulating the secretion of gastric acid and other digestive substances. It also helps to maintain a healthy barrier in the intestinal lining and modulates intestinal immune response (Browning and Travagli 2014; Stakenborg et al. 2013).

THE COST OF DOING BUSINESS:
THE BALANCING ACT IN OUR PHYSIOLOGICAL RESPONSES

At birth, the functions of the sympathetic system and the dorsal vagus system are physiologically available to us immediately. As mentioned in the early part of this chapter, the ventral vagus system takes time to myelinate, meaning we have only limited access to its nuanced functions early in our lives, making us dependent on our caregivers for soothing and co-regulation.

When an infant is distressed and has moved into sympathetic dominance, she needs her caregiver to provide soothing via feeding, touching, making reassuring sounds, and responding to the specific source of distress by changing a wet diaper, or applying lotion to irritated skin, for example. If a caregiver becomes unavailable for extended periods of time, the infant faces increasingly limited options physiologically, in which case:

1. The child will continue to fuss and cry indefinitely, becoming inconsolable even when someone does eventually arrive, or until she is exhausted and falls asleep. This is based on sympathetic arousal.

2. Or the infant will cascade into the survival response of the dorsal system, moving into conservation physiology and becoming quiet and still. This is not immobility without fear, but the freeze physiology activating to conserve resources and preserve life—the tonic immobility that follows unresolved fear. This reaction originates in the dorsal vagus system, producing freeze or shutdown.

In either instance, the infant remains in a physiological state that is affiliated with survival effort. Survival physiology—either extreme sympathetic arousal or dorsal freeze—is meant to be a temporary state that serves the specific survival purpose of preserving life at all costs. These types of physiological responses evolved to provide short-term protection, turning on and off quickly to increase the survival response. They are not intended to function as quasi-permanent or long-term modes of being. When we experience repeated or chronic stress, these responses slowly begin to undermine the maintenance of homeostasis (stability, balance, and constancy in the body's internal functioning).

The term used for this is "allostatic load," a term coined by McEwen and Stellar (1993) that describes the physiological consequences of this stress exposure. One example of allostatic load is the repeated rise in blood pressure that occurs when someone is regularly exposed to stressful work situations. The body makes changes in blood pressure to respond to the stressors, which, in short and infrequent bursts, would help the stressed person adapt to the stressful situation. In the short term, such allostasis helps us adapt to our environment in helpful ways. However, when these blood pressure changes become chronic—because the stressful situation has become prolonged—the physiological changes will produce allostatic overload (McEwen, Seeman, and Allostatic Load Working Group 2009). Porges uses a simple phrase to express this concept: "the cost of doing business" (Porges 2011a, 95).

Individuals cope with challenges in a wide variety of ways, all of them influenced by factors such as genetic predisposition, exposure to early trauma or other life stressors, development of resilience, and lifestyle choices, such as smoking, overeating, or alcohol use. No matter the cause, allostasis comes at a price. The greater the intensity of our physiology in reaction to stressors, the higher the price we pay in wear and tear on our bodies and overall physiology. As the body is forced to adapt to repeated challenges, our physiological reactivity increases, which in turn increases the allostatic load, or the cost of doing business.

The body conducts a constant balancing act, working to allocate its resources to necessary functions without supplying too much or too little energy. Survival physiology uses a greater number of these resources, taxing the body beyond its ideal homeostatic mode. If we remain in sympathetic arousal for extended periods of time, we use more oxygen and nutrients, and secrete more stress chemicals. When the sympathetic system is dominant, we inhibit other functions, such as digestion and immune response, sending the physiological message that we are fighting for our lives. As a result, the functions that contribute to longer-term survival are set aside in order to free up our available physical resources for the active efforts of survival.

Physiologically, this is the equivalent of setting aside a maintenance project like painting the house because the basement is flooding. There is suddenly an emergency that immediately needs our attention, so we divert our energy to respond to that emergency and pause the routine maintenance tasks. Likewise, we will set aside physiological "housekeeping" tasks so that we can respond to the emergency of survival. In this way, we can say that high sympathetic arousal brings with it a high cost of doing business, or a high allostatic load. As other areas of the metaphorical house continue to be ignored, they too begin to deteriorate.

At the other end of the survival physiology spectrum, the dorsal vagus state of tonic immobility also carries a high cost of doing business, but for a very different reason. The dorsal physiology is conservation physiology, and the highest end of that spectrum is the extreme conservation that comes with the death-feigning response. Thinking back to the example of a diving mammal, if we are fully in tonic immobility, the body is responding as if we are under such severe threat that we need to conserve all bodily resources at all costs.

Physiologically, this is the equivalent of setting aside our house-painting project because we lost our job and ran out of money. We are now focused on preserving any remaining resources for food and other essentials, so the maintenance project must be set aside until we have enough resources available to ensure our survival, and enough extra to "spend" on maintenance. We will again set aside "housekeeping" tasks in order to respond to the extreme conservation that the dorsal system demands, creating a high allostatic load.

If we are chronically limiting physiological maintenance functions, such as immune response, uptake of nutrients via digestion, and access to replenishing rest, while at the same time ramping up our survival physiology (which also increases allostasis), then the wear and tear on the physiological system becomes severe. This is how developmental trauma increases the risk of significant health issues over time. The Adverse Childhood Experiences (ACE) Study, discussed in more detail in chapter 6, has clearly demonstrated this correlation.

We believe that at least part of the reason for these outcomes is that developmental trauma tends to induce a greater physiological reliance on survival physiology (high sympathetic arousal and/or high dorsal conservation states), in large part because we have not experienced reliable access to a sense of safety, so the development of the neural platforms for both social engagement and immobility without fear have not occurred as fully as they would have otherwise. The result is somewhat limited access to the physiological platforms that also support critical functions, such as healthy immune response, healthy digestion, and sleep—the hallmarks of good physiological housekeeping and maintenance, and resilience.

In addition to the physiological toll, the lack of healthy development of the full range of ANS response also takes an emotional and psychological toll: "[O]ur research program provides data supporting the hypothesis that the ability to sense and regulate internal physiological state is at the base of competencies in higher-order behavioral, psychological, and social processes" (Porges 1993, 16). In other words, our ability to self-regulate physiologically provides the underlying architecture for more complex behavioral, psychological, and social capacities.

The most highly paced time of development in the human lifetime is the window between conception and three years of age. When we spend too much time during this window in a state of survival physiology, we are not building the neurophysiological architecture that will fully support regulation and connectedness. Knowing the extent to which our very early lives shape our neurological hardwiring, it makes sense that early, sometimes forgotten disruptions in our development can dramatically alter the way we experience the world, ourselves, and others.

5

The Side Effects of
Developmental Trauma

WITHOUT ACCESS TO HEALTHY ATTACHMENT, consistent co-regulation, and the related sense of safety these produce, the neurophysiological platforms for self-regulation may be disrupted, resulting in dysregulation, or impairment of regulatory mechanisms. For our purposes in this chapter, it's important to understand that a lack of regulation is likely to affect all layers of the self: physiological, behavioral, emotional, and social. Symptoms might appear in any, or all, of these aspects of the self. As noted in the introduction, self-regulatory capacity is one of the protective factors affiliated with resilience (Shonkoff et al. 2015).

In the previous chapter, we discussed the role of the ANS in regulating the neural platforms for social connection, perception of safety, and survival response. Although the polyvagal model proposes that response to threat will generally engage different aspects of the ANS, depending on the category of threat—the sympathetic system for active threat response, and the parasympathetic system for either social engagement or the freeze response—Porges himself acknowledges that in actual practice, the mechanisms of threat response will not occur in well-defined phases, but are better characterized by what we might call "transitional blends" (Porges 2011a), with different aspects of the various systems sometimes in dominance, and others engaged in lesser ways simultaneously. Likewise, our social engagement process may include a wide range of blended physiology, depending partly on how active we are during social interactions, or perhaps how stressful we find such situations.

We may see this not only in physiological responses, but behaviorally as well. It's not uncommon to see a child simultaneously clinging to a parent, while also hitting that parent. The child is being angry and aggressive, but also needs connection with and reassurance from the parent.

A great deal of research explores the stress response and ANS function in children in relation to child-parent conflict, marital discord, family conflict, and social stress. We focus here on a specific aspect of ANS function, one that's particularly relevant when working with clients who experience more severe dysregulation, the type that arises when the ANS no longer works within the reciprocal range of response.

FOUNDATIONAL DYSREGULATION

In this section, we focus on what happens when access to safety is so lacking that dysregulation becomes pervasive, to the point that it sets the foundation for the development of the person as a whole—what we are calling *foundational dysregulation*. This would most typically overlap with the disorganized attachment category.

Our description of the ANS in the previous chapter assumes a reciprocal action in ANS responses, as described in figure 3.

When the sympathetic system is in high tone (meaning it's more fully "on"), the parasympathetic system should be in low tone (meaning it's not exerting its braking mechanism on the sympathetic system). Conversely, when the parasympathetic system is in high tone, the sympathetic system should be in low tone, and the result is less activity in the physiology. When exercising, for example, the parasympathetic system should be in low tone, allowing our sympathetic system

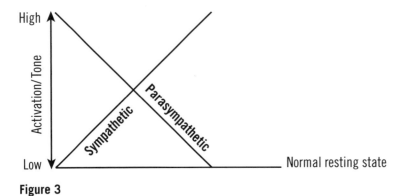

Figure 3

to activate and increase our heart rate, power up our oxygen use, and release nutrients at a higher rate so we can sustain activity. When the ANS is functioning in this way, it's considered to be within a typical reciprocal range of response.

Even within this reciprocal range, there is still room for the stress response, or ANS responses that eventually become maladaptive. For example, harsh parenting, marital conflict, or controlling parental behaviors are linked to children who exhibit chronic low vagal tone, meaning their sympathetic systems remain in a higher activation state on a more ongoing basis, with chronically inadequate braking from the parasympathetic system. This ANS response is in turn associated with anxiety, behavioral issues, and other mental health problems. In the face of chronic stressors within the family environment, the child's sympathetic system may continually activate as part of his threat response, increasing the allostatic load and potentially leading to sympathetically driven behavioral responses like aggression. The initially adaptive stress response, over time, becomes maladaptive and increases the risk that the child will develop physical or psychological health issues (Erath, El-Sheikh, and Cummings 2009; Hinnant, Erath, and El-Sheikh 2015; Krishnakumar and Buehler 2000).

All of this can happen even with the ANS working within its reciprocal range. However, some theoreticians and researchers have extended this bidirectional view of the ANS to include a model that theorizes a more complex responsiveness in the ANS not limited to reciprocal response. Ernst Gellhorn, Gary Berntson, and Peter Levine have all demonstrated nonreciprocal forms of ANS function that can be affiliated with accumulated stress responses (Payne and Crane-Godreau 2015).

Berntson's autonomic space model (Berntson et al. 1994) provides a helpful vocabulary for understanding this nonreciprocal behavior of the ANS. Returning to our graph in figure 3, in that model, the reciprocal range provides coherent signals that create the same directional response in the physiology: sympathetic activation is matched with parasympathetic inhibition, both of which upregulate physiological responses such as heart rate and breathing; or parasympathetic activation is matched to sympathetic inhibition, both of which downregulate physiological responses, creating a more calm and settled reaction. In other words, the physiology is working cooperatively to move responses in a coherent way along the same continuum of either activity or rest.

The nonreciprocal range, by contrast, activates or inhibits the ANS in both directions simultaneously. The terms that Berntson uses are "coactivation" and "coinhibition." *Coactivation* means that both the sympathetic and parasympathetic systems activate at the same time; *coinhibition* means that both decrease action at the same time. Because the sympathetic and parasympathetic systems mediate opposing physiological actions, this version of ANS functioning causes the body to work against itself, trying to accomplish opposing physiological actions simultaneously, creating ambiguous responses physiologically, as shown in figure 4.

Research findings suggest that reciprocal responses in the ANS may indicate that the body's physiology can respond sufficiently in an adaptive way via evolutionarily more advanced forms of responses, as outlined in the polyvagal theory. This means that the more nuanced ventral parasympathetic responses would be readily available. By contrast, nonreciprocal ANS function is most commonly

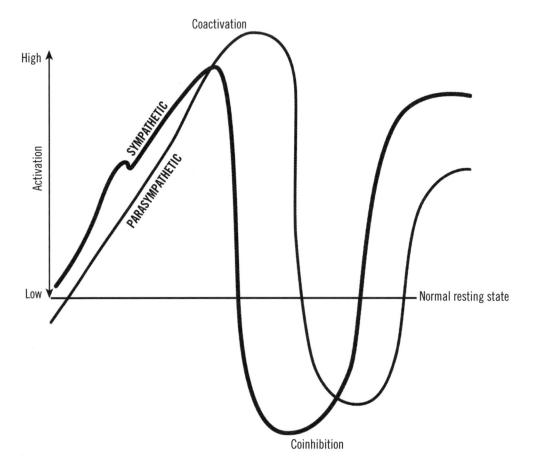

Figure 4

affiliated with a breakdown in regulation in response to accumulated stress, and is implicated in maladaptive behavioral responses in children, as well as a host of health issues (El-Sheikh and Erath 2011). In the following chapter, we will more thoroughly discuss some of the health implications of this form of dysregulation.

Levine's Somatic Experiencing model of trauma recovery describes this form of nonreciprocal ANS function as one of the more challenging versions of traumatic stress physiology. This nonreciprocal physiology tends to produce a self-fulfilling loop of dysregulated responses. It most typically develops in the context of early trauma, connected to events like chronic hospitalizations or family conflict that limit the child's access to healthy attachment and co-regulation. But the dysregulation itself tends to create exaggerated or chaotic responses in the child, so that later attempts at healthy attachment or co-regulation will not be fully effective. The child is unable to attain adequate self-regulation and affect regulation, so circumstances and physiology conspire to destabilize the architecture for safety and regulation. When the early foundation is wobbly, everything built on top of it becomes unstable.

Foundational dysregulation makes it difficult to regulate responses and interactions, in part because the physiology does not support social engagement, connection, or perception of safety. In fact, the responses of the physiology often signal threat or danger—and this is likely happening almost continuously. Lack of regulation causes more extreme responses to frightening experiences (and causes more experiences to be perceived as frightening), causing the amygdala and hippocampus to give higher "value" to those memories and response patterns, essentially creating neurochemical memory markers that make those memories more potent and long-lasting (Janak and Tye 2015). When we then access our memories and their affiliated lessons about past experiences, we effectively "find" more information about threat, which can then reconfirm the idea that our environment is dangerous. We then enter the self-fulfilling loop in which our dysregulation signals threat, our memory of past experiences confirms that a threat is indeed present, and our threat response kicks into gear. At this point, others are likely to respond as if they too are threatened. Friends or family members may adopt defensive or conflict-oriented postures in reaction to us, only confirming our feeling of being attacked or threatened, when it was truly our own behavior that provoked the defensive response in the first place.

In effect, we may be filtering our environment without awareness of it, giving more weight and attention to the smallest possible indicators of threat (or lack of safety) (Janak and Tye 2015). If this has been happening since we were very young, our neuroception becomes "miscalibrated," tuned much more acutely toward perception of threat than perception of safety, even when safety is available. We feel constantly under threat, and we respond accordingly—perhaps with aggression—and those around us react to our aggression and confirm our experience of being under threat. Or we drop into freeze mode and become numb to or dismissive of offers of connection and support, which is soon withdrawn because we failed to embrace it.

Experienced clinicians learn to recognize this form of foundational dysregulation, especially when the physiology isn't operating within the reciprocal range. By itself, this level of dysregulation tends to indicate sufficient challenges to the development of co- and self-regulation that the safest clinical assumption to make is that developmental trauma may have occurred. This will provide the most conservative perspective from which to decide on treatment interventions. If this level of dysregulation is coupled with a known early trauma history, then it is a sure sign that the clinician needs to proceed slowly. There is often difficulty in supporting change because the physiology can swing from high arousal to dorsal freeze very quickly, making it difficult for the client to even process conversation, or to respond to offers of connection and reassurance. Clients will tend to be both reactive to and filtering for threat; they are driven by their survival physiology in ways that can overcome their own best intentions to stay present and connected to their here-and-now experience of safety.

John is forty-five years old and has been married to Maria for more than twenty years, after they met on a blind date while both were seniors in college. They had known each other for only two weeks when they decided to marry. The marriage had many problems from the beginning, but the couple remained together. Maria often says that she married John for better or worse, and this has turned out to be "the worse."

After college, John opened a small travel business. At first, he seemed excited and engaged in the business but quickly began to feel stressed and then developed health issues—in particular, he had trouble sleeping. The economy was changing at the time, and people were choosing to make travel arrangements online. After five years, the business was failing. He was no longer able to pay rent for the office or make payroll for his employees. He found himself drinking more, to try to relax, but the alcohol only further disrupted John's sleep.

John developed severe migraines, which were triggered by bright lights and noise. He lost more than thirty pounds as a result of the stress and the migraines, and his health concerns expanded to include high blood pressure and elevated glucose levels.

After the business went bankrupt, John withdrew, spending most of his time in his room in the dark. He no longer wanted to sleep with Maria and would watch hours of mindless television. He soon stopped bathing and almost completely neglected his basic hygiene. He developed stomach cramps, and began fighting more and more with Maria.

John's physiology was producing the typical mixed physiological responses that accompany foundational dysregulation. He was simultaneously stressed and revved up, but also withdrawn and experiencing low energy. He had trouble sleeping at night, but dozed throughout the day in his dark room.

His sympathetic arousal was activating at different times without any apparent threat, and he then felt unable to settle. He was also feeling drained and overwhelmed. He spoke of feeling hopeless and of wanting to die. At Maria's insistence, John went to see a somatic trauma therapist, who was experienced enough to understand that the symptoms John was experiencing might indicate an early traumatic history. Initially, John became angry and defensive toward the therapist for even asking about his early history, insisting that his symptoms were only about the stress from losing his business.

When the therapist worked with John's arousal level during that session, he then plunged into a three-day sleep binge, with an almost continuous migraine—which he had never experienced before. The therapist then focused more on educating John about the possibilities of what his symptoms might mean in terms of dysregulation, and that helped John recognize some of the swings in his responses that he had been experiencing. In that discussion he revealed that he grew up with an alcoholic father who, when drunk, would hit John's mother in front of John and his brother.

With John more aware of how slowly the work needed to go, he was more willing to take small steps in working with his stress responses, and he had more understanding of what the withdrawal and low-energy states were about. He also had a better understanding of how the early lack of safety in his home situation might be influencing his symptoms.

Although it was clearly going to take a long time to untangle his symptoms and build his capacity for better regulation, for the first time John felt like he had a roadmap for how that might happen.

COMPELLING SURVIVAL PHYSIOLOGY

To differentiate threat physiology from our nonthreat physiology, we use the term "survival physiology" to describe the high-tone sympathetic (high-arousal state) or high-tone dorsal parasympathetic (freeze) physiology that's triggered when we respond to a perceived threat. It helps to think of these two physiological responses situated at the far end of the spectrum in either the sympathetic or parasympathetic response systems. They are meant to be time-limited, and, as discussed in the previous chapter, they take a large toll on us physically, creating a high allostatic load if we stay in these physiological states for extended periods.

The nature of survival physiology is that it's meant to function somewhat like a runaway train. Once it's initiated, we are almost powerless to stop it because we can't afford to deliberate at length about whether there may be a more rational explanation for what's going on, or whether the threat may not be as severe as first thought. We are instead driven by the survival imperative to simply respond immediately. When our own lives are at stake, we can't afford to take chances.

Survival physiology brings urgency and extinguishes curiosity and creativity. As noted in previous chapters, under the influence of high sympathetic activation, we experience significant changes in our physical systems—in our hearing, as well as in the way our brain processes information and memory—that cause us to "filter" our environment for threat and defense. Conversely, under the influence of high dorsal parasympathetic tone, we are numbed to our own sensations and may experience a sense of being disconnected from ourselves and our environment. At the highest tone states of the dorsal system, we will fall into a physiological freeze state.

None of these extreme physiological responses are compatible with logical thought, social connectedness, or a balanced response to our environment and others in it. We are instead driven to act in self-protective ways to resolve the immediate survival challenge. If we've had a healthy beginning, these survival responses will likely be time-limited and happen congruently within the context of the actual survival threat. Our level of response is likely to be well matched, more or less, to the true level of threat. Once the survival task has been accomplished, or we realize that our survival was not in fact under threat, we will return to a balanced physiological state that will support activities other than survival.

Porges describes it this way:

To effectively switch from defensive to social engagement strategies, the mammalian nervous system needs to perform two important adaptive tasks: (1) assess risk, and (2) if the environment is perceived as safe, inhibit the more primitive limbic structures that control fight, flight, or freeze behaviors. Any stimulus that has the potential for increasing an organism's experience of safety has the potential of recruiting the evolutionarily more advanced neural circuits that support the prosocial behaviors of the social engagement system. (Porges 2009, 88)

That is, when we experience a greater sense of safety, we are more able to stay within the social engagement system (ventral vagus), and will be able to inhibit the more primitive survival responses of fight, flight, or freeze.

If, on the other hand, we have not had reliable access to safety, we may not be able to perform the adaptive tasks of accurately assessing risk or perceiving safety in the environment. Our survival physiology may operate as a chronic background state (or filter) for everything we do and experience. We will be more easily catapulted into the urgency of survival effort, and our physiology will respond as if extreme threat is present. We will be more likely to overrespond—or, if our dorsal physiology has become the more dominant physiology, underrespond—to the experience of threat. If our ANS has moved into the non-reciprocal range, our physiology may be chaotic and unable to marshal an organized response to even the smallest stimulation. Our survival physiology may be screaming *run!* and *freeze!* at the same time, overwhelming our ability to sort out these signals so that we can determine what the actual threat might be, and figure out how to respond.

Survival physiology is the equivalent of a sled full of rocks sliding down a snowy slope. The more rocks we have on board, the heavier the sled and the greater the momentum will be. The more extreme the survival physiology, the more it "loads" our responses, the more irresistible it becomes, and the less control we have over our reactions. When our sense of survival is threatened from an early age, our survival physiology may no longer be time-limited; it may become our "normal" physiology. As noted in the previous section, high levels of sympathetic arousal can become our "resting" state, giving us unreliable access to the ventral parasympathetic physiology of social connection. Or we may be numb and apathetic, with our dorsal physiology remaining dominant more than is healthy. In either case, there will be other profound changes in the way we function. It's not just our physiology that's affected—all aspects of the self are impacted when survival physiology usurps our ability to engage with ourselves and others from an internal place that recognizes safety.

When our physiology cannot do its job, survival impulses become distorted in somewhat predictable or identifiable ways, which manifest physically, psychologically, behaviorally, and socially. Without the neural platforms to support healthy social connection, it's very difficult to access co-regulation or self-regulation, or any felt sense of belonging and connection—the very things we need most to help us move out of survival physiology. The maladaptive responses that occur in the absence of healthy regulation then interfere with access to the very regulatory states we are trying to support.

As clinicians, it's important that we understand how survival physiology drives responses in ways that will not make sense when viewed from a nonsurvival perspective. If we can more fully understand the dynamics created by early survival efforts, then we are better able to assist our clients.

LOCUS OF CONTROL

In the 1950s, the American psychologist Julian Rotter developed the model of internal and external locus of control. This model has since been explored more fully in different contexts, and is used in psychology, business, and self-development coaching to help people understand some of the behaviors and belief systems related to their sense of control around the outcomes of events in their lives.

Those with a strong internal locus of control tend to believe they're able to influence the outcome of their experiences, take responsibility for their actions, and take less interest in the opinions of others. They also tend to be high achievers, and attribute negative outcomes to their own failings. Those with a strong external locus of control tend to believe that life is controlled by others, or by external elements they cannot influence, such as fate or luck, and tend to blame others for what happens in their lives. They may also have a stronger sense of faith in letting outcomes rest in the hands of others. Rotter (1975), in his later work, was careful to point out that locus of control lies on a continuum, so that each individual will have a blend of the characteristics associated with each locus. Each has some strengths and challenges. However, those with a stronger external locus of control also tend to be more stressed and prone to clinical depression (Benassi, Sweeney, and Dufour 1988). A sense of self-efficacy and an internal locus of control are both protective factors affiliated with resilience (Shonkoff and Phillips 2000).

We introduce this model here to articulate how clinicians can begin to understand some of the dynamics that typically occur in the wake of early trauma.

For infants, the locus of control is always external. They are dependent on someone else to feed them, change their diapers, and soothe them. In the process of co-regulation and the transition to self-regulation, the infant should experience a reliable caregiver stepping in to attend to disruptions in the internal state—providing a blanket when the infant is cold, for example. Within this state of reliability, the infant is able to move into the external environment with a sense of safety, curiosity, and engagement. As Porges notes, "Response strategies reflect the stage

---

Examples of Locus of Control

Internal Locus of Control

- Is not very interested in what others think or their opinions

- Has a sense of confidence when challenged or confronted

- Typically is healthier physically

- Has a strong sense of self-efficacy; is able to set goals and works hard to achieve them

- Reports being happier and appreciates independence

- Typically works better at her own pace

External Locus of Control

- Frequently blames others for his circumstances

- Is quick to give credit to others, luck, or circumstances

- Has a sense of powerlessness; believes he doesn't have the ability to change his circumstances

- Meets challenges with hopelessness or powerlessness; is prone to learned helplessness

---

when internal needs become less important than external needs—when the baby (fed, burped, and changed) is ready and eager to interact with the world of people and things" (Porges 2011a, 80). When the infant does not have to attend to her internal needs, such as hunger and cold, she is free to become curious about the outer world.

Attentive caregivers who respond appropriately in fulfilling infants' needs support this process of building the continuum of internal to external locus in a healthy way. This allows for the healthy process of co-regulation, which helps the infant/child slowly develop the ability to self-regulate. In this context, the child would eventually develop access to the full continuum of locus of control—a sense of agency in her ability to influence her environment, and an ability to notice that some outcomes are in fact outside of her control and she must therefore adapt to those outcomes without blaming herself for the results.

The same experiences that cause developmental trauma also tend to disrupt the healthy development of locus of control. Disorganized attachment, especially if it's accompanied by nonreciprocal responses in the nervous system, is likely to be affiliated with a disorganized sense of locus of control. Given that developmental trauma occurs during a time when we are developmentally dependent on our care providers—our actual external locus of control—it is not surprising that many of those with early trauma tend to be farther along the continuum toward extreme external locus of control, sometimes feeling that they are being victimized by the outside world, or by specific categories of people who they experience as being in authority—the police, a boss, the government. On the other hand, those with a disrupted internal locus of control may have an extreme sense of responsibility for all experiences in their lives—even those completely outside their control. They may believe that all bad events and outcomes are their fault, or that they are fundamentally bad people who cause (and deserve) bad events and outcomes. We will discuss this important aspect of the side effects of developmental trauma more fully in chapter 7.

We can now see some of the elements that come together to produce maladaptive responses that challenge the restoration of healthy functioning in those with developmental trauma: dysregulation in various systems; survival physiology that drives survival behaviors outside of a survival context; and a distorted sense of control or lack of control. In combination, these will invariably produce compensation and management strategies that we term "defensive accommodations."

DEFENSIVE ACCOMMODATION

In the previous sections of this chapter, we articulated some of the dynamics that produce a real or experienced sense of being out of control—of our own physiology, of our responses to our environment and others in it, and of our own capacity to influence the outcomes of our experiences. Even for an infant or small child, this lack of access to regulation and coherency in experience will feel intolerable. We will create compensating mechanisms and do our best to manage the overwhelming experiences that result when dysregulation and lack of safety are severe. We will develop somatic and physiological strategies, as well as sometimes elaborate behavioral and belief systems, to substitute for genuine regulation.

Rather than some of the terminology more typically used, such as Bernard Brandchaft's "pathological accommodation" (Brandchaft 2007), we prefer the term "defensive accommodation" for these management strategies. When we refer to the management of overwhelming experience, we include not only behavioral but also somatic maladaptations used as survival responses to developmental trauma. Most other models of accommodation address primarily psychological and behavioral responses.

The basic theories about accommodation originated with Sigmund Freud, but Jean Piaget articulated his model of cognitive development in a form that included accommodation in the way it is now more commonly used. Piaget's model articulated how each of us works to integrate our knowledge and experience of the world as we progress through our cognitive development. Piaget used the term "schema" to describe how we organize our knowledge—how we create our own personal worldview, so to speak (Gruber and Vonèche 1977).

Brandchaft (2007) uses the term "pathological accommodation" to describe the deep-seated form of accommodation that develops in the face of early trauma. This form of accommodation, according to Brandchaft, includes all the ways we might unconsciously take on the beliefs and feelings of another, while giving up our own experiences, in order to preserve connection and attachment bonds that have been traumatically threatened. This is seen as originating with the child's attempt to protect himself from "intolerable pain and existential anxiety" (Brandchaft 2007, 667) when parents do not provide access to regulation, and instead demand that the child respond to their (the parents') needs. That is, the parents' own insecure attachment, or lack of self-regulation, prevents them from offering co-regulation to the child, and instead demands that the child respond to and attempt to compensate for these deficiencies. This is, of course, usually driven by subconscious needs and impulses.

Brandchaft describes this dynamic: "Within a secure developmental attachment system, sensitive caregiver responses form harmonious sequences with the child's distinctive experience. Where repeated trauma prevails, the child's natural rhythms and psychological states do not initiate harmonious interaction responses. Instead, the attachments serve as pathways for responses centered in the caregiver's own insecure attachment patterns" (Brandchaft 2007, 674).

We prefer the term "*defensive* accommodation"—rather than "*pathological* accommodation"—because, in the context of early trauma, these accommodations are part of the child's survival effort. The child forms these strategies to defend against the overwhelming feelings of helplessness, terror, or loss of connection that would be too painful to fully experience. Sometimes these accommodations take the form of behavior, as Brandchaft notes, of the type we would see in insecure attachment styles. Sometimes the accommodations manifest physiologically, such as using the dorsal parasympathetic system to dampen our arousal.

As we mature, we carry these dynamics into adulthood, where they interfere with our ability to maintain healthy behaviors in relationships, and where they continue to disrupt healthy physiological responses. Brandchaft accurately captures the compulsivity that accompanies defensive accommodations deriving from early trauma. Because the accommodations are directly linked to our experience of survival threat, they carry with them the same compelling urgency that all survival physiology incites. "There is a basic conflation here," Brandchaft writes, "in that no distinction is drawn between compulsive attitudes of accommodative submission and voluntary wishes to please, and these are being indiscriminately regarded as characteristic of 'love.' Accommodation out of love, with a respect for the legitimate needs of one's partner, is the successful outcome of healthy development and remains the sine qua non of any wholesome relationship. Pathological accommodation shows the continuing influence of traumatic developmental attachment experience and is marked by its essentially compulsive quality" (Brandchaft 2007, 670).

This is where we begin to see the intersection between perceived locus of control and defensive accommodation. The more we experience and/or perceive a lack of agency, or an inability to influence the outcomes of our experiences, and the more our environment is experienced as threatening, the more forcefully our defensive accommodations will arise.

"The further outside the range of the normal experience and the more life-threatening an experience, the more difficult it will be for the normal mental mechanisms to work efficiently to process and master that experience," writes Bruce Perry (2002, 6), describing the impact of early traumatic experiences. Developmental trauma can make even the most basic needs, like being cared for and nurtured, seem outside of normal experience, and their absence is indeed life-threatening.

We are reminded again that when trauma occurs in the nonverbal development phase of life, the trauma literally imprints on the patterning of neurons, creating a template for the neural systems that provide a frame of reference for future experiences. Compare that to traumatic experiences in adults, who already possess a supportive neural system—the trauma may alter that system, but a strong foundational architecture is already in place. Trauma typically will not undo years of neural patterning. It will disrupt that patterning, but a healthy foundation built during infancy, childhood, and the teen years has created something like a sturdy table. Whatever sits atop the table may be dramatically altered, but the table remains intact and better allows for rebuilding. In contrast, with developmental trauma, the table was not properly leveled or was built without much attention or craftsmanship, and therefore, everything resting on the table is unlikely to have the support it needs.

In healthy neural programming, our physiology is "designed" to achieve homeostasis. Under the influence of developmental trauma, there will be notable adaptive changes in cognition, affects, behavior, neurophysiology, and physiology. Developmental trauma does not have the same impact on all children and adults. The two primary responses to developmental trauma in children are hyper-arousal response or dissociative response, and the majority will utilize both. Descriptive terms like "oppositional," "defiant," "distant," "acting out," and "resistant" are often used to describe the fearful adult or child. These types of behaviors tend to anger, frustrate, or mystify others and bring about greater separation for the adult or child who deploys these behaviors, which produces the opposite of the desired result. These behaviors can be difficult to understand, as the child may be overreading the nonverbal cues of angry adults, and this can move her toward a more primitive or disorganized state in her behaviors and responses.

The more we know about developmental trauma and the impact of early trauma on the neural development of an individual, the greater our ability to show compassion and understanding toward the child or adult. Even a basic understanding of developmental trauma can allow for greater possibilities in our interactions. Understanding the effects of faulty neural platforms and the formation patterns of defensive accommodations to threat is the key to healing. It's important to understand that defensive accommodations are driven by deep survival urges and perhaps a foundational lack of regulatory capacity, to the extent that an individual likely feels out of control of her own body and responses.

Imagine putting a pot of water on the stove and setting the burner with the expectation that the water will reach the perfect temperature for a cup of tea and then bubble along on its own. You're anticipating the friendly conversation you'll have with your visiting relative as you sip your lovely cups of tea together. But suddenly, the water begins to boil over and you rush to the stove at lightning speed to turn it off, burning yourself badly as you do this, which means your relative needs to take you to the emergency room to get care. As a result of that experience, you decide that it's simply too dangerous to ever have a cup of tea because it brings the risk of being burned. Furthermore, your relative probably won't want to come for a visit because those visits clearly end in disaster, so it's probably better simply not to invite your relative to your home again. You can think of this as a metaphor for a certain kind of defensive accommodation, just one way our nervous system can manage activation or respond to overwhelming experiences so that we can move forward in our lives. Oftentimes, the attempt to protect or defend ourselves is taken to extreme ends and results in isolation or separation. Defensive accommodations, by their very nature, tend to bring with them limitations in terms of our ability to grow and live our lives fully.

When looking at defensive accommodations in relation to developmental trauma, we are looking at more primitive forms of accommodation. The more primitive these accommodations, the less effective they become as we mature, as our peers expect more predictable, "normative," and sophisticated behavior. In the category of defensive accommodations, we can also include behaviors such as self-harm, eating disorders, compulsive behaviors—anything that substitutes for regulation, or anything that helps support a sense of control, safety, or connection.

Frank is an eighth grader who is struggling socially at school, where he doesn't have any friends. Frank's parents were killed by a drunk driver when he was two years old, and he has since been living with his aunt and uncle. Frank doesn't seem to have any of his own memories of his parents but relates stories about them that he's heard from relatives.

After his parents died and he moved in with his aunt and uncle, his uncle began sexually abusing Frank after he went to bed at night. Frank was too afraid to tell anyone what was happening to him, because his uncle threatened to put him in an orphanage if he ever mentioned it to anyone, and so the abuse continued for several years.

Frank no longer has a felt sense of peace or quiet in his body. He started having nightmares and began failing his classes. He is frequently sent to the principal's office for disruptive behavior. He tried smoking pot and using other drugs but couldn't find the sense of relief he was seeking until one night when he tried cutting. At first, he made small cuts on his arms. The reaction was immediate: In that one moment, or a few moments at most, Frank felt no emotional or physical pain in his body. He was at peace.

Frank continued to cut and increased the frequency and intensity of the cuts. He continued cutting his groin, legs, armpits, and arms. His skin became scarred by the cuts. Even though this level of defensive accommodation was effective for helping him settle for brief periods, it didn't last, which caused him to cut more frequently.

Frank hungered for calm and ease, and found a method that seemed to accomplish that, but of course provided only temporary relief. His cutting helped him manage his overwhelming sense of agitation and stress, but until he received support for more genuine regulation, it would be difficult to give up this defensive accommodation.

The cutting Frank depended on is just one example of many possible defensive accommodations our clients may develop as they seek to regulate their nervous system, calm their agitation, and escape overwhelming feelings of panic and confusion. Table 1 outlines various types of accommodations and how they can manifest, particularly those that fall into the more primitive category, which is most common in relation to developmental trauma.

Table 1: Defensive Accommodation

ACCOMMODATION	DESCRIPTION	EXAMPLE
Denial (primitive)	Blocking external events from awareness; refusing to accept reality or facts; acting as if a painful event did not exist because it's too much to handle and/or experience.	Someone who uses alcohol to the point that it interferes with his daily life, but he insists he doesn't have a drinking problem.
Regression (primitive)	Going backward to a psychological time in which the person was faced with the original threat or stress.	When a child starts school, he becomes activated, and starts to wet his bed again.
Acting Out (primitive)	Finding an extreme way to express feelings that seem impossible to express in other ways.	Feeling a surge of almost uncontrollable anger and driving one's car recklessly at high speeds.
Repression (primitive)	Happens unconsciously to prevent disturbing or threatening thoughts from becoming reality.	A student who feels her teacher is being unfair but refrains from showing aggression toward the teacher.
Dissociation (primitive)	Often felt as a floating sensation that comes with a loss of time or awareness. This escape prevents the person from experiencing threatening or dangerous events firsthand. In severe cases, dissociative types can develop distinct and different personalities.	Someone who might dissociate at the dentist's office to avoid feeling the pain from having a cavity filled.
Compartmentalization (primitive)	Someone who lives in two or more realities where separate sets of values or morals are kept.	A person who has strong religious beliefs and moral values but also cheats on his spouse with prostitutes while remaining unconscious of the cognitive dissonance.
Projection (primitive)	The act of transferring or ascribing your negative thoughts and impulses to another person who doesn't share those same thoughts; a type of misguided blame.	A parent may be angry with a child for leaving the lights on even though the parent also leaves the lights on from time to time.

ACCOMMODATION	DESCRIPTION	EXAMPLE
Reaction Formation (primitive)	The act of forcing unwanted or angry thoughts into their opposing form.	A person is angry with her boss yet continues to bring the boss homemade donuts.
Intellectualization (between primitive and mature)	Using intellect and reason as a defense to avoid unconscious internal or emotional conflicts; a way to avoid by overthinking.	A person who has just been diagnosed with an incurable disease then avoids the additional stress response by focusing his energy on researching the disease.
Rationalization (between primitive and mature)	The cognitive distortion of the "facts" to make an event or impulse less threatening.	A parent hits her child, and then says it's for the child's own good.
Sublimation (mature)	Finding satisfaction with a substitute in a socially acceptable way; done purposely to convert a negative feeling to something that feels positive or beneficial.	Being angry at your boss, then going home and cleaning house.

These types of accommodations are often perceived by others as habits or personality types, rather than self-protective responses. Because they function on the subconscious level, they are often challenging for those whose lives are intertwined with people who've experienced early developmental trauma. What's important to understand is that for those with developmental trauma, defensive accommodations have literally helped them to survive. These accommodations are highly effective for immediate or short-term effects.

Take, for example, one of the more primitive forms of defensive accommodation—denial. For a small child, sequestering the event away, pretending it never happened, or allocating it to something that is part of a fantasy is likely to provide relief from the terror of the overwhelming experience. Even adults rely on more primitive accommodations most often. Again, taking denial as an example, it may combine in an adult with something like alcohol abuse to numb experiences of distress, but then denial of the alcohol abuse as problematic. We expect to see these more primitive defensive accommodations in those adults who seem stuck in a negative loop or in chronic activation, whose ability to learn new and more effective techniques has been hindered.

When evaluating or examining defensive accommodations, it's important to understand that these defenses were developed to aid/facilitate/ensure survival. These accommodations more than likely are set in motion and have always occurred on a primarily subconscious level, rather than in the more logical pre-frontal cortex. In other words, these accommodations are not selected intentionally. Rather, they are the direct result of a perceived threat to survival.

Defensive accommodation frequently leads to maladaptive behaviors. In the context of developmental trauma, it's not unusual to find extreme versions of maladaptive behavior, because the underlying need for these accommodations is the management of overwhelming survival impulses, often coupled with an out of control physiology.

SOMATIC MANAGEMENT STRATEGIES AS DEFENSIVE ACCOMMODATION

We have focused primarily on defensive accommodations that are predominantly behavioral or psychological, but these types of strategies can easily veer into somatic and physiological efforts to create a sense of control. In some cases, this happens as the result of a coupling between a somatic/interoceptive experience and a stressor.

For example, a caregiver responds harshly when her small child asks for something to eat, shaming the child for wanting food, and then forcing the child to finish an oversized meal. The child may then begin to affiliate the feeling of hunger with the arrival of a frightening caregiver, and he will manage that anxiety by limiting food intake and numbing himself to feelings of hunger. He has now created a defensive accommodation that includes both behavioral and somatic triggers and responses.

As noted in the "Compelling Survival Physiology" section of this chapter, we can also be forced into maladaptive physiological responses by chronic stress exposure. In this case, it's not an unconscious behavioral change, but rather a physiological change that develops over time in response to the same types of stressors that create defensive accommodations.

A common example is the overuse of the dorsal parasympathetic braking mechanism. In the absence of reliable co-regulation with a caregiver, a child develops a mechanism for managing overwhelming activation when distressed. Because the dorsal physiology does dampen sympathetic arousal, the child may learn—somatically and physiologically—to cascade into the dorsal freeze state as a trigger response to general overstimulation. Over time, this becomes the primary somatic management strategy used for responding to any overly stimulating experience—even when the stimulation might be positive, like the anticipation of a birthday party. Essentially, our physiology has now created a new construct for how to respond to excitation. Rather than developing a range of responses that include excitation of a positive nature, we overrespond to any excitation by shutting down and numbing.

Any maladaptive somatic strategy will tend to increase allostatic load and negatively impact our long-term health. In the next chapter, we will discuss in more detail some of the side effects of the physiological and somatic impacts of developmental trauma.

PART II

Regulation and Resilience:

Recognizing and Repairing Developmental Trauma

THE MATERIAL IN PART II is designed to help clinicians understand the side effects of developmental trauma, and how to recognize the signs that indicate developmental trauma may be influencing a client's symptoms. It provides an orientation to the ways in which developmental trauma impacts the autonomic nervous system, compromising access to experiences of safety, and taking a tremendous physiological toll.

In addition, the information in part II explores the mechanisms of chronic traumatic stress physiology, which are different from other forms of trauma, and how ongoing experiences of survival effort create symptoms and disrupt the ability of clients to respond with ease and spontaneity to life challenges, ultimately compromising resilience.

In the final chapters, we present information about what clinicians need to understand and take into account in their interventions with their clients, and how to include a regulation-informed model of working somatically to support clients to build greater capacity for regulation and resilience.

6

Repercussions of Adverse Childhood Experiences (ACEs)

PART I FOCUSED on understanding the foundations for healthy development under ideal conditions, and some of what can go awry in that development, particularly in relation to developmental trauma. In part II, we focus on some of the critical side effects of developmental trauma, and how those side effects will manifest in our clients. It contains some of the technical material needed when working with the deeply somatic disruptions that occur in the wake of early trauma.

Many clinicians experience that their clients who have had challenging childhoods often arrive for their first appointment with hopelessness in their voices, unsure of where to turn or what to do next. Their resources may be nearly depleted, and some will feel isolated and disconnected from the world. Though reaching out for help is rarely easy, for those who've lived with the consequences of early trauma all their lives, it can be especially challenging. This may be their third or fourth—or twentieth—attempt, and they are likely to feel that no one has seen or heard or believed them during any of their prior efforts to find answers and make changes.

The typical client with developmental trauma has spent a lifetime developing strategies to cover up or hide his early challenges. But as we begin to peel back the layers beneath his presentation, we see what's behind that hopelessness—the feeling that he has "been here before," that he has fruitlessly sought other ways to find relief or change his behavior, that there is an inherent futility in the expectation that this time will be different. Yet the mere fact that he has come in for therapy shows that he hasn't completely abandoned hope for the future.

For adult clients, the reason for seeking support varies, and the list of possibilities is long. Those seeking psychotherapy may be experiencing feelings of overwhelm, anxiety, isolation, or loneliness, or may be struggling with addiction, feelings of abandonment, or difficulty with commitment—or myriad other psychological/emotional issues. Sometimes the issues manifest in more physical or somatic ways, which perhaps bring a client to a health care provider. These can include muscle pain, migraines, or gut discomfort, or even cognitive problems, such as difficulty concentrating or learning.

Often a client has some sense that her current difficulties may be related to earlier life experiences, but cause-and-effect correlations are not readily apparent. As noted in chapter 3, epigenetics could be a hidden contributing factor, but there could be other experiences in the client's early history that would not be obviously considered as developmental trauma, such as difficult birth events, substance use by the mother during pregnancy, neonatal hospitalization, surgery, or illness. Yet, many clients show up needing help and have no sense whatsoever about what happened to them or when. The common theme in their stories is that something interrupted normal growth and development.

Children also enter therapy for a wide range of reasons—usually a parent has reached the end of her rope and doesn't know where to turn. The inability to parent a child with developmental trauma often comes with a deep sense of shame for one or both parents, which may have delayed their attempt to seek help longer than they would have otherwise. Without understanding of how early trauma can powerfully change a child's behavior, parents often feel it must be something they've done, or a failure to have done things differently. Children may act out in school, have trouble sleeping, refuse to listen to their parents, or become aggressive. This, in turn, causes more worry and shame as parents fear what the future may bring for their children. As occurs with adults, children may also be brought to health care providers for the same types of physical symptoms: digestive difficulties, trouble sleeping, unexplained pains, and cognitive or learning issues.

But we now know, thanks to an extensive study of adverse childhood experiences, that both psychological and physical issues can be traced directly back to early trauma.

THE ADVERSE CHILDHOOD EXPERIENCES (ACE) STUDY

In 1985, Kaiser Permanente researcher Dr. Vincent Felitti noticed a puzzling and paradoxical trend in his obesity clinic: participants who were having the most success with weight loss were dropping out of the program before completion, only to later regain the weight.

Curious about the reasons for this pattern, he interviewed nearly 300 participants and stumbled upon another surprising pattern: almost all of those who left the program early shared in common some form of early childhood trauma.

That initial study grew into a public health study, a collaboration with Dr. Robert Anda and the Centers for Disease Control and Prevention (CDC) that still continues, involving the evaluation of more than 17,000 participants. Using a simple survey developed for and administered during physical examinations, the researchers asked a series of eight questions to evaluate whether the participants had been subjected to specific experiences in childhood, while also gathering information about the participants' current behaviors and health status. The results were—and continue to be—staggering, transforming the way we view childhood trauma and its impact on adult health; it has led to a paradigm shift in the way physicians, psychologists, psychotherapists, schoolteachers, and social workers view and treat patients, clients, and students.

In 2007 Dr. Anda created the ACE Score Calculator, which allocated numerical values to the answers to the ACE questionnaire, and provided clinicians with a way to assess risk factors based on the total score. As the use of the ACE questionnaire evolved to include other areas of focus, such as evaluating at-risk children in the home setting, or taking a client history in preparation for therapy, the questions have also evolved. There are different versions of the questionnaire now in use, the most common being the one presented here, which includes the ten questions Dr. Anda uses.

It's important to note that reading the questions on the test or filling out the questionnaire can cause distress. We encourage readers to attend to their responses and discontinue taking the questionnaire if they find themselves disturbed by it.

The ten adverse childhood experiences (ACEs) included in the questionnaire measure whether or not someone has experienced any of the listed conditions in a household prior to age eighteen. Even though the age range exceeds the range used for the definition for developmental trauma (which is trauma that occurs prior to age five), we feel that, overall, this study has yielded important information about long-term outcomes for our clients. Exposure to a single category of experience counts as a single point. The number of incidents themselves are not measured in this questionnaire. Each "Yes" counts as one point. The total points determine the ACE score.

ACE Questionnaire

1. Did a parent or other adult in the household often or very often . . . Swear at you, insult you, put you down, or humiliate you? or act in a way that made you afraid that you might be physically hurt? No___ If Yes, enter 1 ___

2. Did a parent or other adult in the household often or very often . . . Push, grab, slap, or throw something at you? or ever hit you so hard that you had marks or were injured? No___ If Yes, enter 1 ___

3. Did an adult or person at least five years older than you ever . . . Touch or fondle you or have you touch their body in a sexual way? or attempt or actually have oral, anal, or vaginal intercourse with you? No___ If Yes, enter 1 ___

4. Did you often or very often feel that . . . No one in your family loved you or thought you were important or special? or your family didn't look out for each other, feel close to each other, or support each other? No___ If Yes, enter 1 ___

5. Did you often or very often feel that . . . You didn't have enough to eat, had to wear dirty clothes, and had no one to protect you? Or your parents were too drunk or high to take care of you or take you to the doctor if you needed it? No___ If Yes, enter 1 ___

6. Was a biological parent ever lost to you through divorce, abandonment, or other reasons? No___ If Yes, enter 1 ___

7. Was your mother or stepmother: Often or very often pushed, grabbed, slapped, or had something thrown at her? or sometimes, often, or very often kicked, bitten, hit with a fist, or hit with something hard? or ever repeatedly hit over at least a few minutes or threatened with a gun or knife? No___ If Yes, enter 1 ___

8. Did you live with anyone who was a problem drinker or alcoholic, or who used street drugs? No___ If Yes, enter 1 ___

9. Was a household member depressed or mentally ill, or did a household member attempt suicide? No___ If Yes, enter 1 ___

10. Did a household member go to prison? No___ If Yes, enter 1 ___

Now, add up your Yes score: _____ This shows your ACE score.

There are, of course, many more types of early trauma that are not listed in the study. Anda and Felitti chose specific types of early trauma because these appeared most frequently in the research. This does not mean other forms of trauma are not significant, just that they did not fall into the most commonly reported categories.

Other fairly common types of trauma that were not mentioned in the study include: witnessing a sibling being abused; experiencing the loss of a parent or significant grandparent in the family; not having a place to call home, or actually being homeless; living through a severe accident; seeing one parent abuse another, or a grandparent abuse a parent; being separated from a parent too early due to premature birth (extended periods in a neonatal care unit with limited contact with caregivers); undergoing early surgeries, hospitalizations, or other medical trauma; and, in some cases, being adopted.

The outcome of the ACE Study revealed five main discoveries, which are listed on the ACES Too High website (a news site that reports on research related to ACEs):

- ACEs are common. Nearly two-thirds (64 percent) of adults report at least one.

- They cause adult onset of chronic disease, such as cancer and heart disease, as well as mental illness, violence, and being a victim of violence.

- ACEs don't occur alone. If you have one, there's an 87 percent chance that you have two or more.

- The more ACEs you have, the greater the risk for chronic disease, mental illness, violence, and being a victim of violence.

- ACEs are responsible for a significant share of workplace absenteeism, and for costs in health care, emergency response, mental health, and criminal justice. So, the fifth finding from the ACE Study is that childhood adversity contributes to most of our major chronic health, mental health, economic health, and social health issues. (ACES Too High 2017)

The possible ACE score ranges from zero to ten. Each type of trauma counts as one point on the scale, no matter how many incidences of that trauma have been experienced. The higher the ACE score, the higher the probability of related risks. "People with an ACE score of 4 are twice as likely to be smokers and seven times more likely to be alcoholic. Having an ACE score of 4 increases the risk of emphysema or chronic bronchitis by nearly 400 percent, and suicide by 1200 percent. People with high ACE scores are more likely to be violent, to have more marriages [and divorces], more broken bones, more drug prescriptions, more depression, and more autoimmune diseases. People with an ACE score of 6 or higher are at risk of their lifespan being shortened by 20 years" (ACES Too High 2017).

What's particularly startling about the study was that the 17,000-plus participants were mostly white, middle and upper-middle class, and college educated, and all had jobs and access to great health care (all were members of Kaiser Permanente). This is not the population that had traditionally been considered at risk for developmental trauma, so it was an eye-opening finding.

It has long been known that poor minority communities also tend to have poor health statistics. In a 2012 radio episode of *This American Life* (episode 474: "Back to School"), San Francisco pediatrician Nadine Burke Harris spoke of her work in Bayview-Hunters Point, a poor minority neighborhood in San Francisco, where she saw daily how those poor health statistics took a toll on the community. Initially, she thought that providing the more usual public health services, such as immunizations, obesity treatments, and asthma treatments, would make the needed difference.

What she found instead was that this was not the primary need. In her intake sessions with the families, she realized that children in the community were experiencing danger on a nearly daily basis—witnessing violence and domestic violence, having their homes broken into, and so forth. Burke Harris began to make the connection between these experiences and the symptoms she was seeing, and the ACE Study provided her with the explanation that she needed.

As Burke Harris explained to Ira Glass, the host of *This American Life*, the mechanisms and effects of traumatic stress arise from this type of chronic exposure to survival stresses. She offers an example of what would normally happen if you were faced with a specific survival threat, summarized here: If you're in a forest and see a bear, a very efficient fight-or-flight system instantly floods your body with chemicals, such as adrenaline and cortisol, that effectively shut off the thinking portion of your brain—the cognitive part that would naturally stop and take the time to consider other options. This is very helpful if you're in a forest and you need to run from a bear; you don't want to spend time thinking about it. The problem, Burke Harris added, "is when that bear comes home from the bar every night."

She goes on to explain that if a bear threatens you every single day, your emergency response system is activated again and again and again. You're always ready to fight or flee, and a key analytical part of your brain—the prefrontal cortex, which helps you diagram sentences or calculate math equations, for example—becomes chronically stunted.

For Burke Harris's patients, many of whom had four or more categories of adverse childhood experiences, "their odds of having learning or behavior problems in school were thirty-two times as high as kids who had no adverse childhood experiences," she told Glass, who noted in his reporting of the story, "What is holding children back is not poverty—it's stress." What we would add to that statement is that this type of stress would fall more accurately into the category of traumatic stress.

What the ACE Study demonstrates is that it is not poverty per se that is the problem; it is all that typically accompanies poverty: lack of safety, exposure to violence, neglect, diminished access to health care, and learning difficulties. Those same factors can also be present in the absence of poverty.

The ACE Study provides a clear indicator that we have been viewing developmental trauma through a distorted lens, that we must change our assumptions about the context within which it occurs, and that we must change our assessment and delivery of care practices. As Burke Harris discovered, it's not enough to treat the health issues in isolation. Working with the root cause of those issues—trauma—is the more fundamental need.

It's important to underscore the study's finding that a higher ACE score points to greater *risk* of poor physical and mental health, and of facing negative social consequences later in life, not a guarantee of those negative consequences occurring. What we know from resiliency research is that there can be protective factors at play that will support the resilience that promotes positive outcomes in spite of adversity. It's also important to note that the question of developmental trauma is not simply yes or no. It's a question of degree. It's not a given that a high ACE score for any specific individual will absolutely lead to the side effects indicated by the study results.

The ACE Study continues to produce staggering results about long-term effects of early trauma. As illustrated in the pyramid in figure 5, adverse childhood experiences disrupt neurodevelopment in its very early stages, and those disruptions then continue, evolve, and deepen through the maturation process with continued negative impacts, including a higher risk for early death.

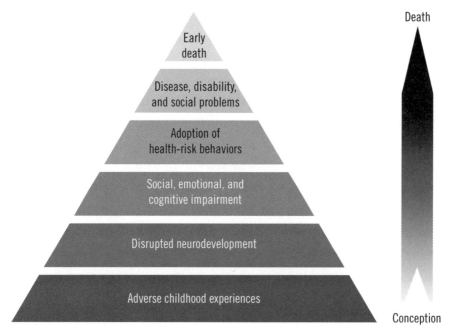

Figure 5 Source: Centers for Disease Control and Prevention. 2012. www.cdc.gov/violenceprevention/acestudy/ace_graphics.html.

Many of our clients have suffered for years from disease, disability, and social problems. As adults, many are isolated and unable to work; as teenagers or children, they may be stuck in a cycle of self-defeating behaviors. It is also definitively clear to the authors of this book that adverse childhood experiences of the mother can affect infants, even fetuses in utero, by disrupting attachment and thus altering a client's sense of security and safety throughout development, although we still don't fully know the impact of ACEs across generations via epigenetics.

The original study is now completed, and the CDC is no longer seeking individual participants for the study. The ongoing longitudinal data is being collected from twenty-eight states that joined in the data gathering; this data set is maintained by the Centers for Disease Control and Prevention. The CDC also conducts outreach to providers and states to further trauma-informed health care and education, now that it has become evident that developmental trauma is having lasting, negative effects on health and well-being. This research and data collection continue to examine the prevalence of ACEs and reinforce the connection between ACEs and negative behavioral and health issues. Because of its scope and depth, the ACE Study has allowed us to better understand the future of those who have experienced early childhood abuse and neglect.

Although an ACE assessment can tell us a lot about an individual's past, it can't tell us everything about a person's present. It is only a guidepost for statistical probabilities that someone will develop symptoms or direct repercussions related to his early history. We can see the ACE questionnaire as an inventory of lack of safety or belonging; and we know that the less safety and connectedness a child experiences in his early years, the higher the probability of poor outcomes.

By necessity, studies deal with large numbers of individuals and general trends toward different probabilities of outcomes. Those of us delivering care directly to individuals deal with the effects of these experiences on individual human beings. That means our experience with our individual clients may not directly reflect the statistical probabilities in the ACE Study. We may see different trends or outcomes (compared with the ACE Study) in the small sample of clients we see individually as therapists. Certainly, the ACE Study can't tell us everything we need to know about our clients.

There are, of course, many factors that will influence the impact ACEs may have for any given client. Fortunately, as has been noted previously, there are some protective factors that may mitigate the effects of such challenging early histories. Most notably, factors that instill a sense of safety and belonging tend to reduce the impact of ACEs.

In 2006, the Resilience Questionnaire was created as a companion to the ACE Study. This questionnaire, updated in 2013, was not created for research, but for clinicians who work with children to help them identify some of those potentially protective factors that might be present in the child's life. Mark Rains and Kate McClinn of Southern Kennebec Healthy Start came up with the fourteen statements included on the survey, which is scored much the same way as the ACE Study (Rains and McClinn 2006).

As noted in previous chapters of this book, developmental trauma has a very particular impact on our ability to perceive safety, to develop reliable regulation in our physiology, and to function as reliable witnesses to our experiences. It's important for practitioners to understand how deeply the life experiences cataloged in the ACE questionnaire can impact our clients' ability to utilize the interventions we offer them in our attempts to help.

When our clients come to us for treatment, we need reliable methods for assessing how their histories and presenting symptoms may be interrelated; and how to apply all of this knowledge (the ACE Study and developmental trauma theory) and make it relevant, practical, and useful to our individual clients as we support them in their recovery. Understanding the somatic impact of early trauma will better enable clinicians to work effectively with developmental wounds.

Resilience Questionnaire

Please circle the most accurate answer under each statement.

1. I believe that my mother loved me when I was little.

   Definitely True/Probably True/Not Sure/Probably Not True/Definitely Not True

2. I believe that my father loved me when I was little.

   Definitely True/Probably True/Not Sure/Probably Not True/Definitely Not True

3. When I was little, other people helped my mother and father take care of me and they seemed to love me.

   Definitely True/Probably True/Not Sure/Probably Not True/Definitely Not True

4. I've heard that when I was an infant someone in my family enjoyed playing with me, and I enjoyed it, too.

   Definitely True/Probably True/Not Sure/Probably Not True/Definitely Not True

5. When I was a child, there were relatives in my family who made me feel better if I was sad or worried.

   Definitely True/Probably True/Not Sure/Probably Not True/Definitely Not True

6. When I was a child, neighbors or my friends' parents seemed to like me.

   Definitely True/Probably True/Not Sure/Probably Not True/Definitely Not True

7. When I was a child, teachers, coaches, youth leaders, or ministers were there to help me.

   Definitely True/Probably True/Not Sure/Probably Not True/Definitely Not True

8. Someone in my family cared about how I was doing in school.

   Definitely True/Probably True/Not Sure/Probably Not True/Definitely Not True

9. My family, neighbors, and friends talked often about making our lives better.

   Definitely True/Probably True/Not Sure/Probably Not True/Definitely Not True

10. We had rules in our house and were expected to keep them.

    Definitely True/Probably True/Not Sure/Probably Not True/Definitely Not True

11. When I felt really bad, I could almost always find someone I trusted to talk to.

Definitely True/Probably True/Not Sure/Probably Not True/Definitely Not True

12. As a youth, people noticed that I was capable and could get things done.

Definitely True/Probably True/Not Sure/Probably Not True/Definitely Not True

13. I was independent and a go-getter.

Definitely True/Probably True/Not Sure/Probably Not True/Definitely Not True

14. I believed that life is what you make it.

Definitely True/Probably True/Not Sure/Probably Not True/Definitely Not True

THE SOMATIC EFFECTS OF DEVELOPMENTAL TRAUMA IN ADULTS

Margaret has a history of early childhood trauma, which has impacted every aspect of her life. Both of her parents were alcoholics—her father was violent and abusive, and her mother was passive, withdrawn, and prone to serious and extended bouts of depression. After her father abandoned the family when Margaret was three, Margaret's mother made a series of suicide attempts. These were followed by hospitalizations, which sent Margaret and her two siblings into and out of foster care for most of their childhood years. In some cases, the foster homes contained more abuse than the children experienced at home.

As an adult, Margaret experiences frequent panic attacks, various phobias, severe social anxiety, trouble sleeping, and a multitude of health issues, including food and environmental sensitivities, digestive issues, and fibromyalgia. Nevertheless, she managed to put herself through college and holds down a job as an accountant in a small firm.

What we now know from the ACE Study is that symptoms like Margaret's, and the limitations she has struggled with throughout her life, are not unusual given her childhood. Contained in the ACE questionnaire is the story of many thousands of people who have experienced developmental or early childhood trauma. Our physical and physiological responses to trauma are inseparable from our emotional and psychological responses. It's worth pointing out that only two of the ten questions on the ACE questionnaire include physical abuse of the child—all other questions relate to emotional neglect or abuse, witnessing the abuse of others, or feeling unloved. Yet, many of the side effects of developmental trauma are somatic, deeply held within the physical systems of the body. In addition, as we know from the ACE Study, developmental trauma increases the probability that we will engage in health-risk behaviors, such as smoking or drug use, further strengthening the connection between developmental trauma and its effect on our somatic selves. Because the physical symptoms are in fact directly related to early trauma, they are inextricably entwined with, and the result of, the client's psychological and emotional health. We now know that incontrovertibly.

And yet, current treatment models are still catching up to the true complexity of developmental trauma and its impact on the complex systems of neural patterning. We still tend to separate delivery of care for physical and somatic issues from the psychological and emotional issues that also arise from early trauma. In the story told above, Margaret saw doctors for years as she tried to address her physical symptoms, but as long as the underlying emotional and psychological issues—the trauma issues—went unaddressed, the physical symptoms could not be fully alleviated.

The simple act of answering the ten questions on the ACE questionnaire alerted Margaret to the possibility that her childhood may be relevant to her current experience. She answered "Yes" to nine of the ten questions on the survey. Once she understood that the severe lack of safety and stability in her childhood undermined the development of her ability to regulate her responses—her own physiology—she began to feel relief from the shame she had carried for so long. The knowledge that her symptoms are known by-products of a disordered, unstable childhood allowed her to entertain the possibility that she was not alone in facing her challenges, and that help was indeed possible. All the times she felt her heart racing, or desperately wanted to flee a situation—that was her young self fighting for her own life! The sensations she thought would kill her were simply evidence of how hard she'd fought all along to survive.

As stated earlier, the ACE Study focuses on developmental trauma directly related to neglect and abuse in our early lives. As noted, one can also see the questionnaire as an assessment of lack of safety. However, as also previously noted, the categories listed on the survey are not the only possible sources of developmental trauma. Extended hospitalizations for the child or care provider, early surgeries, or severe injuries—experiences that occur within the context of psychologically healthier families—can also lead to similar symptoms. Our bodies do not differentiate between a threat we might consider "normal"— like being in the hospital, away from care providers, where we're subjected to repeated painful procedures—and threats that are more obviously dangerous, like violence in our own home. We still respond physiologically as if the bear is at our heels. Our survival physiology is triggered no matter the source of the threat.

Once children reach adulthood, they can flee their environments and put themselves in places where they no longer face actual threats, but having spent so many years of childhood feeling unsafe, the traumatized physiology is now primed to move toward self-protection; it will lean in that direction even without much in the way of a trigger. Something as fleeting as a stray thought might provoke such a response, causing the heart to race and a sudden urge to flee. This can cascade into freeze mode, where an individual can no longer think, rationalize, or respond.

As we discussed in chapter 5, survival physiology is meant to be compelling and unstoppable. It drives particular responses in our physical and behavioral systems that are organized around safety and survival. When we grow up "under the influence," so to speak, of our survival physiology, we grow up with survival as a driver for many categories of responses. Our exteroception (perception of the outside world) is tuned more toward perception of threat to our survival. A common example, noted in chapter 2, is the change in the middle-ear muscles, which emphasize perception of lower-frequency sounds when we are in high-activation states. This adjustment would help us if a tiger were stalking us, but when there is no tiger, the result is a difficulty discerning the sound of the human voice from background sounds. Therefore, even a calm, rational reassurance from a trusted friend can fall on deaf ears.

This is a significant—and very real—change to the physiology and somatic systems that affect a client's ability to comprehend the therapist's verbal interventions, and must be accounted for in the way we approach communication and treatment.

Likewise, interoception (perception of our inner somatic experience, which informs our experience of self) is also disrupted—tuned more toward survival-oriented information and limiting our ability to notice more subtle states that may be affiliated with well-being and pleasure. This could mean that a client is deriving unusual or unexpected meaning from normal sensations and may be unable to accurately report what she feels.

In survival physiology, both the inner and outer worlds of self-communication are hyper-tuned to sort information for signs of danger and threat. A client cannot afford to be curious and exploratory when he feels his very life is in danger. As a result, neuroception, or perception of safety, is deeply undermined, and often a client is an unreliable witness to his own experience.

While this happens, he is also subject to the sometimes wildly fluctuating physiological responses that are the hallmarks of developmental trauma, especially if that physiology is no longer reliably functioning within the reciprocal range in the ANS. These physiological responses are in turn reflected in the multitude of physical symptoms affiliated with high ACE scores. The idea of foundational dysregulation, which we discussed in the previous chapter, describes one of the fundamental challenges when working with clients who experienced severe developmental trauma: how to understand the somatic and experiential narrative when the physiological information that helps build the narrative is ever-changing and unreliable.

The physiological and somatic drivers of response that develop in the context of developmental trauma are so potent that we cannot leave them out of the picture when considering the effects of early trauma. If nothing else, the ACE Study makes clear that it's not possible to address physical symptoms as if they are unrelated to the early trauma experiences—the client's somatic systems are just as affected by early trauma as his psychological and emotional systems.

As clinicians, once we understand the unique dynamics and interplay between somatic and other symptoms of developmental trauma, those symptoms begin to make sense. They become less difficult to account for in our treatment planning, and we can better meet our clients where they are on their path to change and recovery.

In the next two chapters, we will provide more specific signs to help you recognize the specific symptoms that often accompany developmental trauma. The following is a list of some of the most common somatic side effects of early trauma that clinicians are most likely to encounter. This is by no means an exhaustive list, but many of these categories of symptoms will be familiar to those who work regularly with clients with high ACE scores.

COMMON SOMATIC SYMPTOMS AND RESPONSES

Somatic symptoms related to developmental trauma often have the quality of changing into new variations of the same symptom, or evolving into new symptoms altogether. One of the hallmarks of somatic symptoms related to developmental trauma is this changeability. Symptoms also tend to be seated in critical physical systems, like the heart, lungs, circulatory system, nervous system, and immune system.

As clinicians, if we can understand the physiological patterns that typically evolve from the survival demands of early trauma, we will be better equipped to deliver effective and appropriate care for our clients, and we will be better able to educate them about their own symptoms, histories, and "operating systems."

Common Symptoms

- Somewhat unexplainable symptoms that don't easily fit into specific diagnostic categories of any kind.

- Complex, unexplainable combinations of responses that can present as syndromes, meaning there is no specific test for diagnosis, but meet multiple criteria, sometimes for multiple syndromes—i.e., may fit the diagnostic criteria for fibromyalgia, chronic fatigue, and lupus.

- Paradoxical responses to medications and other treatments; side effects occur at subclinical doses.

- Extreme sensitivity—to light, sound, tactile stimulation, and/or smells.

- Difficulty tracking their own experience from the inside.

- Terror at going inside themselves with their attention.

- Uncontained and strong responses to small stimuli.

- Sometimes have been identified as malingerer or hypochondriac—seems symptoms are imagined; can't find basis in specific physical cause.

- Their physiology tends to play a big role in their response system—get easily stimulated into high-activation states, or plunged into deep freeze states; have strong physical responses, even with minimal emphasis on physical states.

- Precipitous responses—i.e., pain suddenly escalates to high levels with little warning.

- Delayed responses to interventions—may seem to have tolerated the intervention very well, but after a day or two may have severe worsening of symptoms.

The ACE Study provides a wealth of information about the types of symptoms that are affiliated with early trauma. Helping clients understand their symptoms through the lens of early trauma goes a long way toward lifting the shame many clients feel about their inability to control their symptoms and their own bodies.

One final note: The ACE Study results articulate the side effects of developmental trauma in adults. Children, on the other hand, may be in the midst of experiencing developmental trauma, but the side effects noted in the ACE literature typically take time to develop, so those side effects most accurately describe adult expressions of those early experiences. Children don't show the same symptoms noted in the outcomes of the ACE Study, because they haven't yet had time to develop the related symptoms—their physiology is still evolving. But that doesn't mean there aren't other symptoms and indicators that should raise alarm. In addition to using the ACE questionnaire to assess risk for children, we can also pay attention to the symptoms that indicate possible effects of developmental trauma.

THE EFFECTS OF DEVELOPMENTAL TRAUMA IN CHILDREN

The period from conception to around age five has tremendous long-term impact on life. This window of early childhood is considered a chiefly nonverbal or pre-memory period, so the history that can be retrieved often comes secondhand from a parent or other adult. But, in some cases, such information can be difficult to assess, particularly if caregivers or other adults in the family don't remember or are unwilling to discuss unpleasant experiences. In the case of adopted children, the information can be lost entirely as the child transitions from one family to another.

As we've noted, the brain is not fully developed at birth. Approximately 80 percent of brain development occurs prior to age three, yet the brain will continue to change throughout life, being molded by a child's experiences, upbringing, and environment. In fact, the brain is constantly influenced by life experiences. We call this ability of the brain to constantly change its "plasticity." Early brain development is most influenced by experiences, especially the relational experiences with caretakers and others involved in the child's growth and development. At this phase, much of that early development is based on unspoken communication. These early experiences are essential to creating the blueprint for thoughts, feelings, and behaviors. However, this nonverbal period can be the most challenging to penetrate and understand through cognitive or verbal approaches.

Bruce Perry of the ChildTrauma Academy in Houston, Texas, designed a chart (adapted in table 2) to illustrate the effects of early trauma on the child. He incorporated the fight, flight, and freeze responses to show what happens physiologically in a child during moments of stress or discordance. It's also important to note that children who live in constant terror can have a reduction in IQ of up to forty points compared with their peers. This directly affects and impedes the child's ability to learn new skills (including self-management skills) and create healthy early relationships (Perry 2004a). See the sidebar for a common list of symptoms in children.

Table 2: The Threatened Child: How Fear Alters Thoughts, Feelings, and Behavior

Internal state	Calm	Alert	Alarm	Fear	Terror
Brain systems	Neocortex	Cortex	Limbic	Midbrain/ brain stem	Brain stem/ ANS
Plans for the future	The rest of your life	The next seven days or twenty-four hours	The next few hours or minutes	The next few minutes or seconds	No sense of time
Ability to think	Uses abstract thought; thinks and reflects	Thoughts are concrete	Highly emotional thinking	Reacts instead of thinking	Blames others, and thoughts seem to loop
Hyper-arousal; fight or flight	Able to rest	Becomes hypervigilant	Becomes resistant; oftentimes tearful	Becomes defiant; often has tantrums	Becomes aggressive toward others
Freeze/dorsal/ dissociative	Able to rest	Becomes avoidant	Becomes overcompliant like a robot	Can engage in fetal rocking back and forth	Can faint from the thought of the terror
Cognitive awareness and developmental stage	Regresses to fifteen- to thirty-year-old behavior, between adolescent and adult behavior	Regresses to eight- to fifteen-year-old behavior, between childlike and adolescent behavior	Regresses to three- to eight-year-old behavior, like a young child or toddler	Regresses to one- to three-year-old behavior, like an infant or toddler	Regresses to newborn to one-year-old behavior
Responds to interaction	Able to talk and discuss ideas	Able to talk and engage in learning	Able to play, can engage in learning	More reactive doing and some cues	Can give non-verbal safety cues
Cognitive aptitude (IQ)	Normal	Decreases 10 points	Decreases 20 points	Decreases 30 points	Decreases 40 points

Common Symptoms: Children

- Anxiety

- Low self-esteem

- Anger or aggressive behaviors toward others

- Physical attacks on others

- Behaviors that are needy in ways that don't accurately match the current developmental age

- Inability to deal with stress and adversity

- Lack of self-control; impulse-control issues

- Inability to develop and maintain friendships

- Alienation from and opposition to parents, caregivers, and other authority figures

- Antisocial attitudes and behaviors

- Difficulty with genuine trust, intimacy, and affection

- Negative, hopeless, pessimistic view of self, family, and society

- Lack of empathy, compassion, and remorse

- Behavioral and academic problems at school

- Incessant chatter

- Difficulty learning and behavioral issues in the classroom

- Depression or apathy

- Obsession with food: hoards, gorges, refuses to eat, eats strange things, hides food

- Repetition of the cycle of maltreatment and attachment disorder in their own children when they reach adulthood

For children who have experienced early trauma, we know that one of their greatest needs is to be seen, heard, and believed. They have a complicated association with memory, because the brain development that supports explicit memory does not occur until about age three. (The impact on self-narrative that occurs with developmental trauma is discussed more fully in chapter 8.) Because of early developmental ruptures and their high level of stress, the children affected often respond with parts of a story put together to appear true. This use of implicit memory—instead of explicit memory—is a commonly shared trait.

Children may also exhibit many of the same somatic symptoms we see in adults, although more typically in an acute form rather than the more chronic manifestations.

Table 2, based on the chart Perry formulated, shows the impact of perceived threat on children, and the associated behaviors that may be interpreted as "immature." These behavioral markers are often signs of regression toward a less mature style of functioning. Table 2 shows the effect of external fear stressors on internal states, including the effects on the brain and the ability to learn. It also points out the external behaviors observers may witness when the child is in the midst of a fight-or-flight response. The chart flows from left to right, showing first the internal state or plan and then what happens as the stressor increases from calm/normal to terror. Each stage shows the emotional and educational costs for the individual. These regressive stages can also be seen while working with developmental trauma in the treatment room. Table 2 could also be read as moving from regulated states to extreme dysregulation.

TRAUMA SPECTRUM DISORDERS

Clinicians have developed a new vocabulary for better articulating the complexity of symptoms related to severe trauma, particularly trauma that occurs early in life. The multiple clinical features of trauma—ranging from acute psychotic, panic, dissociative, and depressive features on one end of the spectrum, to narcissistic and antisocial personalities on the other—have prompted clinicians and researchers to view trauma along a continuum. The term "trauma spectrum disorder," or "posttraumatic spectrum disorder," is beginning to replace a more simplified interpretation of PTSD.

James Beck and Bessel van der Kolk (1987) and Lawrence Kolb (1989) identified psychotic manifestations following trauma, including delusional thinking, various types of hallucinations, disorganized thought processes, confusion, poor reality contact, and other formal thought disorders.

In developmental trauma, we often find greater levels of autonomic nervous system dysregulation, most notably in activation states, which in turn demand more complex strategies for managing the experience of being out of control. When adults or children have limited access to basic physiological and affect regulation, we expect to see symptoms intensify under stress, even normal daily stress. Effectively, the additional stressors or triggers exceed the person's ability to actively manage and limit her symptoms, her defensive accommodations fail, and the symptoms can possibly rise to the level of psychosis and appear dangerous or threatening to others.

One of the most common features of the trauma spectrum is depression. A depressive state can arise from the client's original sense that the world is not a safe place. Some of the features ascribed to depression in the *Diagnostic and Statistical Manual of Mental Disorders* (DSM) are a sense of helplessness, poor concentration, lack of interest, insomnia, and suicidal feelings. When we begin to look at depression as part of a spectrum related to developmental trauma, the symptoms can be viewed in a different context—they may be expressing the foundational dysregulation that often results from early trauma, but they also express the very helplessness that was integral to the traumatic experiences themselves.

Helplessness plays a significant role in dissociation, a natural defense mechanism used to divert one's awareness away from pain, lack of agency, and potential loss of self or life that occurs in trauma. Clients report a sense of losing time, drifting, or floating. Dissociative identity disorder has a strong correlation with severe childhood trauma (Ellason, Ross, and Fuchs 1996).

In therapy, we view dissociation as a management technique, which likely had a functional role in the response to severe early trauma. This is also one of the most controversial aspects of trauma. Dissociation is viewed by therapists both negatively and positively in the treatment of early trauma, but we expect to see clients dissociate less as they develop a greater sense of regulation and can, to a greater degree, inhabit their own bodies and minds during times of conflict or stress.

Many of the features on the trauma spectrum, such as borderline personality disorder, are now believed to result from untreated early trauma. A borderline personality can be seen as a reaction to severe early trauma, in which the client's attachment appears disorganized, with greater challenges forming relationships. These clients live in a constant state of loss, and "separation distress" seems amplified. They seem more anxious to connect and will connect with those who provide a negative impact on their lives, if only to establish at least some sense of connection. These features in a client can be seen by some therapists as the most challenging to encounter and treat. The effort to create a safe place in the therapist's office, with the therapist functioning as the secure base of attachment, can be difficult to maintain for many therapists, given the intense need for a sense of connection and constant reassurance that many such clients have.

Learning to identify the signs of developmental trauma from the outset of treatment informs everything that follows, from the treatment plan to the pacing of sessions. In the coming chapters, we will present more detailed information about how to recognize the strategies that clients have developed to manage not only their symptoms, but also the underlying dysregulation that is the hallmark of early trauma. As clinicians, if we are well oriented to the manifestations of early trauma, we are better able to support the development of healthy regulation and greater resilience in our clients.

7

The Window of Tolerance
and the Faux Window

"WINDOW OF TOLERANCE" is a term coined by Dan Siegel to describe the optimal window within which we can respond to a stimulus without becoming overly aroused, and then be able to settle naturally. This isn't about timing, but about a psychological and physiological setting in which we are capable of "cooling down" after being activated by a stressor. As an example, consider experiencing a close call while driving. The driver may feel her heart racing, her breathing accelerating, and her muscles bracing in reaction, but when she realizes the danger has passed, she will settle back to her normal driving behaviors. The driver did not become so frightened that she had to stop driving, nor did she become paralyzed in her response to the stimulus of the near miss. This is one way we might define regulation, and it would also be a marker of resilience.

When we have access to a healthy Window of Tolerance, we benefit from a self-correcting system that can respond to experiences, even somewhat challenging experiences, and come to rest again. Within that window, we avoid provocation into either dysregulation or an extreme threat response. There isn't a single "correct" Window of Tolerance for everyone—there are many different ways that healthy responsiveness can manifest. Each person has a different range of capacity that functions as their "window." In the context of trauma, the Window of Tolerance tends to be associated with the ventral parasympathetic system, which supports social engagement behaviors, awareness of self, and an experience of relaxation that still allows awareness of our surroundings.

The concept of the Window of Tolerance has now become ubiquitous in the trauma field and within the field of psychotherapy generally. The idea is most often discussed in the treatment of trauma, but also offers a way of interpreting our reactions to experience more broadly. We can think of the Window of Tolerance as the zone where we effectively process environmental signals without becoming too reactive or too withdrawn, given the circumstances. This model is based on the normal development of the nervous system.

The Optimal Arousal Zone, as shown in figure 6, is associated behaviorally with the ability to respond with forethought and attention to self and others—typical functions supported by the ventral parasympathetic physiology. Functioning within this zone allows us to be present in the here and now—our brains

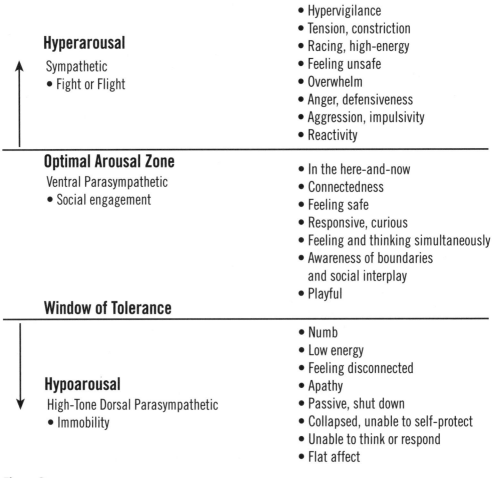

Figure 6

can function in such a way that we process information and experience effectively. Because the Window of Tolerance model is most commonly used in the context of trauma or stress response, it would not usually include the low-tone dorsal physiology often dominant during sleep and healthy immobility without fear, such as nursing/bonding behaviors. In such states, the physiology is not in survival mode, but in rest/digest/replenishment physiology. We don't think of this as "arousal," but it falls within the regulatory range indicating healthy self-regulation, which is what the Window of Tolerance ideally reflects.

In the Window of Tolerance framework, we can see sympathetic dominance (hyper-arousal) taking us over a threshold and placing us outside our Optimal Arousal Zone, as shown in figure 7, which in turn means we must likely take active measures to settle ourselves, or we will feel compelled to respond to the arousing stimulus with active threat responses, such as fight or flight. When we are functioning outside our window in hyper-arousal—or in physiological sympathetic dominance, where we feel too much arousal—we will exhibit signs of the sympathetic activation system, such as fear, trembling, feeling overwhelmed, or hypervigilance.

Dorsal parasympathetic dominance, by contrast, would take us outside of the window in the other direction—with hypo-arousal (the dorsal parasympathetic/freeze response, or too little arousal), as shown in figure 8. In that case, we experience the effects of dorsal dominance, such as numbness, a sense of disconnection, or lack of energy. As we know, both the hyper- and hypo-arousal

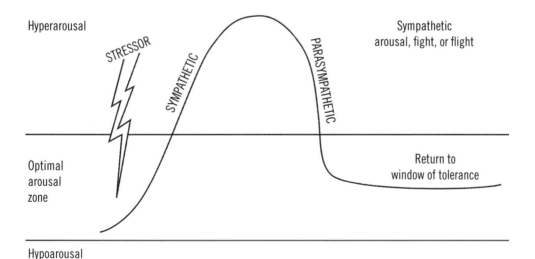

Figure 7

zones are affiliated with survival physiology. They tend to evoke threat-response behaviors, including the freeze response, or they require active effort, such as self-soothing behaviors, so that we can steer ourselves back into the Window of Tolerance.

When we slip outside of the Window of Tolerance and into survival physiology, the subcortical regions of the brain become more dominant, inhibiting our access to the executive function of the prefrontal cortex. We are more likely to be over-powered by our own survival responses, losing access to the more rational and logical thought processes that are mediated by the cortical regions of our brain.

One possible goal of therapy for the trauma survivor is to expand his Window of Tolerance, increasing his capacity to respond to greater and greater challenges and stimulation, while remaining within a range of self-awareness and regula-tion that does not provoke survival physiology. This capacity would arise from an increase in the client's access to healthier self-regulation and a greater felt sense of safety. Often this is initially accomplished by exposing the client to var-ious tools that assist with self-regulation and self-soothing. Later in this chapter,

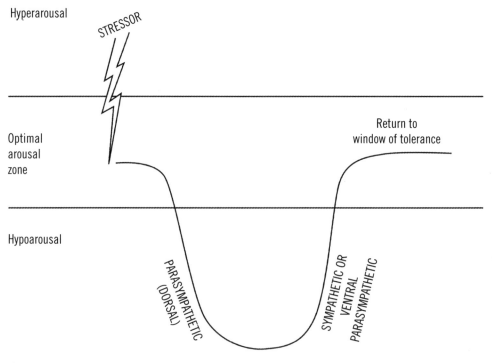

Figure 8

we will discuss other ways the clinician can support expansion of the client's Window of Tolerance.

When we function within the Window of Tolerance, we are able to connect with others, because we are feeling safe enough to seek out connection, and we are within a physiological state that supports such connection. When we are regulated within this window, we are better prepared for learning experiences—we are capable of receiving, processing, and integrating information—and we are more fully able to respond to the demands of everyday life with greater ease.

As noted above, the Window of Tolerance theory is based on normal development of the nervous system. When a client has experienced developmental trauma, his ability to self-regulate or co-regulate within the Window of Tolerance is likely to be more limited. That typically means the client will function in a chronically activated state (sympathetic arousal), or perhaps a mild state of the freeze response (dorsal parasympathetic), or what we might call "functional freeze." In this case, the dorsal physiology is more dominant than is healthy, though the client is still able to function; he is not in such a deep state of freeze that he cannot support at least some level of daily activity. In the following sections of this chapter, we will present a variation of the Window of Tolerance model that addresses the varying dynamics of developmental trauma.

Dr. Daniel Siegel, after spending years polling many thousands of health care and medical professionals to create proper, accurate definitions of the "mind" and "mental health"—but not finding any consistent definitions within that community—finally developed this definition of the mind, which was met with agreement by his colleagues: "The mind is an embodied and relational emergent process that regulates the flow of energy and information" throughout the body (Siegel 2014, 1). In this definition, Siegel differentiates the mind—the function of complex and interrelated systems—from the brain itself. He, among many others who study the mind, proposes that the mind—and the self, for that matter—are not simply extensions of the activity of the brain. In his concept of "mindsight," he proposes that humans require healthy development not only of the brain, but of the mind, and of our relational capacity, in order to develop fully and function in such a way that we can create satisfying lives for ourselves. "Studies are very clear: When we help others, we all win. Compassion and empathic joy are the outcomes of integration. And these are the realization of the fact that our 'self' is both embodied and relational—we are more than the boundaries of our skin" (Siegel 2014, 1).

When the mind and our relational capacity develop in a healthy way, a responsive and flexible Window of Tolerance and healthy self-regulation are the natural side effects. The human experience of "energy and information flow" to which Siegel refers—the ability to access a sense of connectedness and safety—will be more fully available if all aspects of "self" development have been in place in a healthy way from the earliest formation of the self. As Siegel notes, we develop not only a sense of *me,* but of an interconnected sense of being part of a larger *we* through our social connections, an integrated *MWe* (Siegel 2014). When things go well during our development, the self is seen as part of a plural entity, able to connect with others and reap the benefits of that connection.

Trauma during early development ruptures the sense of the *MWe,* blocking the possibility for such a concept to develop in our consciousness (or unconsciousness). The result, often, is a general and prolonged sense of isolation and an experience of the self as singular, as apart from the outside world. Trauma can instill in survivors an inability to reach out for connection when in need, and an inability to reap the benefits of belonging to the greater *we.* If this has been our experience during our developing years, then our Window of Tolerance is likely to be quite narrow. It will take very little to push us outside our Optimal Arousal Zone, and we will likely find it rather challenging to bring ourselves back within that range.

However, when our Window of Tolerance functions within a healthy range, we experience the benefits in three areas: somatic, mental-emotional, and behavioral:

- **Somatically,** regulation supports us in our ability to learn and to connect with others. It provides a general sense of ease throughout our entire system, giving us a greater sense of groundedness and connectedness in our inner experience. Even our pain receptors are calm, and we likely experience less pain and discomfort.

- **Mentally and emotionally,** we experience a greater sense of calm. We become increasingly more curious about discovering and learning new things in the world around us. We interact in a more playful and relaxed mood. We seek out others and want others around us to share our experiences relationally.

- Cooperation with others is a clear sign of **behavioral** regulation. Because of our interpersonal connections, we feel more motivated to pursue our goals, accomplish what we set out to do, and finish projects, rather than leaving them incomplete. We are likely to be more open to spontaneous activity and capable of feeling a deeper sense of empathy toward others. Our creativity emerges, and our gift of sharing with others becomes more profound.

Our early life experiences profoundly impact how our Window of Tolerance develops, and how we are able to tolerate activation and distress. Fortunately for most, the Window of Tolerance develops so that we can negotiate our ever-growing and ever-expanding lives. However, for some, an expansive and well-regulated Window of Tolerance is unfamiliar, even foreign. Such clients need support in order to expand their capacity and develop a greater sense of resilience, as well as regulation.

LOCUS OF CONTROL

Julian Rotter's earliest research in the 1950s focused on the concept of personality, and eventually led to the development of an idea he called *locus of control of reinforcement,* which we touched upon in chapter 5. Rotter was focused on the role of personality in social learning theory. His construct was based on the theory that personality is related to a person's interaction with her environment, that our early experiences and interactions will affect our future lives and choices. The concept of locus of control is integral to the information presented in this book in relation to regulation and resilience. Healthy development of our locus of control parallels healthy development of our capacity for self-regulation, which in turn contributes to a healthy Window of Tolerance.

Rotter believed that it was not possible to consider someone's personality without also considering the environment in which the person developed. He believed that one should take into account a person's history of her individual learning, experiences, and environment, as well as the stimuli she is aware of and responding to, when considering how the personality has developed. Rotter believed that personality is a set of stable potentials for responding to situations in a specific way (Mearns 2017).

We know that our early experiences affect our health and relationships throughout our lifetimes. Results of various studies, such as the ACE Study, as well as other social and psychological studies, have proved that correlation. Rotter was probably ahead of his time in thinking there was no specific window of development where personality was formed and locked into place. He saw the brain as more plastic and ever-changing. He *did* recognize that the more prolonged a person's exposure to certain experiences, and the longer she held certain beliefs, the harder it became to change the person's way of thinking and the expression of her beliefs.

Rotter explored the construct of personality from a more generalized behavioral perspective, rather than a trauma perspective, to better understand what motivates a person, how he experiences a sense of satisfaction, how he perceives his sense of control over outcomes, and how he understands and processes reinforcing events. In the decades since Rotter began his investigation, more advanced research has been conducted around locus of control and how it's shaped by maltreatment or trauma. This has greatly expanded our view of how trauma influences the allocation of a sense of control (Roazzi et al. 2016), and of how locus of control is related to resilience.

Locus of control is viewed as a continuum, rather than a set of discrete options or possibilities at one end of the spectrum or the other. The continuum includes everything from extreme internal to extreme external locus of control, as illustrated in figure 9.

Extreme External  Extreme Internal

Figure 9

Those with an internal locus of control believe strongly that they are responsible for their choices and, ultimately, that they are responsible for their own sense of reward or accomplishment and the interpretation of events—known as "reinforcements" in the locus of control model. Those with this mindset see themselves as the captains of their own ships. They look inward for responses to situations and experiences, and allocate responsibility to themselves (rather than others or random circumstances) for their successes and failures in life.

At the opposite end of the spectrum, those with an external locus of control believe in fate and give credit to external forces for their life circumstances. They are more likely to allocate responsibility for successes and failures to luck, chance, or other people in their lives to whom they ascribe power. It is difficult for them to imagine that they bear any responsibility for their own reinforcements.

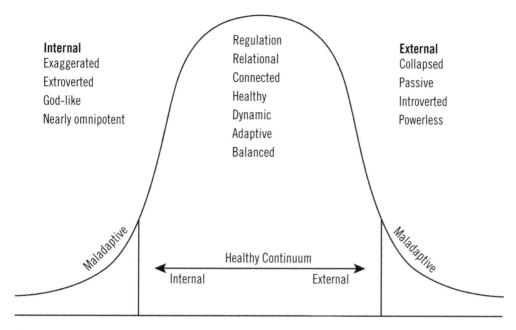

Internal
Exaggerated
Extroverted
God-like
Nearly omnipotent

Regulation
Relational
Connected
Healthy
Dynamic
Adaptive
Balanced

External
Collapsed
Passive
Introverted
Powerless

Maladaptive

Maladaptive

Healthy Continuum

Internal   External

Figure 10

In figure 10, we can see that locus of control can be graphed as a bell curve, with a healthy range in the middle, where movement between the experience of internal and external locus of control can occur on a continuum. Any individual might fall toward one end of the spectrum or the other as a general expression of her personality. Within a healthy range, we would find the capacity for recognition that some things are truly beyond the realm of our control (and we must find ways to adapt), whereas other things are within our control (and require us to take responsibility).

At the far end of the spectrum, on either side, are the extreme versions of locus of control, which are considered maladaptive. An extreme internal locus of control might produce the perception of being all-powerful and god-like, and would certainly include sociopathic behaviors. Another version of internal locus of control could manifest in feelings of responsibility for all bad things that happen, even those that are clearly outside of our control. We might have an exaggerated sense of our own importance and our ability to influence events, and may exert almost obsessive levels of effort to control such events.

An extreme level of external locus of control might produce a sense of powerlessness, the feeling that we are unable to accomplish anything due to all-powerful "others," such as the government or our bosses, that we have no say in what happens to us, and that we should simply surrender to fate. We might lack the ability to recognize the relationship between what happens in our lives and our own responsibility for it; we are simply victims of circumstances or outright maliciousness. We may tend to blame everyone else for whatever happens, even for things that clearly arise from our own behavior. What we know from more current trauma research is that those with greater access to a healthy sense of internal locus of control tend to fare better in life, whereas those with a tendency toward external locus of control are more prone to clinical depression, for example (Benassi, Sweeney, and Dufour 1988).

Rotter cautioned against making broad interpretations based on locus of control. He continually urged practitioners to take the circumstances of the environment into account, including how people respond in different situations. Even though the concept can be generalized and used as a predictor of behavior, to a certain degree a person's locus of control can change with her environment.

When considering locus of control in relation to developmental trauma, it's important to look at the first six weeks after birth. Infants are born completely helpless and have a developmentally appropriate method of survival that requires an external locus of control. If the caretaker is consistently meeting the needs of the infant, the infant will experience an increasing sense of internal locus of control, even though the care is coming from an external source. Much as healthy co-regulation will naturally build self-regulation capacity in the infant and child, responsiveness on the part of the caregiver slowly builds an experience of agency in the infant and child. It fosters an unspoken sense that the infant or child has the ability to influence the outside world, first through the ability to influence the caregiver's response to the infant's needs. When the child has not experienced that sense of agency, he is less likely to fully develop a sense of internal locus of control.

We can also draw a correlation here between internal/external locus of control and anxious/avoidant attachment styles. Someone who is anxious in his attachment style could be seen as having an external locus of control that is farther along the continuum toward the extreme, whereas a person who has an avoidant attachment style could be seen as having an internal locus of control that is farther along the continuum toward the extreme. The person with an anxious attachment style is more likely to rely on the other person in the relationship to provide comfort and a sense of security, and may even expect that person to function as his source of regulation. In the absence of a direct sense of connection with that person, those with an anxious attachment style are more likely to feel unable to manage their own responses. Those with an avoidant attachment style will tend to find comfort in their own company and won't experience a sense of needing, or even wanting, anyone else's input into their lives.

Melinda lived at home with her mother, Gloria. Melinda was fifty-five years old and Gloria was in her late eighties. They had always lived together. Melinda's father was killed in a self-inflicted hunting accident when Melinda was six months old. Gloria remained enmeshed in Melinda's life and became anxious when Melinda would go to school or to her friends' houses. Once Melinda was an adult and working, she had to call Gloria two to three times per day from work, or Gloria would begin phoning her repeatedly to find out if Melinda was okay.

Gloria blamed God and the world for the death of Melinda's father, even though he had pointed the gun toward himself while reloading. Gloria was never able to accept that her husband had any responsibility for the accident and never took responsibility for her own situation. She blamed the insurance company, and later Social Security, for not paying her enough money to survive on her own. Her attachment style was anxious, and her locus of control was external.

Melinda, on the other hand, would find quiet and peace in her reading and would spend hours sitting alone in her room. If she didn't get that time every day, she would begin to feel anxious and nervous about going to work or leaving the house. While in her thirties, she met Tom at work. He found her interesting and funny and asked her out on dates. Their romance grew, and he wanted Melinda to marry him. He complained that he wanted to spend more time with Melinda, but she needed so much quiet, alone time that it was difficult to find enough time together. Between her mother and Tom, Melinda felt overwhelmed.

Tom was offered a promotion at work that came along with a relocation to another state. He wanted Melinda to move with him and start a life together. Gloria became angry and distraught, blaming Tom for her sadness and despair. She finally managed to convince Melinda to cancel her wedding plans and stay with her, convincing Melinda that Tom really didn't understand Melinda. Melinda's avoidant attachment style fed into her mother's manipulation as Gloria kept pointing out that Melinda would grow to hate Tom because she would have no time to herself to sit and read.

Gloria's anxious attachment style and external locus of control had interfered with her ability to recover from the loss of her husband, and in turn influenced Melinda's ability to "launch" into adulthood and develop her own healthy external locus of control. Melinda's avoidant attachment style can be seen as a defensive accommodation to the constant anxiety that Gloria brought to her role as a mother. Unable to manage her own activation and stress without withdrawing into extended periods of isolation, Melinda had difficulty sustaining a relationship outside of the enmeshed relationship with her mother.

As noted above, the healthy development of our locus of control is also part of what influences the healthy development of our Window of Tolerance. When we have a sense of agency in our ability to influence what is happening to us, but can also understand when circumstances are effectively beyond our control and therefore we must adapt to those circumstances as best we can, that is one of the signs of resilience. It also influences how we manage our responses when we move out of our window into hyper- or hypo-arousal, as we will discuss further in the next section.

THE FAUX WINDOW OF TOLERANCE

We can extend the Window of Tolerance model to include the understanding of how clients utilize various strategies for managing their dysregulation and uncontained responses when they leave the Window of Tolerance and enter into hyper- or hypo-arousal states, particularly if they are chronically unable to access the Optimal Arousal Zone (the ventral parasympathetic and low-tone dorsal physiology). In such cases, defensive accommodations develop to manage chronic levels of hyper- and hypo-arousal states. On top of the Window of Tolerance model, we can overlay what we have come to call the Faux Window of Tolerance. The model of the Faux Window provides a representation of what occurs when someone is chronically outside of his Window of Tolerance, and has developed defensive accommodations that effectively provide him with the experience of being within his Optimal Arousal Zone—when, in fact, he is operating chronically outside of that zone.

In this representation, in figure 11, the Window of Tolerance is shown as being narrowed, making it very challenging for the client to stay within that window once any sort of stimulus appears. This is what typically occurs in the face of developmental trauma. The chronic dysregulation that commonly accompanies early trauma usually forces this narrowing of the Optimal Arousal Zone to the point that almost anything bringing challenge to the system will push someone over the threshold of the window. In figure 11, we can see how this would occur with chronic hyper-arousal.

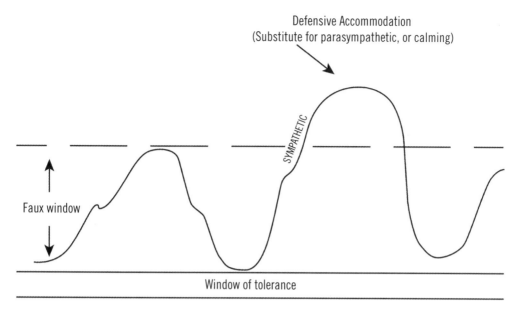

Defensive Accommodation
(Substitute for parasympathetic, or calming)

SYMPATHETIC

Faux window

Window of tolerance

Figure 11

The Window of Tolerance is at the bottom of the diagram. On the hyper-arousal side of the Window of Tolerance, we have indicated an additional window, which we term the Faux, or artificial, Window. In this range, the client manages her hyper-arousal states with defensive accommodations—self-soothing behaviors like dissociation or compulsive eating—that hold her responses within a range that she experiences as manageable. The movement in and out of the Faux Window will occur much as it does within the Window of Tolerance, but the client may not actually reenter the Window of Tolerance, only stabilizing as best she can within a hyper-arousal state that is "workable" or "manageable" for tolerating her sympathetic activation symptoms and responses.

As with the Window of Tolerance, there can be a Faux Window on the hypo-arousal side of the true Window of Tolerance. In this case, the client will manage his hypo-arousal states with defensive accommodations that would substitute for either the ventral parasympathetic system (social engagement) or the sympathetic (active response) system—perhaps by using stimulants, acting out, or entering hyper-sexuality—to keep his experience of the low-energy states of the dorsal physiology within a range that feels tolerable. Again, the defensive accommodations may not be sufficient to move the client back within the Window of Tolerance, instead stabilizing as much as possible within the collapsed, disconnected dorsal physiology. Figure 12 shows this version of the Faux Window.

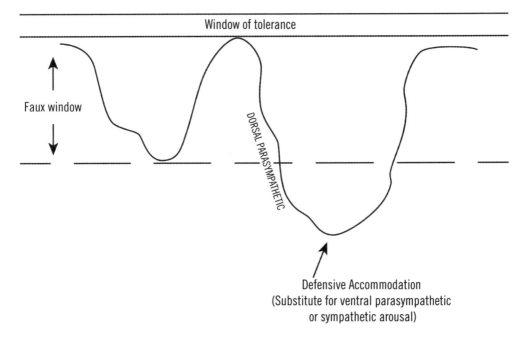

Window of tolerance

Faux window

DORSAL PARASYMPATHETIC

Defensive Accommodation
(Substitute for ventral parasympathetic
or sympathetic arousal)

Figure 12

This is not regulation, but it will sometimes feel that way to clients who have not experienced genuine and sustained self-regulation. Many clients who have experienced developmental trauma have never fully developed a Window of Tolerance—they chronically operate beyond their threshold of regulation. Because they don't have access to genuine self-regulation, they will come as close as they can by applying defensive accommodations.

For ease of discussion, the Faux Window for both hyper- and hypo-arousal responses has been overlaid on the Window of Tolerance in figure 13.

Let's look at the hyper-arousal portion of the Faux Window, in the instance of chronic arousal that developed early in life. Under such conditions, when the sympathetic system rises, the ventral parasympathetic response lacks the capacity to adequately reduce activation and restore equilibrium, or a return to the Window of Tolerance. Perhaps the ANS is operating outside the reciprocal range, and there is now *coactivation* of both the sympathetic and parasympathetic systems. In that case, as the sympathetic activation rises, so too will the dorsal parasympathetic, provoking simultaneous but contradictory physiological responses. The result is the felt sense that our bodies, our responses, are out of control.

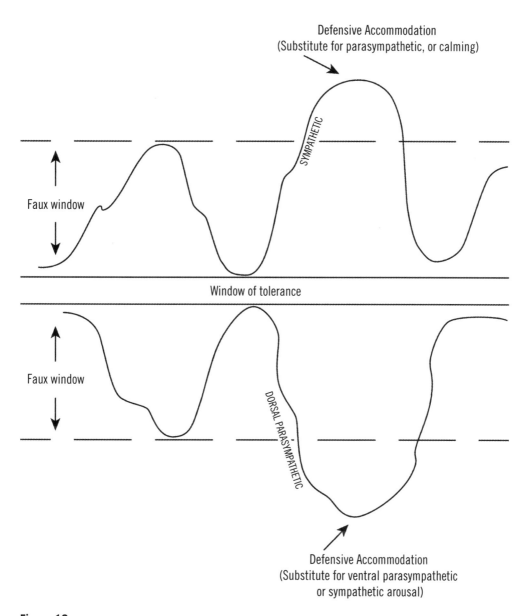

Defensive Accommodation
(Substitute for parasympathetic, or calming)

SYMPATHETIC

Faux window

Window of tolerance

Faux window

DORSAL PARASYMPATHETIC

Defensive Accommodation
(Substitute for ventral parasympathetic
or sympathetic arousal)

Figure 13

As a substitute for actual regulatory capacity in the parasympathetic system, we will likely develop some type of management strategy, or defensive accommodation, to address the hyper-arousal. It's unworkable to live and function in a constantly elevated state of arousal, so we find ways to manage that activation and create some form of secondary equilibrium—the Faux Window.

As noted in chapter 5, defensive accommodations can take many forms. They may be physiological, behavioral, mental-emotional, or relational. We consider attachment styles, for example, to be a type of defensive accommodation. Obsessive self-soothing behaviors, such as uncontrolled eating, might be another type.

Overusing our dorsal physiology and moving into collapse and numbing is another common physiological strategy related to early trauma. The high-tone (freeze) dorsal physiology is not meant to be used on a chronic basis, but if we have limited access to the ventral parasympathetic system, we sometimes learn (physiologically) to use the dorsal system as the primary control mechanism for the sympathetic system. As noted in chapter 4, the low-tone dorsal physiology is dominant when we are experiencing immobility without fear, which occurs during sleep, quiet bonding behaviors, and other resting states. However, in the absence of healthy co-regulation, we may have experienced limited exposure to the ventral physiology, and so we used what was available to us at the time—the dorsal physiology. Having successfully used this "trick" once, the body may again utilize that same neurological route under similar circumstances in the future, and again repeatedly over time. Once the pattern is formed, we may chronically use immobility responses and conservation physiology to dampen sympathetic arousal the moment we feel any level of activation at all. However, this is still conservation physiology, which does not provide proper support for social engagement, activity, or the full range of self-regulation responses, and so it carries a high allostatic load. In other words, the physiological defensive accommodation of overusing the dorsal physiology brings a high cost of doing business. It holds us within a physiological range that is more affiliated with the survival response, which means we have less energy available for other critical physiological functions and we begin to deplete ourselves.

This overuse of the dorsal physiology is one of the common physiological strategies that develops in response to early trauma, and is implicated in some of the symptoms the ACE Study has linked with early trauma. Learning to work effectively with the dorsal physiology is a critical aspect of supporting clients in the development of regulation, which in turn supports greater resilience. Later in this chapter, we present more information on that topic.

In the upper range of the Faux Window, we may reach the edge of anger or rage. We verge toward panic or other responses affiliated with hyper-arousal. Because the Faux Window is often well outside the Optimal Arousal Zone, we need to understand as clinicians that within that Faux Window, the client is not in fact within a regulated state and does not have reliable access to the ventral physiology that supports social engagement behaviors, as well as regulation. Instead, the client is overstimulated, even when appearing to function within his Window of Tolerance.

Even strong defensive accommodations may not be sufficient to return us to the Window of Tolerance. They may be just enough to return us to the Faux Window, but, again, that is not within the self-regulation range, and someone who has had little experience with self-regulation may mistake the Faux Window for actual regulation. This maladaptive regulation system feels normal to him—it's all he knows.

The clinician may also be fooled by defensive accommodations if the client's capacity for managing her responses is effective and well developed. A clinician can easily misunderstand or misjudge the client's capacity to tolerate more stimulus. A client's return to the Faux Window may be mistaken for a return to regulation, and the clinician may proceed with further interventions that only serve to strengthen the client's defensive accommodations as she struggles to manage her overstimulation.

The same process can occur in the mirror image of the Faux Window, on the hypo-arousal side. In this case, as we move into dorsal parasympathetic dominance, neither the ventral parasympathetic nor the sympathetic systems have enough capacity to restore equilibrium and return the physiology to the Optimal Arousal Zone. As may be true with the upper range of the Faux Window, we may be operating outside the reciprocal range of the ANS, in this case with *coinhibition* occurring. When the parasympathetic system reduces its effect, so too the sympathetic system reduces its effect, again creating contradictory impacts in the physiology.

Jerry is fifty-six, single, and employed as a typesetter for a local printing company. He works the overnight shift with one other employee. Jerry was born prematurely and spent the first two months of his life on a respirator in the neonatal intensive care unit. Jerry's mother and father were not able to touch Jerry until he was almost six weeks old. He was surrounded by machines without the nurturance of loving touch for nearly two months. Jerry's mother and father were farmers, and he was the fifth of eleven children. Because of their work on the farm, they were able to visit Jerry in the hospital only one day a week. This separation was not planned, but had long-term consequences for Jerry and his emotional development.

Jerry was considered a "good" baby when he came home. His mother remarked that he slept most of the time and rarely cried until he was two years old. Jerry's mother was expecting Jerry's younger sibling before Jerry was three months old. Jerry's mother did not have the energy necessary to care for Jerry's needs, and she often propped up bottles to feed him and rarely interacted with him.

By age three, Jerry seemed wild to his family. He frequently ran away from the family and broke toys without reason. When he entered school, he was labeled ADHD and placed on medications to regulate behavior and mood. He struggled to learn and had no meaningful relationships.

In middle school, Jerry refused to take his medication any longer, complaining that the side effects were too disturbing. His mood changed drastically, to constant high arousal and agitation. He began to drink his father's vodka to help himself relax. It wasn't long before he added pot to the mix and would drink and smoke pot several times a day. He was passed through school by teachers who didn't know what to do or how to help him.

During high school, Jerry had several run-ins with the law. He was arrested for intoxication and for possession of marijuana. He continued to drink and smoke pot. It was only when Jerry was high or intoxicated that he could tolerate being around his family. He would get very quiet, and no one noticed his emotional pain. He was reenacting the role that his parents seemed to love the most—the quiet, sleeping infant who didn't cry.

Jerry had several short-term relationships after high school. The relationships all ended because of Jerry's substance abuse, or his rage, which would surface from time to time. Women would say they were afraid of Jerry and where his anger could lead. Jerry struggled to keep jobs and lived on the edge of society until he found his current job as a typesetter.

Jerry seemed to do his best working alone at night. He was able to drink and smoke pot and still hold down a job, but he often became angry during his shifts and screamed at his coworker. His coworker confronted him about his alcohol and drug use, but Jerry had one response: he was not addicted, and he denied being an alcoholic.

Jerry used denial and substances as defensive accommodations. During his younger life, he used medications as an artificial parasympathetic brake for his sympathetic arousal. He rarely had the experience of his parasympathetic response coming on naturally—his ANS was out of sync with itself. Jerry blamed others for his problems, but desperately wanted to be accepted and loved by his family. He had never experienced a natural Window of Tolerance, but existed only in a Faux Window. This Faux Window at one edge was dark and quiet, and, at the other, filled with anger and rage. He used substances to manipulate his regulation within the Faux Window.

With his lack of access to co-regulation and soothing during his first weeks of life, Jerry's physiology tuned more toward overuse of the dorsal conservation physiology. Once home with his family, his quietness was misinterpreted as his being a "good" baby who never cried. Because his mother was already overwhelmed with child care, she felt relief at having a baby who seemed to need so little from her.

As Jerry matured, that fundamental lack of regulation began to show more in his inability to manage his own responses, and he began to use substances as a defensive accommodation to support what felt like a "smoother" experience, rather than the wild ride he had when he wasn't using his medication.

In Jerry's case, working to help him stay within his Window of Tolerance, offering attachment repair and consistent co-regulation, is likely to make a big difference in his ability to regulate his responses. Because of his tendency to overuse his dorsal physiology, he has as much defensive accommodation on the hypo side of his physiology as he does on the hyper-arousal side.

As occurred in the hyper-arousal side of the Faux Window, defensive accommodations will be used as a substitute for the regulatory functions of the sympathetic or ventral physiology. This could include the use of stimulants or self-stimulating behaviors that bring us out of the lethargy and numbing that typically accompanies the dorsal freeze states. It could also manifest as hyper-sexuality or other almost obsessive attempts to experience a sense of social connection. By contrast, such defensive accommodations might include the avoidance of social situations that feel too stimulating. But this avoidance can plunge us further into numbing and lethargy.

On the hypo side of the Faux Window, we may be on the edge of complete collapse, struggling with a sense of depression and hopelessness. We may spend an inordinate amount of time managing our energy, limiting our exposure to stressors, and finding ways to conserve our limited physical resources.

Again, the defensive accommodations themselves tend to occupy even more of our life's energy, further narrowing our Window of Tolerance and provoking more defensive accommodations. Already, we can see how some of the symptoms affiliated with early trauma, as seen in the ACE Study, for example, can arise from these dynamics of responses related to the Faux Window.

As with the hyper-arousal range of the Faux Window, if defensive accommodation strategies are well developed and effective on the other (hypo-arousal) side of the Faux Window, both the client and the clinician may misinterpret the client's state and believe she is within the Window of Tolerance. The clinician may therefore prepare for further interventions that might ultimately challenge her response system rather than restore it.

Another common physiological "habit" that may develop in the face of developmental trauma is an oscillation between high arousal and a deep dive into the dorsal physiology. We would typically see this in the context of foundational dysregulation, as discussed in chapter 5. In this case, one would see a client who alternated between the upper and lower ranges of the Faux Window, showing symptoms related to each, and having a complex system of defensive accommodations.

Any version of the Faux Window can be affiliated with somatic symptoms related to overuse of survival physiology, the types of symptoms we see with patients who score higher on the ACE scale.

Most people who operate within the Faux Window are not aware that they are not actually within a regulated state. If this is all they have ever known, this is as close to regulation as they can get, and they are likely to have normalized the Faux Window to the point that they would say they are relaxed and settled, even when they are well outside the Optimal Arousal Zone. With experience, clinicians can learn to recognize these defensive accommodations, and recognize when a client is operating within her Faux Window, rather than within her Window of Tolerance, and adjust interventions accordingly.

BUILDING CAPACITY TO HANDLE STRESSORS AND EXPANDING THE WINDOW OF TOLERANCE

From the clinical perspective, awareness of the Faux Window allows us to change our interventions with clients so that we are not simply strengthening the need for their defensive accommodations. If we are working with clients who are constantly outside their Window of Tolerance and making the assumption that they have enough regulatory capacity to handle stressors as they arise, we are likely doing little more than reconfirming their defensive accommodations.

Part of learning to work well with developmental trauma is learning to recognize defensive accommodations and understand them as signals that the client is beyond or below the threshold of his Optimal Arousal Zone. Rather than considering what we may need to *add,* we more likely must consider what should be *reduced* or *removed* to decrease overstimulation and diminish the need for defensive accommodations. In such cases, we need to limit the interventions we use to those that help the client remain within his Window of Tolerance, and reduce how frequently we provoke the need for defensive accommodations.

At the same time, we should also provide support to increase the capacity for self-regulation, which will in turn expand the Window of Tolerance, thereby reducing the need for defensive accommodations. We will discuss the support for regulation more fully in subsequent chapters.

For those clients who have limited access to social engagement physiology, or for whom people are frightening, we may need to understand that the demand for social engagement and connection—or even the offers of connection that we might think of routinely offering as part of our therapeutic interventions—may be too much for the client and may actually strengthen his Faux Window responses.

As clinicians, if we have the habit of overtly offering support and opportunities for connection, we may actually be driving that type of client even beyond her Faux Window and increasing her hyper- or hypo-arousal responses. Instead, we may make more progress by taking pressure off the client to respond. We may need to wait until she gently offers connection—a passing reference to how she thought of us when she saw a painting similar to the one in our office—and respond only when her capacity has increased enough to make this small invitation to connect. We may need to work first with this type of client from a more directly physiological perspective before we can work relationally.

We can expand the Window of Tolerance through regulation work, by repairing attachment, by creating safety, and by using small, incremental, and gentle challenges to the regulatory capacity of the client to expand her Window of Tolerance. One of the ways we can support expansion of the Window of Tolerance is by working effectively with the dorsal parasympathetic physiology.

WORKING WITH DORSAL PHYSIOLOGY

As noted previously, overuse of the dorsal conservation parasympathetic physiology is one of the common ANS responses to early trauma. In such cases, the dorsal physiology is not operating within the low-tone range of "immobility without fear," but has become chronic at the farther end of the spectrum, closer to the freeze response, or what can be considered *functional freeze*. Alternatively, the ANS may be outside the reciprocal range, creating chronic coactivation or coinhibition, thus providing physiologically mixed responses.

Chronic freeze physiology, as well as chronic nonreciprocal ANS physiology, are both associated with some of the ACE symptoms discussed in chapter 6. We can see this aspect of physiological range as a physiological defensive accommodation, a substitute for genuine regulation. Rather than having access to the full range of responses within the Window of Tolerance, we instead narrow the window by continually using the dorsal system to keep any arousal in check, creating a Faux Window that doesn't tolerate any stimulation.

The challenge for the clinician is that clients with this form of dysregulation will often "fall" into the dorsal physiology with even the smallest stimulation, or may habitually live in a somewhat numbed and low-energy state, almost seeming serene or undisturbed. The dorsal physiology is often more dominant in clients who are dissociated, because the natural numbing and sense of disconnection that accompanies the freeze physiology tend to support dissociative states.

This chronic dorsal state is the mirror image of a chronically high level of sympathetic arousal in a client. With sympathetic arousal, the client will tend to be visibly unsettled, often anxious, with physiological symptoms that indicate more high-energy survival responses, such as fight or flight. By contrast, the dorsal physiology is usually more difficult to recognize. Because the client is often numbed to her own experience, she may be reporting that she feels fine and doesn't feel activated.

As with sympathetic activation states, however, any further stimulus or challenge to the client's system will likely cause even greater movement along the spectrum of response. For the dorsal system, that means the client would move even more deeply into a freeze response, or, conversely, be more out of control if she is in the nonreciprocal range of the ANS.

This chronic dorsal physiology is often present because, in her early years, the client lacked reliable access to the co-regulation needed to fully develop the ventral parasympathetic physiology. The nonreciprocal ANS physiology is often affiliated with the disorganized attachment style, as well as with high ACE scores. That, in turn, often means the client views other people as the source of—not the solution to—her stress states. The type of client who sees humans as threatening will typically not find social engagement or offers of connection to be settling. In fact, the idea of even simple eye contact might be terrifying. The client can't move into social engagement to access her parasympathetic system, and she may rely on the dorsal system as the regulating influence for her sympathetic arousal, which moves her into functional freeze to manage activation.

As Porges has noted with early trauma, our orientation systems may get "miswired" toward dorsal physiology, precipitating a dive into the high-tone dorsal physiology even as we try to scan our environment for danger. The very act of trying to search for potential threats will precipitate the freeze response. This is a deep physiological response that must be accounted for in interventions used by the clinician. With this type of client, the typical therapeutic interventions we might use to communicate safety may actually backfire. Invitations to make eye contact, to notice that the therapist is present and available, to look around the room and notice what's there—these may actually drive the client more fully outside of his Window of Tolerance and more fully *into* his defensive accommodations, both physiologically and behaviorally. He may disconnect further, dissociate, or drop even more deeply into conservation physiology.

From the perspective of clinical interventions for this type of client, we need to consider that offers of social engagement are not workable strategies for inviting further development of the ventral parasympathetic physiology. We will have to "titrate" our invitations into social engagement and connection—scale them back, offer them in very small doses, and carefully study our client's responses as we tiptoe into new therapeutic territory. We can do this by employing the dorsal system to begin accessing safety (immobility without fear) and inviting the client into the low-tone range of the dorsal physiology, by letting him be quiet, without asking him to engage with us. As noted previously, we are considering *what can be taken away* to relieve a feeling of pressure on the client's social engagement system, rather than *what we are adding* by way of a demand for response from the client.

For example, the clinician can simply let the client rest in good company. This might include actual napping, if the client feels safe enough to do that, or it might include a sense of quiet co-regulation, allowing moments of silence, without the clinician asking too many questions of the client. This can be done without physical contact, but if the client feels comforted or reassured by having gentle touch applied, then that can be included. This method can often be experienced by the client as being allowed to rest while the clinician "keeps watch." This provides a safe haven and secure base while the client explores his ability to let down his guard and settle into the low-tone dorsal physiology, as opposed to freeze physiology. The clinician may need to gently "coach" and help the client notice if he begins to dissociate rather than rest, gently inviting him back into the room.

If the clinician is "standing watch," the client may feel safe enough to doze or go inside himself to notice his internal sensations. Ideally, the client may gain a sense of the clinician being attuned enough but not intrusive.

Alternatively, the clinician may share some "parallel play" with the client, asking the client to make a drawing of something that happened in the past week that was pleasant, and leaving the client to do that with only an occasional comment from the clinician. Or, perhaps, the client and clinician can listen to some music together that the client requested. Of course, these experiences must also be titrated, and it needs to be clear that the client is at ease with this process.

As clinicians, we can sometimes undervalue these subtle forms of intervention. The implied client contract is often that we be more apparently active in guiding the process. However, if we consider that our primary intervention in working with any form of developmental trauma is the offer of co-regulation, then any opportunity to create that dynamic, no matter how quiet or small, will often produce benefits for the client and the therapeutic relationship. This approach can help repair attachment disruptions by providing a sense of safety with the clinician and access to deep, somatic co-regulation. This can go a long way toward allowing the client to safely connect with himself, in whatever way feels manageable.

Slowly, as the client feels more comfortable and gains greater access to the quiet, nonfear range of the dorsal physiology, the clinician can gently make more offers of ventral connection, of social engagement. The focus should be on keeping the client within his Window of Tolerance, easing into social contact, titrating incrementally into access to the physiology of social engagement, and gently expanding his capacity.

BUILDING MORE ACCURATE INTEROCEPTION

Those with early trauma experiences, particularly if those experiences were severe and extended over long periods of time, have, out of necessity, learned to pay attention to the world primarily through a lens of potential threat. As noted earlier in this chapter, in order to expand a client's capacity and increase resilience, we need to first work within his actual Window of Tolerance rather than within his Faux Window.

Because the purpose of the Faux Window is to create a secondary equilibrium that substitutes for a true Window of Tolerance, the client is most often unaware that the Faux Window is not actual regulation. In addition, it is relatively easy to overstimulate this type of client to the point that he moves outside of the Faux Window as well, which will inevitably precipitate strong survival responses. Trying to work within a range that allows the client to return to his Window of Tolerance, and stay within it, is not easy when there is so much volatility in the client's responses. One of the tools that can be helpful is to support the client in building more accurate interoception. This will allow him to more carefully track his responses, enable him to learn to notice when he is outside of his Window of Tolerance, and provide more accurate feedback about interventions.

One of the common biophysiological methods used when working with trauma is that of having the client track her own sensations. As clinicians, we may take for granted that the client is able to differentiate between different categories of sensations, or that she can accurately report the sensations she is noticing. However, those apparently simple tasks may not actually be available to the client.

Each of us has developed our own language of the self—the somatic language we use to tell ourselves how we are, and perhaps even who we are. That language developed directly from the context of our early experiences of self, and our early experiences of self in relation to other. When those early experiences occurred within the context of trauma, our somatic conversations with ourselves also occurred within that context.

We might then develop a somatic vocabulary that is well attuned toward sensations of pain, distress, danger, watchfulness, or other survival-related forms of attention. But we might have a very limited somatic vocabulary for positive experiences—for noticing when we are safe, when we are enjoying the taste of something, or when all is well. If we haven't achieved a state of ease in many years—or ever—such a state is impossible to recognize.

Without the properly attuned interoceptive language, we cannot recognize the felt sense of safety, we cannot recognize the signs that tell us we are within our Window of Tolerance, and we cannot recognize regulation when it is happening. Some of the most basic things a clinician may rely on from the client's reporting of experience may be reported inaccurately, or be so unavailable to the client that he essentially doesn't understand the clinician's inquiry. An apparently simple question like "When was the last time you felt safe?" may be almost completely befuddling. The client will try to peer inside himself, search for the information, but come up empty. "Um, I'm not sure if I've ever felt safe."

One of the key elements in the treatment of developmental trauma is helping the client build healthier and more accurate interoception. The most common way this will occur is through a process in which the clinician "compares notes" with the client about what is being observed. When the clinician notes a change in the client's physiological or somatic systems, she can mention that to the client, and the client can compare her own experience: "I notice that you just took a deep breath. Did you notice that? What did that feel like?" If touch is being used, the clinician can report what she notices, and make the same type of inquiry to the client: "I notice your muscle just seemed to relax under my hand, and I can now feel your breath moving through that area. What did you notice from the inside?"

Considering that the client, in early childhood, should have received plenty of feedback from caregivers about her somatic states ("Yum, that tastes good, doesn't it?"), then this simple process of comparing notes can be seen as part of the essential somatic "reparenting." "This is what I'm noticing from the outside. From the inside, what are you noticing?" This is one of the important elements that should have been present in early co-regulation: "I'm feeling like this. How are you feeling?"

Another way clinicians can support healthier and more accurate interoception is by helping the client understand what different types of sensations signify in terms of his own state of mind and physiology. This may be particularly important in relation to positive sensations. If someone has spent the majority of his time attending to things that might be dangerous, he may be limited in his ability to notice the things that aren't. From a survival perspective, it's much more critical to notice what might harm us, so more of our attention will be trained to do exactly that.

Clinicians may need to coach clients in how to notice which feelings are pleasant, which feelings they like, or, perhaps, if that's too big a leap, which feelings are "less bad" than others. In this regard, exploring how the client names and categorizes sensations is often important. What may sound from the client's report to be an unpleasant sensation may actually be the sensation of something "normal" happening. A client who has been overusing her dorsal physiology—chronically staying within a slightly numbed experience of self—may have little experience feeling much of anything inside her body. Even something as simple as feeling her stomach growl from hunger may be alarming, simply because it's an unfamiliar sensation and the client doesn't quite know what to make of it. If someone has been so disconnected from her body to the point that normal sensations of bodily processes have been essentially unavailable, as clinicians we need to understand that such clients may not recognize "normal" when they feel it, and may interpret these sensations through the lens of potential danger.

Again, this categorizing of sensations—especially when differentiating between threat and excitement—is what should have occurred in the social and bonding interactions that take place in a healthy early experience of self and other. Together we create a communal, somatic language we share in order to name how we feel together, or how we agree or disagree about preferences. For example, one of us likes the sensation of our stomach dropping when we ride a rollercoaster, but another doesn't. We learn that not everything we dislike is inherently bad or dangerous; it's merely a preference. We learn not to be alarmed by every uncomfortable sensation, and we learn how to notice what we do like.

If this has been missing for us, then we need to literally learn the language of self-conversation. As clinicians, that may be one of the important forms of support we offer: helping the client explore sensations from a perspective of curiosity and experimentation. Even though this is a simple and, in many cases, playful task, it can help the client expand her range of possible interoceptive meaning-making. As we will discuss in the next chapter, changing our somatic narrative is a critical element in recovering from trauma and moving toward greater resilience.

8

The Trauma Map: The Narrative of Developmental Trauma

CREATING NARRATIVE is one of the ways we make sense of our lived experience, our history, and our responses to that history. These stories help us to conceive of our own personal evolution, our lineage, or the creation of our current selves. We make meaning for ourselves around our cultural identities, gender identities, memories, and life experiences. We form the "story" of our lives that connects various aspects of our lived experience into a cohesive whole. One of the symptoms of trauma, and some forms of mental illness, is a diminished ability to form or remember a cohesive or positive narrative (Charon 2001; Gold 2007).

Self-narrative is a critical part of both psychological and medical practice, informing diagnosis, treatment, and recovery (Hirsh and Peterson 2009). The trauma narrative, in particular, is important for the recovery and healing of a trauma survivor (Levine 2010). This narrative includes more than the verbal recall of events and emotions; it reaches deeper into our physiological system and can potentially wreak havoc on our overall well-being if healing has yet to occur. For some clients, therapy may be the first opportunity to tell this story to another person. As clinicians, we will of course be listening to the words and the story, but also looking for clues as to how the client experiences that story somatically in the telling and construction of the narrative. This chapter explores both verbal and somatic narratives and their importance in helping clients reclaim their narrative and move toward improved regulation and healing.

VERBAL NARRATIVE

One key to understanding verbal narrative is the knowledge that early challenges in a client's life can affect multiple layers of his development, including how memories are integrated, and how the brain processes experience. Humans have two forms of long-term memory: implicit memory and explicit memory. Implicit memory is formed and used unconsciously, but can affect the way we think and behave. One of the most common forms of implicit memory is called *procedural memory,* in which the repetitive performance of a task eventually means we can perform that task without even thinking about it. By contrast, explicit memory (also called *declarative* or *autobiographical memory*) requires conscious thought, and is the intentional way we remember facts and experiences.

Our earliest memories are considered implicit, meaning they contain only impressions, a selection of details, or snippets of events, but form no real or distinct, explicit recall of events. The explicit or autobiographical memory does not come on board until around age three, when the left brain is further along in its development and providing the capacity for more logic and reasoning. This means that in our early experiences, we are not neurologically capable of forming memories in the same way we do when our brains are more mature. This has a profound impact on how we carry our narrative of those early experiences. We will not be able to form a verbal, autobiographical narrative for these early experiences, but may have strong feelings and responses associated with them. In particular, we may have strong somatic responses, which is why somatic narrative becomes so important in relation to early trauma.

In these early developmental times, adults sometimes misinterpret children's different processing of memory—the snippets, impressions, and metaphors that will be used to express feeling states—and consider them to be misrepresentations of the truth. This sometimes occurs in a different context in therapy, when the clinician assumes the client is not providing an accurate report of his history—the jumble of implicit memory can be mistaken for error in reporting when it is actually an honest expression of the developmental age at which the experiences occurred. Implicit memory does not provide a clear, sequential narrative. It also includes an emotional quality that may have been linked to the experience the child recalls, and therefore may seem exaggerated or unrelated to the "facts" of what occurred, particularly when compared with an adult's experience of the same event.

We know from extensive research into the relationship between trauma and memory that, during high activation, the brain processes memory differently (van der Kolk 1998). Under the influence of traumatic stress, even in adults, current experiences will be combined with snippets from implicit memory and other unrelated events, and all of these will be stitched together into a narrative that may seem coherent, but is in fact a conflation of various events that may have happened at widely varying ages. In children, this conflation of events and feelings is a normal part of early development, but trauma intensifies this process.

To complicate matters further, the pre-attachment phase—the first six weeks of life—is the time when we are most vulnerable to the longer-term impacts of developmental challenges. As noted in chapter 4, during the first six months of life, we are particularly vulnerable to experiences that challenge our physiology, because our ventral vagus nerve has yet to fully myelinate, reinforcing our dependence on caregivers for regulation. These earliest weeks and months of life are the time when an infant should begin to develop the feeling of safety and connection. A child at this very early stage of life is vulnerable to a caretaker's ability to connect and meet the child's earliest needs. If the caregiver lacks capacity for nurturing and connection, the child will have diminished access to co-regulation, which is likely to lay down early implicit templates for a sense that safety is lacking or unreliable. There may be some level of repair that occurs later, but the basic template may still be present in a way that later influences self-narrative.

The nonverbal memory period can last up until age three, so it would be normal for us to have very little explicit memory of those early years. For some, particularly those who have experienced early trauma, there is essentially no explicit memory of any childhood events. It's as if we were dropped onto the planet as an adult with little awareness of childhood, except perhaps some sense of themes or generalized feelings, such as fear or loneliness.

It is our opinion that clinicians working with developmental trauma should receive a client's narrative with this foundational belief in mind: *I see you, I hear you, and I believe you.* No matter the verbal narrative presented by the client, it's essential that clinicians listen, and that we believe and validate the story. We are not considering narrative as a factual representation of specific events, but rather an articulation of the client's *experience of* and *response to* those events. As with a biophysiological model of trauma, which holds that trauma is not inherently contained in the event, but in the response to the event, we can consider that narrative contains both implicit and explicit information about the impact of our history and experience. As clinicians, we need to attend to how the implicit narrative also informs the explicit one—what the client has difficulty saying may be more important than what he has figured out how to say and organize into his more coherent narrative.

Leila Levinson (2011), an expert on transgenerational trauma, argues that telling our stories helps us heal. The process of piecing together and sharing that narrative releases some of the energy created by the experience and allows us to externalize that experience, moving the emotional energy outward. In the telling of difficult personal events, in giving the story to another, the story becomes shared—it is no longer ours alone. A listener receiving our story offers understanding and empathy. We begin to move away from the sense of isolation fostered by the experience and into community, which is one of the elements required for healing.

We can consider narrative from the perspective of Bowlby's concept of the secure base. The caregiver functions as the safe place the child turns to when she is looking for resources or learning new things for herself. This is the safe person the child seeks for protection and security. When working with narrative from this perspective, the therapist takes on the role of the secure base, the keeper of the secrets, a container for the story of traumatic experiences. Safety and protection are offered, regardless of the narrative's specific content, or its "believability." As the client progresses through therapy and feels more able to expand her capacity, her story will begin to change and take on new meaning. A clear sign of improvement for the client is the creation of a new narrative.

Verbal narrative is only one part of the healing cycle for the client. In the context of developmental trauma, the concept of narrative must be expanded to include the many ways trauma can reveal itself. We may need to consider, for example, the responses within the physiological systems—a physiological self-narrative—as one of the ways a client may express her history. We also need to look for and detect signs of chronic stress during narrative formation, even when there may be nothing else in the verbal narrative to indicate distress in the nervous system.

As was discussed in the previous chapter, assessing the client's ability to operate within his Window of Tolerance—versus the Faux Window, where defensive accommodations are at play—will give us a great deal of information about early experiences that may be so normalized the client doesn't know how to include them as part of his self-narrative.

Likewise, we can see attachment styles as part of the defensive accommodations established for the infant or child as he tried to manage overwhelming survival needs when care providers were unavailable. The attachment styles themselves can help inform us about the clients' early stories of safety or lack of safety.

As noted previously, the most basic definition of developmental trauma tells the story that will often appear in clients' narratives of trauma: when we were young, bad things happened, and those who should have been there to help and care for us could not, or did not, come to our rescue or help us to navigate the situation. There are a multitude of variations on that essential form of early trauma. There are many possibilities for bad or frightening experiences: different reasons why our care providers couldn't, wouldn't, or didn't comfort us, protect us, or love us; different ways our care providers tried to help but did not succeed; different ways our care providers were instead the source of fear or pain. Although these possibilities may form the underlying "factual" experiences of trauma, a client's narrative may not directly match that experience. Perhaps a client's story describes a great childhood with warm and loving parents, but now she struggles with relationships or feels a sense of dissatisfaction, or constantly feels unsafe—adult experiences that don't match the narrative she has of her early years.

It's rare that you will hear a child express blame toward his biological parents. He will most often create a narrative that shifts blame elsewhere, to some force outside the family, a medical condition, or even toward the fantastical, such as a story that the child was taken from his biological parents. As we mature, we may develop the capacity to integrate our experiences and early challenges into our narratives more directly, and our narratives will change accordingly.

Because developmental trauma, by its very nature, occurs when we are experiencing more nonverbal stages of development, the underlying narrative of that essential story is often hidden and intertwined with later experiences that mask the foundational impact of the events of our early lives. Yet the underlying narrative often permeates the themes that play out in our lives. It drives our responses and behaviors in ways that are important but unavailable to us in a conscious way.

The narrative of developmental trauma is inextricably interwoven with our physiology, our experience of safety or lack of safety, and our experience of connectedness or isolation with our somatic selves. Often it is also intertwined with a deep sense of shame, shame that feels like an essential element of self, an important component of early trauma we will discuss in more detail later in this chapter.

The narrative of developmental trauma is a three-dimensional map of our histories, but one that sometimes limits our abilities to explore new territory. Clinicians need to know how to read that complex map so they can help clients create new, healthier maps—new narratives that include experiences of safety, connectedness, and resilience.

SOMATIC NARRATIVE

As we have noted throughout this chapter, one of the significant aspects of developmental trauma is that it occurs before our verbal skills are fully developed. In the case of very early trauma, we are still in a developmentally preverbal stage. Our brains aren't fully developed in such a way that would allow memory to form as it will later in our developmental lives. Our ability to create narrative, as that term is commonly used in psychotherapy, will be at least somewhat limited. We may later overlay narrative on those early experiences, making meaning of them and finding a way to fit them into our sense of personal history, but at the time the experiences occurred, we were not building a narrative in the way we are able to as mature adults whose more developed brains can support language.

As we know, our earliest experiences are primarily lived somatically. Our bodies are like antennae gathering awareness from our experiences. Our brains are not yet sufficiently developed that we can rely on cognition or higher-order thinking and reasoning as a way of understanding our lived experiences. We are instead having somatic conversations with ourselves through our interoceptive and sensory experiences. We may be cooing and burbling with our care providers, but much of our experience of connection and safety is happening through our direct somatic experiences of contact and soothing. As we grow a bit older, our social experiences and the feedback from our social group will become more important. But in our earliest stages of development, we are neurological and somatic sponges, absorbing experiences all at once without filtering them through a fully conscious mind. We are not yet making narrative that arises from more cognitive awareness, or bringing self-reflection into play.

This means that the narrative of developmental trauma is primarily a *somatic narrative*. Our lived experience occurs in deeply somatic ways, through our sensory systems, our interoceptive awareness of our internal states, and our direct sense of comfort and discomfort. If we are making meaning, it will tend to be fairly primitive and "chunky," not nuanced. Any meaning will center around very basic survival needs: am I hungry, warm, connected, loved, afraid, or safe?

Somatic narrative is not linear, nor is it sequentially organized in the same way a more verbally, language-oriented narrative can be. Although a somatic narrative may be coherent, it cannot always be verbally articulated. Somatic experiences are multimodal, with simultaneous experiences of different sources of information all clamoring for our attention at one time. Somatic narrative tends to be more diffuse, with qualities that might be described as a *sense of*, rather than something more recognizably defined, or cognitively available. Terms such as "felt sense" are often used to describe this somatic version of narrative, the felt sense of safety or lack of safety being common themes related to trauma. We would be hard-pressed to define exactly what, in detail, gives us that felt sense, but we tend to know it when we feel it.

This is exactly the challenge with a more somatically based narrative—we feel we *know* it. Somatic narratives tend to have a sense of being factual, of being something we simply *know*. Humans are living, breathing, self-referencing systems. When asked to peer inside ourselves and notice how we are feeling, we report, for example, on a bad day, that we are feeling anxious, like we're going to die. How do we know we are feeling anxious and going to die? Well, because we are feeling anxious, like we are going to die! As clinicians in this circumstance, we may try to help a client clarify her state by gently suggesting, "So, when you go inside and feel all those sensations of being anxious, you have the thought that you are going to die." To this, the client will likely reply, "No, it's not a thought. I'm actually feeling it."

Part of the challenge when working with developmental trauma is working with this deeply somatic form of narrative. Think of it this way: Traumatic experience leaves behind a neurological footprint, a series of breadcrumbs that help us visualize a larger, more complete map of how we navigated (and survived) our early experiences, and how we integrated that survival process into our experience of self, other, and environment. Over time, this map becomes the territory within which we understand how to function—it is a constant reference point for new experiences. All of us create these maps, or narratives, about our lives and lived experience. When developmental trauma has occurred, that map, or narrative, may be organized around the trauma—the trauma is its governing philosophy.

The somatic narrative may be so powerful that it essentially becomes the life narrative. Alternatively, as with illness narratives, it may be a short and explanatory narrative for what we are feeling in this moment, related to our symptoms, for example. We may update our narratives to provide context for ourselves for current events.

In the previous chapter, we discussed how important it is for clients to develop more accurate interoception. One of the reasons for this is that without accurate interoception, it is difficult for clients to update their somatic narratives. Changing the somatic narrative is one of the key elements in building resilience in clients who have had limited access to regulation and healthy functioning, so the clinician's job is to triangulate information from verbal and somatic narratives while helping the client also refine and strengthen her interoceptive capacity.

UNDERSTANDING THE RELATIONSHIP BETWEEN VERBAL AND SOMATIC NARRATIVES

Narrative is multilayered and will have formed over time as we continued to integrate and make meaning of our life experiences. In the context of early trauma, the verbal and somatic narratives help form the overall trauma map, an intricate and often delicate map that colors our physiological and behavioral responses, as well as our belief systems about ourselves, others, and the external environment, all of which are likely to be deeply influenced by those early trauma experiences.

Narrative is a way to organize our experience so we can access it and find our way within our own lived experience, creating a referencing—or mapping—system for ourselves to help us understand who we are. The map is accurate for the current territory because it is the description we have formed to explain that territory. The narrative is always inherently "correct," just as our own story of our lives is correct as we experienced it from the inside. It is an accurate representation of our subjective experience, whether that lines up with what others might see from the outside or not. For the clinician, the narrative can provide greater understanding of the client's experience, helping to set in place the most critical foundational element of work with developmental trauma: *I see you, I hear you, and I believe you.*

That's why we speak of "remapping" as part of the repair process that will eventually lead to greater resilience within the client. We aren't saying the old territory isn't valid, just that a new map might provide some improved options for exploration. If we keep using the old map for reference, we will constantly find ourselves in the old territory, with the same disappointments, hurts, and frustrations.

Rodney is the youngest of three siblings. One of his brothers is a doctor, the other a research scientist. Rodney's parents have always put a lot of pressure on their children to excel. Although Rodney did well in school, he did not have the same interest in science that his brothers had, which was a disappointment to his parents. The parents' home is decorated with several photos of Rodney's brothers, but none of Rodney. Rodney's experience in his family, his ongoing narrative, is one of never being good enough, of never living up to his parents' expectations. He has always had a background level of anxiety and stress, which sometimes escalates into panic attacks, but is usually experienced as a constant companion of low-grade anxiousness, with a focus on trying to "get it right," no matter what he's doing.

Rodney has been working with a somatic therapist to address these issues, but has been struggling to notice anything but his stress symptoms. When his therapist invites him to notice his breath, for example, he wonders if he's breathing the way she expects him to, and then notices that his breathing feels constricted. When his therapist asks him to notice if he feels settled, he can notice only if he feels less stressed or more stressed. He again just feels as if he's always getting it wrong, even when his therapist assures him that whatever he notices is fine.

Finally, after doing regular homework of noticing when something positive happens, and then noticing how he feels inside, Rodney is becoming able to notice small differences in his stress level. He can't yet say he feels relaxed or settled, but he does feel like he's able to notice his sensations without so much self-judgment about whether he's doing it "correctly."

With developmental trauma, the trauma map becomes the foundational referencing template, so the client will refer back to that template in order to orient for new sensations and experiences—all are filtered through a trauma orientation. Because the survivor has likely had limited access to experiences of safety, regulation, and resilience, his referencing system may be more calibrated toward traumatic stress responses as the norm, and the new sensations of increasing regulation and resilience may feel wrong, causing him to react against the very changes he has been trying to accomplish. Like using our well-worn, familiar map of Los Angeles to navigate while in Indianapolis, the old, familiar map won't match the new terrain, and we are likely to feel baffled and lost.

As clinicians, we may need to devote significant time to helping clients become aware of the new skills they have developed: the ways in which they can now stay within their Window of Tolerance even when feeling challenged, the reduction of defensive accommodation strategies, the development of their capacities for self-regulation, and the development of a more accurate interoceptive vocabulary for their own experiences.

External locus of control, one such defensive accommodation, frequently appears in trauma-oriented narratives: I can't change my internal state because of what's happening outside; sensations are coming from outside sources, or a disease, or toxicity in the water, or allergies. These narratives about day-to-day reactions, along with physiological and behavioral responses, will often tell us what our clients *can't* do: Because the music in the restaurant was so loud, I couldn't settle. Because there was so much bright light, I wasn't able to think.

This client is telling us she feels powerless to settle unless external conditions are exactly right. To support a remapping, we likely need to help her develop skills and strategies for regulating her responses, *even though* the music is loud, and *even though* there is a lot of light. What we're looking for as we attempt to "redraw" the trauma map is the creation of a new referencing system that will help the client arrive more directly at the feeling of being settled without having to feel limited by her external environment.

Illness narratives are also a common component of the narrative of developmental trauma. They are almost invariably a combination of somatic and verbal narratives. As we saw in chapter 6, early trauma is strongly linked to later development of diseases and health issues. Illness can also become inextricably linked to deeper metaphors and narratives that can explain the client's experience of helplessness, powerlessness, lack of safety, or dysregulation. Illness narratives often focus on a specific "storyline," so to speak—the story of our symptoms, how they began, and how they have progressed. An illness narrative may also include our beliefs about how we may, or may not, recover. A somatic narrative might provide one of the threads in the illness narrative, holding the sensations that we affiliate with our illness and symptoms, bolstering our beliefs about the potential seriousness of our health challenge and possible outcomes. Illness narratives, or short-term explanatory narratives, will often be a part of the overall trauma narrative that we have formed to try to explain why we are struggling.

In our modern medical system, clients' illness narratives are often received with skepticism, in part because it's understood that they are not necessarily medically accurate: they do not provide a reliable source of information, as would medical tests. If considered at all, the narrative may be considered the client's "story" of their illness rather than an accurate report of specific symptoms or the history of those symptoms or of past treatment. Medical tests and impartial clinical data are relied on most heavily for diagnosis and decision-making in the medical context.

There are many important reasons medical practitioners should be skeptical of illness narratives. Research in this field has shown that illness narratives are strongly influenced by a multitude of factors: family members' responses to the patient's symptoms or diagnosis; larger cultural constructs and ideologies related to illness; the patient's denial of symptoms, or need for hope of a positive outcome; the patient's desire for attention; the patient's misunderstanding of her symptoms; and so on. However, as some narrative medicine scholars point out, this skeptical approach can place the patient's story at risk of being marginalized, of being perceived as inaccurate, untrustworthy, or perhaps even untrue (Shapiro 2011).

As we have come to rely more heavily on technical approaches to diagnosis, we have inadvertently lost the potential richness that comes from exploring the illness narrative itself as being important. For clients who have experienced early trauma, the potential denial of the validity of their narratives can be a reenactment of earlier trauma experiences. For this reason, offering our clients the experience of focused attention and active interest in the illness narrative can be settling and validating for them.

Physical illness is one of the potential side effects of early trauma, as the ACE Study has shown. As noted in earlier chapters, if the dorsal parasympathetic physiology is chronically overactive, for example, we will function day-to-day in full-time conservation physiology. This can easily lead to illness narratives that explain low energy, poor digestion, or low blood pressure as part of a more substantial disorder for which the client might repeatedly seek medical attention. While it's important to ensure that client symptoms have been properly attended to medically, we must also be aware that a deeper narrative may need exploration.

We can see some of the ACE-affiliated symptoms as part of a somatic narrative that may yield valuable exploration with the client, partly as a way to educate the client about how he may want to remap his understanding of his symptoms. For some clients, learning about the relationship between high ACE scores and potential health impacts can be empowering. As happened for Margaret in her story in chapter 6, it is sometimes helpful for clients to expand their understanding of their symptoms to include the possibility that the symptoms are related to early trauma history.

It is also possible that illness narratives themselves are directly related to the client's defensive accommodation and maintenance of a Faux Window. Especially when there is a more extreme external locus of control, clients may find it more reassuring to allocate uncomfortable sensations to an illness, rather than ascribing them to feelings of dysregulation. Again, it's always important to ensure that any potential medical issues have been attended to.

In working with developmental trauma, it is almost guaranteed that clinicians will encounter these intertwined forms of narrative, not just verbal narrative alone.

TRAUMA MAP: PHYSIOLOGY AND BEHAVIOR

We don't usually think of physiology or behavior as part of a client's narrative. But in developmental trauma, the lived experiences of trauma are deeply embedded in our physiology, in our behaviors related to survival and defensive accommodation, and in our most fundamental beliefs about ourselves and the world around us. These elements should be actively included in the clinician's understanding of the narrative—the trauma map of each client. As clinicians, we must be aware that certain types of physiological responses, and certain types of behaviors, are expressions of a client's trauma map.

Because developmental trauma is so inextricably linked with early states of survival threat, primitive survival responses may be lurking underneath our more mature behaviors. Trauma physiology drives particular categories of behavior, notably defensive and self-protective behaviors, adding to them a sense of urgency. That makes it more difficult for the client to bring curiosity and creativity to the change process, and to explore a different narrative, somatic or otherwise. What began as helpful responses in a survival context may have become maladaptive and now stand in the way of recovery and change. Survival physiology is potent, and potentiates any narrative to which it becomes attached. We could say, for example, that any particular somatic narrative feels factual, and survival physiology makes that narrative feel *importantly* factual.

Anything affiliated with survival effort will often play an important role in any form of narrative, and anything affiliated with our earliest survival efforts is likely to be somewhat hidden in our narrative, simply because it occurred during what was a primarily nonverbal time of our development when implicit memory was our primary mode for recording our experience. We will not have a cognitive memory or clear story to ascribe to those experiences, and may be searching for ways to explain the aftereffects of those defining events. They will permeate our historical sense of lived experience and will play out in themes that emerge over time, often related to the type of survival responses that become the hidden drivers of our narrative.

The classic model of threat response includes defensive and self-protective behaviors that fall into three primary categories: fight, flight, or freeze behaviors. Porges's polyvagal theory more recently prompted researchers to include social engagement in the broader understanding of threat response. In this view, the hierarchy of threat response begins with behavioral attempts at social engagement to mediate threat, and if those don't work, we then turn to more physical modes of protection (fight, flight, freeze). Several more recently developed models, such as the Sensorimotor Psychotherapy model, break those social engagement options down into more specific categories, such as submission behaviors or attempts to connect with attachment figures for protection. This emphasis on the importance of social engagement as part of the defensive system provides a more complete articulation of potential threat response in social animals because it also includes the social and relational aspects of survival effort.

As noted previously, the ANS and its related physiological systems provide important components of physiological support for survival responses: mobilization, immobilization, and social engagement. When our physiological systems are working well and have developed in a healthy way, they will support our capacity for self-protection in an appropriately contextual way. As we discussed in chapter 4, the neural platforms for the different categories of self-protection will support those categories of behavior. We will have access to the ventral parasympathetic physiology to support social engagement, access to the sympathetic physiology to support flight or fight behaviors, and, if needed, access to the freeze response of the dorsal parasympathetic physiology to ignite the deep conservation physiology that may be needed in extreme times of survival stress.

By contrast, if our physiology has developed in the context of traumatic stress, it may drive behaviors and modes of thinking that are more likely based on the "trauma map"—unresolved survival efforts that evolved into maladaptive response patterns. For example, we might cascade into the freeze response when stressed, rather than reaching out for help and support. If we have the physiological pathways of collapse and helplessness well-worn into our response systems, it will be very challenging to override those earliest neural platforms that provoke collapse. Healthier attachment behaviors will be beyond our reach, making it more of a challenge to move toward connection.

These physiological and behavioral response patterns in turn inform our narratives of ourselves, increasing the accumulated experiences that reinforce our trauma map.

Jonelle is a forty-seven-year-old mother raising four children with her husband, Bob. Jonelle was raised in an abusive family. Her mother was more concerned with her own relationship with Jonelle's stepfather than with Jonelle. Her mother met Jonelle's basic needs—food, water, and changing diapers—but rarely spent time exploring language and playing with her. Jonelle grew up with core issues of feeling unwanted and unloved.

In high school, Jonelle met Bob, who was supportive of Jonelle during her outbursts at school and at home. Bob understood that, after these outbursts, Jonelle would need to rest for several days, but she would return to the Jonelle he loved.

Later, Bob asked Jonelle to marry him, and they had two children together. Everyone was happy, despite underlying stress and tension. Jonelle continued to require "time-outs" from her family to restore. She often felt anxious and overwhelmed, and her time-outs helped her recover her equilibrium.

Jonelle heard about two children who were up for adoption, both of whom had rather severe trauma histories. She saw this as an opportunity to help others, and she and Bob decided to adopt the two girls. Very quickly after the girls came to live with them, frustrations increased, and Jonelle felt she had made a critical mistake in adopting the children, partly because her relationship with her own children was suffering.

One night at the dinner table, with the girls acting out and arguing constantly, Jonelle's sympathetic arousal rose beyond her Window of Tolerance. She was furious with everyone at the table and felt as if they were all attacking her. Without stopping to think, Jonelle picked up the kale from the bowl and began throwing it at everyone at the table while screaming. As quickly as her response occurred, Jonelle went into collapse, weeping and apologizing, filled with shame for having acted out so aggressively toward her family.

Bob had to help Jonelle to bed that evening. She was overwhelmed and drained from the experience. It took several days for her to recover.

Jonelle's early experiences left her ill-equipped to manage her survival physiology when she moved outside of her Window of Tolerance. Her behavior provided a narrative of its own about the lack of help she had received in learning to manage her hyper-arousal states. Bob had been extremely helpful for Jonelle, understanding her need for time-outs and recovery from these outbursts, but this event with her family caused her to seek professional help to get a handle on these long-standing patterns.

In chapter 5, we discussed defensive accommodation, which is a form of maladaption that evolves from efforts to manage overstimulation, fear, overwhelming experiences, and other survival-driven responses. Repeatedly moving beyond the threshold of our Window of Tolerance produces the defensive accommodation strategies we use to stabilize ourselves within our Faux Window. This is part of how our map is drawn—our management strategies are often invisible to us, so we operate from a specific template without actually realizing it. We reference back to our maladaptive physiological and behavioral responses, but we have no way of understanding them within a broader trauma perspective.

SEEING NARRATIVE THROUGH A NEURODEVELOPMENTAL LENS

Another aspect of our physiological systems that contributes to the underlying architecture of our narrative is our early neurodevelopment. Human babies are not immediately able to volitionally support some of the critical functions of survival, such as feeding themselves. Early reflexes support necessary functions for survival, such as coordinating our breathing and swallowing to avoid choking, managing movements that help us seek and literally hold on to connection, and responding to our environment. Like other elements of our somatic systems, these reflexes can be disrupted by early trauma, and that disruption can manifest in hidden ways in our future development.

Our earliest reflexes provide the underpinnings of our later development. If those reflexes are disrupted, then the development that is typically built upon those reflexes can also be disrupted. Some reflexes, such as the gag reflex and startle reflex, persist throughout our life. Others are present when we are very young—such as the rooting reflex, which causes the infant to turn his head toward the side on which his cheek is stimulated—and as we mature and integrate the critical functions of those reflexes into our behavior and responses to the environment, the reflexes are extinguished, or disappear within natural gestures, movements, and responses to the environment. Some reflexes are present at birth, and others activate during a particular developmental stage. See the sidebar for a list of some of the reflexes that are important to consider when working with developmental trauma.

Such reflexes essentially substitute for volitional movement until the infant has matured and learned enough to make more conscious choices about purposeful effort and movement. These early reflexes are referred to as *primitive reflexes*—automatic movements that originate in the brain stem and occur without cognitive involvement. As the brain develops and becomes more sophisticated, the need for these automatic responses decreases, and the reflexes integrate into the somatic self. When a primitive reflex does not integrate fully, we say that it is *retained*.

Primitive reflexes can be disrupted by physical experiences, such as falls, head injuries, extended hospitalizations, anesthesia, exposure to toxins, and other severe stressors on the infant. Sometimes primitive reflexes are disrupted by genetic abnormalities. Developmental trauma is also one of the stressors that can disrupt primitive reflexes.

The majority of primitive reflexes are integrated within the first year of life. When that doesn't happen, these disruptions in neurodevelopment can cause later difficulties with social, academic, and motor learning. Retention of reflexes can be directly related to an inability to learn, and can negatively impact interoception.

Neurodevelopment in the brain is hierarchical, developing from the bottom up—from the least complex (the brain stem) to the most complex (the limbic and cortical areas). This development is sequential, which is why the term "neurosequential development" is applied when assessing whether neurodevelopment occurred in a healthy way. Neurodevelopment is a finely organized system in which each section develops at a different time, independently of each other, with independent functioning, but with different elements of the system connecting and coordinating between one another.

These foundational neural networks must be almost completely organized in utero to ensure a functional birth. By contrast, cognitive development occurs over many years. When neurosequential development hasn't unfolded in the way it should, then all future development is built on a shaky foundation.

Our neurodevelopment can provide a window into our early development overall. The events and factors that cause developmental trauma are the same events and factors that disrupt neurodevelopment. Later development of the

Primitive Reflexes

The **Moro reflex** is related to primitive fight-or-flight response. It is a primitive version of the startle response, with arms first spread, and then retracted. It appears at birth and usually integrates within two to four months after birth.

Possible Signs of Retention: Hypersensitivity, hyperreactivity, low impulse control, sensory overload, and social and emotional immaturity.

The **rooting reflex** is an automatic response to food and to stimulation of the cheek. The baby turns her head toward the side on which the cheek is stimulated, to support feeding behaviors. This appears at birth and fully integrates within three to four months of age.

Possible Signs of Retention: Picky eating, dribbling of saliva or other liquids when drinking, speech and articulation issues, and thumb sucking or thumb picking.

The **Palmar reflex** is an automatic flexing of the fingers to grab hold of something and not let go. It appears at birth and fully integrates within five to six months.

Possible Signs of Retention: Difficulty with fine motor skills, poor manual dexterity, and messy handwriting or dysgraphia.

The **asymmetrical tonic neck reflex (ATNR)** assists the baby through the birth canal and helps the child develop contralateral (cross-pattern) movements after birth. It activates during birth and integrates within the first six months of life.

Possible Signs of Retention: Poor eye–hand coordination, difficulty with handwriting, trouble crossing vertical midline, and poor visual tracking for reading and writing.

The **spinal galant reflex** spinal galant

Possible Signs of Retention: Poor concentration, poor short-term memory, unilateral or bilateral posture issues, bedwetting, and fidgeting.

The **tonic labyrinthine reflex (TLR)** aids with head management and postural stability using major muscle groups. It activates in utero and integrates within three and a half years of life.

Possible Signs of Retention: Low muscle tone, walking on tiptoes, decreased sense of balance, motion sickness, and spatial orientation issues.

The **Landau reflex** is assists with posture development. It activates within four to five months after birth when the infant begins to sit up on her own. It integrates within one year.

Possible Signs of Retention: Poor motor development.

The **symmetrical tonic neck reflex (STNR)** assists the infant in preparation for crawling. It usually activates between six and nine months.

Possible Signs of Retention: Low muscle tone, poor eye–hand coordination, a tendency to slump while sitting, and an inability to sit still and concentrate.

brain depends on what has happened in the early stages of development. The earlier the disturbance, or rupture, in development, the more severe the repercussions are likely to be. If all is well and the system is working as it was designed to, then later development occurs without incident. However, if a child experiences a rupture in the development of the lower brain, everything that follows developmentally will be built on that ruptured foundation.

Timing is an extremely important component when exploring developmental trauma. When viewed through a neurodevelopmental lens, we can see that timing determines the long-term consequence of early ruptures. The same trauma that occurred at one month of age will affect a child differently than if it had occurred at three years of age. This is because the child is in different phases of neurodevelopment at one month compared with three years. The trauma will rupture either a more primitive system (at one month) or a more developed and mature system (at three years). If the trauma is repeated for the same child, the child becomes more vulnerable to future ruptures. Just as more positive experiences through the developmental stages will have a stronger and more positive effect on the child's future relationships and learning abilities, so too will challenges to their development have a more negative effect.

The development of the brain is seen as use-dependent. Early adverse experiences affect the use-dependent development of the brain. The system alters itself to meet the challenges in the environment, "resetting" in a way that heightens awareness of threat, keeping the child always on alert (Perry and Pollard 1998; Perry 2004b).

Early neglect (whether intentional or unintentional) often means early needs were not sufficiently met to support healthy neurodevelopment. To ensure healthy development for the young child, there must be an adequate frequency of interaction with the caregiver, along with correct patterning and timing of the interactions. This can be seen as a critical part of the attachment process that supports healthy development of the infant. There must also be adequate stimulation of the right kind, and in the context of safety, to support healthy neurosequential development. This produces what is termed "core capacity," our internal ability to co-regulate and self-regulate. Core capacity strengthens our ability to have healthy interactions (Perry 2004b, 2006). The timing and pattern of developmental rupture influence our final functional outcome and our level of functioning in the world.

The primitive reflexes are activating and integrating primarily during our preverbal period of development. Disruptions, then, also occur when we are still incapable of processing the disruptive experiences within autobiographical, or declarative, memory. We will likely have no specific narrative for the disruption of the neurodevelopment itself, but we may have developed narratives for the *side effects* of the disruptions.

As can be seen in the sidebar, common side effects of retained reflexes include learning issues, poor balance, and low muscle tone. In children experiencing even one of these difficulties—and developmental trauma can impact multiple aspects of neurosequential development (Perry 2009)—the self-narrative is likely to include a negative self-reference (feeling stupid, incompetent, different, or "other"). Bullying and teasing by peers may happen because the child is not coordinated enough to easily participate in physical activities, or because the child is experiencing learning challenges. Disruption in neurosequential development is often linked strongly with chronic somatic shame. The experience of being unable to meet basic environmental challenges, and challenges in learning, can deeply etch a sense of inadequacy into our sense of self.

Viewing our clients through a neurodevelopment lens will help us as clinicians to understand the signs of disrupted neurodevelopment and develop a plan for healing. When working with adults, we will notice the adaptations that were formed to compensate for the missing elements of development. It's rare that someone knows their neurodevelopment has been disrupted. Perhaps if the disruptions are severe enough, the client may have been diagnosed. Most commonly, however, the disruptions are embedded in the client's "mapping" system and remain invisible to him. Learning difficulties may be linked with shame experiences, and the resulting conclusion is "I'm just stupid." The narrative then evolves to include the neurodevelopmental disturbance, but without any knowledge of what fuels the meaning-making, creating the felt sense that something is wrong.

Working with developmental trauma can be a bit like working in the dark—we don't have reliable cognitive memory or narrative to guide us in our clinical interventions. Somatic memories and responses are often our best guides, because they can provide a narrative that is accessible even without cognitive memory or verbal narrative clues. As clinicians, we must develop our ability to observe and distinguish various sources of information about how things went awry in the client's early history. Once we understand the fundamentals of neurosequential development, this can guide us in assessing our clients' needs for repair. But if neurodevelopment is severely disrupted, this may limit the interventions we can use, at least until the client has undergone appropriate work to integrate his neurodevelopment more fully.

ATTACHMENT: DEFENSIVE ACCOMMODATION AND BEHAVIORAL SYSTEM

As part of our observations of clients' trauma "mapping," we can also consider their attachment styles, or attachment behaviors, as part of their narratives about their survival efforts. By observing how the client manages stressors related to relational connection, we can add more information to our overall sense of her narrative. In this way, we can again see behavior—in this case, behavior in relation to attachment figures—as a form of narrative.

Bowlby's original work focused on research about the intense amount of stress infants experience when the caregiver is unavailable or separated from the infant. Separation can be defined as physical separation from the infant, such as leaving the room, or the caregiver being preoccupied or unavailable to connect with the infant. In Bowlby's study, infants responded by crying, holding their breath, screaming, and frantically searching for their caregivers in anticipation of reconnection with the missing caregiver. Even though the common belief at the time was that the behavior was associated with emotional pain, Bowlby noted that not just humans express this fear, but other mammals show similar distress as well (Bowlby 1973).

Bowlby saw these behaviors as adaptive responses to separation from the caregiver, who offers support, protection, and a sense of compassion and empathy toward the infant. This need for proximity reflected the child's dependence on the caregiver for food and other needs. From an evolutionary perspective, this proximity increased the chances that the infant would survive to an age when she would be capable of reproducing. Bowlby saw the process as emerging from the motivational system of survival to bring about proximity of the caregiver. He later referred to this system as the attachment behavioral system.

The attachment behavioral system views attachment styles as part of the response to survival need. This system linked together the ethological models of human development and the modern theories on emotional regulation and personality. Bowlby saw the attachment system as concerned with one primary focus—survival. How close is the attachment figure? Is the caregiver available, accessible, and attentive to the infant? These survival questions formed the underpinnings of the concept of proximity maintenance.

When safety and security are consistently available to the infant, she develops what is categorized as secure attachment, which supports healthy relationships and sufficient confidence to explore the external world. We expect those with secure attachment to also have a foundational capacity for self-regulation and to meet the criteria for healthy resilience.

If safety and security are not consistently available, the child is likely to develop more anxious or ambivalent attachment styles. We can see these attachment styles as attempts to manage the survival stress that arises when the caregiver does not reliably provide a sense of connection and safety. In this context, we can see attachment styles as a form of defensive accommodation.

If the infant has a failed sense of connection with the primary caregiver, the infant moves to a state of fear/anxiety or toward defensiveness. In fear and anxiety, the infant moves toward begging or pleading for the caretaker to meet his needs or concerns. This anxiety of searching for the caregiver leads to a more defined anxious attachment style, with constant effort to maintain proximity to the caregiver to soothe anxiety. This is also affiliated with a more extreme external locus of control.

Conversely, if the child moves more often into defensiveness, he utilizes a more avoidant attachment style. The child will try to maintain proximity to the attachment figure without showing a desire for connection. This disorganized attachment style arises from two dueling impulses—the need for connection to reduce anxiety, but also fear of the anxiety produced by connection.

Using these defensive accommodations, the small child learns to manage his survival stress when his caregiver is not available consistently enough for co-regulation.

It is important to understand that these defensive accommodations continue to grow as the infant or child continues to search for proximity with his primary caretaker. If he cannot reestablish that connection, he can move into a sense of collapse. Bowlby later referred to these states as despair or depression.

SOMATIC SHAME

The common vocabulary around shame has not yet fully evolved. For some researchers and scholars, "shame" means only unhealthy, chronic, or toxic shame. Other words, such as "guilt" or "remorse," are then used to describe healthy elements of social learning that support prosocial behavior. For other researchers, the terms might be "healthy shame" versus "toxic shame." In this discussion, we use the simple vocabulary of healthy, prosocial shame versus shame that is chronic or maladaptive.

Shame, like many human survival responses, comprises a spectrum of meaning. Healthy shame experiences fall at one end of the spectrum, and unhealthy or maladaptive forms of shame sit on the other. There is currently an abundance of information available about the role that shame and shame cycles play in our lives and culture. Brené Brown has done a tremendous amount of research to bring shame into broader awareness, and there are numerous helpful resources now available about how clinicians can work with shame in the therapeutic setting.

Here we discuss another element of shame: *somatic shame*. David de Rosenroll, a counselor, educator, and instructor for the Somatic Experiencing model, coined the terms "somatic shame" and "identity trauma" to describe the deeply held experiences of chronic shame that can permeate our somatic experiences or become inextricably woven into our basic sense of self (de Rosenroll 2017). Chronic somatic shame can produce a sense of shame that we may *cognitively* understand as unfounded or illogical, yet we may be unable to change or remove the shameful feeling. Panic attacks and phobias can often produce this sense of somatic shame. We cognitively understand that our fears may be exaggerated or unrealistic, but we still feel them and can't control our responses to their triggers. We may even feel shame around thinking about the triggers.

Identity trauma posits the idea that our basic sense of identity and most essential somatic experiences of self are organized around shame experiences. Transgenerational trauma can produce this type of experience, as can gender diversity or neurodiversity that gives rise to a sense of being different or "other," even at a very young age, particularly if that has been coupled with active shaming from those around us. There are unfortunately many different ways in which essential and chronic shame experiences can become deeply entwined with our sense of self. Developmental trauma is one of those potential sources.

Somatic shame, identity trauma, or other forms of chronic shame can produce a deep, body-based experience of shame. *I am bad, I am the problem, I am unlovable, I am incompetent.* The experience of disconnection and lack of belonging supplies a mistaken sense that the lack of belonging is the result of being unwanted, or unworthy, of not deserving to belong in the first place. Rather than experiencing healthy shame, which clearly indicates that our behavior is the cause but that we still belong and are loved, unhealthy shame makes it seem as though *we* are the issue, *we* are the problem.

Dr. Allan Schore has provided helpful information about the importance of the caregiver's response in helping children recover from shame experiences. He also offers useful insight into the relationship between healthy shame/recovery and the development of healthy affect regulation (Schore 2013; Burgo 2012).

Shame is affiliated with the inhibitory physiology of the parasympathetic system. In its healthy social manifestation, it is meant to inhibit antisocial behavior and support prosocial behavior (Porges 2011a). When the infant and small child have proper access to repair and restoration of connection with their attachment figures, shame can support development of awareness of social rules, and can actually increase a sense of belonging and safety by having the child learn that he can recover from the shame experience and return to connectedness with caregivers and the social group as a whole by taking certain actions (accepting responsibility, making an apology, and altering future behavior) (Schore 1991).

In this context, we need to understand that healthy shame more accurately falls into the category of survival need. The inhibitory nature of the shame experience has to be strong enough to inhibit even our own self-interest. The experience of healthy shame should be so strongly negative that—as we slowly learn to internalize our prosocial experiences—we begin to self-inhibit. If all goes well, we eventually internalize the healthy rules of our social group, such as limitations on violence toward others, and we no longer struggle to understand how to behave as a good citizen within our circle of connection and belonging. The initial healthy shame experiences have been transformed into prosocial, altruistic behaviors that support social connection.

Particularly in primitive societies, acceptance by others in the group was pivotal for survival of its members. Shunning, or being expelled from the tribe that provided food, shelter, and safety, sometimes resulted in death. The role of shame in promoting prosocial behavior can be seen clearly, in this context, as part of the survival need of the individual, as well as that of the group. Even in modern cultures, we need acceptance from our community. Acceptance and belonging are fundamental to feeling safe in the world. Research shows that children lacking acceptance by a healthy "clan" that validates and supports them during and after a traumatic experience will more likely develop feelings of hopelessness and overwhelm (Ludy-Dobson and Perry 2010).

Shame can link with trauma through the inhibitory physiology that accompanies shame experiences. Sometimes that inhibitory physiology is unexpectedly "useful" for managing high-activation states. Shame can be an effective defensive accommodation that inhibits high activation, especially if the activation tends to manifest on the fight side of the survival response. A common narrative that might arise in this context is that of a client who is afraid he will kill someone if he ever lets his true self emerge. Shame can act as a regulator for that sense of uncontrolled aggression by inhibiting what the client has framed as his "true self," when what is more likely happening is that shame has become linked with inhibition of aggression. Shame might even work to inhibit what may be healthy and appropriate fight responses. For some, shame has become an integral part of the Faux Window, providing substitute access to regulation.

Healthy shame should be time-limited and followed by reconnection and reconfirmation of belonging and love. After the mother shouts "No!" when her child is about to touch a pot of hot water—and her shout causes him to cry—she then rushes to him and cuddles him, perhaps even apologizing for raising her voice. This cycle of correction followed by confirmation of connection mimics attachment cycles; responsiveness and repair are included as part of the natural rhythm of learning how to be safe and mutual in our relationships. Shame occurs in the context of social connections, whether in its healthy or unhealthy forms, and is repaired in the context of social connection.

Unfortunately, shame can be deployed in unhealthy ways that may cause us to inhibit healthy behaviors. In abuse situations, we may be taught that appropriate boundary-setting, saying "No," or exerting our autonomy is grounds for punishment. In such cases, we learn to inhibit reactions, objections, and appropriate aggression. We often turn the shame inward, where it becomes chronic, unhealthy, and toxic.

Early experiences of lack of belonging and acceptance can promote unhealthy shame experiences that can manifest as a sense of being *essentially* unworthy, unlovable, and bad. Likewise, epigenetics (transgenerational trauma) can bring with it a core sense of shame. These deeply held somatic templates for shame can be challenging to resolve. Helping the client find a healthy sense of belonging and connection can be difficult, especially when the ideas of belonging and connection have been so strongly affiliated with the shame experience.

What is critical for clinicians to understand is that shame, particularly somatic shame, retains the potency of its survival imperative, its inhibitory function, even when it has been coupled in unhealthy ways and has become maladaptive. It tends to link strongly with distorted meaning about self and behavior.

Shame experiences can begin as cognitive experiences—our initial reaction may be to assess what we've done wrong, what happened that triggered the other person's response to us. But, very quickly, shame can cascade into the inhibitory physiology. If we have the physiological "habit" of overusing the dorsal physiology, shame will very quickly plunge us into our primitive response system—our reptilian brain—shutting down our ability to support cognitive processing. In this way, that dorsal physiology can become the "keeper of secrets," holding the shame experience, but not clear content.

This is another part of the client's "mapping" system. For many clients, shame is an integral part of their narratives, and it's deeply embedded in their somatic responses. Shame becomes something like a substitute for regulation. Rather than accessing inhibitory physiology, we move into shame experiences, which bring with them an inhibitory function. This is another form of maladaption or defensive accommodation that can strongly impact the client's health, as we see in the ACE-affiliated symptoms.

WORKING WITH SOMATIC SHAME

Because the trauma, and the shame experiences associated with trauma, occurred when we were not developmentally differentiated—from our caregivers, or within ourselves—they occur within an inherently undifferentiated context. That increases the probability that the shame experience will be misallocated. Rather than understanding our feelings of shame because of something we did, we are more likely to feel a sense of shame for who we are. In some cases, abuse includes active shaming of the child, so those around us are purposely using shame to punish, exclude, humiliate, or keep us quiet.

Valeria is a forty-two-year-old Hispanic woman who was sexually assaulted by a group of neighborhood boys when she was thirteen while walking home from middle school. Her trauma narrative remains strong even twenty-nine years after the assault. Although Valeria has been successful in life, becoming a therapist and working within the immigrant community as an activist, she frequently experiences a deep sense of shame about the rape, and feels it has shaped her sense of self in ways that continue to challenge her.

> I never feel safe. Ever since the rape, I'm afraid to be alone. And I'm ashamed of being afraid. I check and recheck the locks on the doors and windows of my apartment. I was never a popular girl in school. I was teased for being fat and Hispanic (although those were not the words they used), and most of the kids wouldn't even sit with me in the cafeteria.

> On the days when I can leave my apartment, I can barely tolerate the fear I feel. I can't even walk around the block in my own neighborhood. I feel like a prisoner. Even if one of my friends is walking with me, if I hear a sound like the one the boys made—like a horn blowing—I am thrown into a state of complete fear. I feel like it's all going to happen again.

> Even though I've gotten better over the years, I still feel like I'm sitting on a ledge, waiting to fall off. I can barely sleep at night, and relaxing seems very alien to me. I think maybe I just don't deserve to be happy, to have the life I want. I feel like my life is a scary movie. As I'm watching my life, my palms get sweaty, I can feel my heart pound, and I'm sure something bad is going to happen. I am still full of shame, wondering what I did to make those boys hurt me.

> Each time I begin to experience success in my work, I drop into a kind of inertia, almost a kind of depression, where I stop pursuing the things that have been interesting to me, and that have helped me fulfill my dreams for my career.

With her therapist's help, Valeria explored the somatic sensations that accompanied each of the symptoms she had been experiencing (anxiety, hyperresponsiveness to certain sounds, a sense of not being safe even when she has locked doors and windows, a powerful sense of contraction into shame, a sense of inertia and apathy). As this type of work proceeded, Valeria's inhibitory physiology became less automatic for managing activation, and began to allow the higher levels of the brain—the limbic or midbrain—to receive greater access to the processing of the shame experience. As this occurred, it was important for Valeria's therapist to understand that Valeria may then also have access to the "secrets" that were too overwhelming for her to process, that she may then more potently feel what she has been unable to feel previously.

In Valeria's case, as she slowly and methodically explored each element of the sensations and their associated meanings, her physiological responses, and her *thoughts, she began to feel an even deeper sense of rejection and fear. In particular, she explored the deep somatic shame narrative that had defined her experiences since she was thirteen years old. She began to find echoes of earlier experiences that she had forgotten about from her childhood.*

> *When other kids would tease me, it reminded me of how my father used to tell me I was ugly. As early as I can remember, I felt my father didn't like me, that he was angry with me. He would yell at me and pinch me, saying I was a wicked girl. I never really understood what I had done to make him hate me so much. I felt like, somehow, the other kids knew something about me that I didn't, that I was a bad person. I withdrew, which seemed to incite them into more teasing. I felt there was no way to escape from constant humiliation.*

> *When I was still young, my father left us, and I always felt that was some-how my fault, even though now I know that's not true. My mom struggled to provide a home for me, and many times we went without eating. I barely remember my dad now, and I had forgotten about those early times with him, how he was so mean to me. When I think of the rape experience, I feel the same rush of shame that I used to feel as a very small child—like I was being punished for being a wicked girl, and somehow I deserved to feel that way.*

For Valeria, the early experiences of her father's disgust and anger had linked strongly with her later rape experience, making the feelings of shame that much stronger, confirming for her the belief she held as a little girl that she was indeed wicked, and that she somehow brought on the rape experience. But those shame experiences were hidden, not consciously available to Valeria so that she could connect them to the rape itself. She repressed her experiences with her father, ban-ishing them almost entirely from her narrative. As she reconnected those elements of her early history, her inability to recover fully from the rape experience was less of a mystery to her.

She also realized that her identity as a Latina had also been negatively influenced by those early shame experiences. Her Latina identity had been actively used by her classmates to bully and shame her, and those experiences also linked back to her earliest feelings of shame, further damaging her sense of her value, her sense that she deserved a happy life.

For Valeria, there was no way to separate the rape event from the early trauma she experienced from her father—they were inextricably interwoven, but without her awareness, and those early experiences potentiated the impact of the rape experience. Working with her therapist to explore the complex links between her early history and the later rape provided greater access to a sense of resolution, and helped to change her narrative in a way that more accurately reflected her genuine capacities and strengths.

Helping a client understand how shame dynamics can become such a deep part of the "mapping" of his early experiences will begin the process of changing the trauma narrative of shame. Teasing apart the underlying healthy survival impulses from the shame that inhibits the client is often helpful. In chapter 11, we will more fully explore the dynamics of how trauma experiences link, or couple, and the ways in which we need to work with those coupling dynamics to help the client recover.

9

The Need for a New Map: Regulation, Regulation, Regulation

IN THIS CHAPTER, we invite clinicians to consider what could be called a *regulation-informed* approach to working with those living with the symptoms of, or the defensive accommodations related to, developmental trauma. This type of approach is particularly important for clients with high scores on the Adverse Childhood Experience questionnaire, or for those who no longer have access to the reciprocal range in their autonomic nervous systems—whose ANSs coactivate or coinhibit rather than working within the usual balancing dynamics of the healthy reciprocal range.

Of the 17,000-plus participants in the ACE Study, two-thirds had experienced at least one of the ACEs. Of those two-thirds, 87 percent had experienced more than one, so even those without severe developmental trauma may still have felt some of the same effects (ACES Too High 2017). Because of the potential volatility in a client's responses, especially with foundational dysregulation and the possibility of reenactment, it's recommended that a regulation-informed approach be administered in small increments, allowing for more subtle changes in the client's symptomatology. The intention is to build a support scaffold for the client, who can then increase capacity and regulation in order to continue with her recovery.

Approaching treatment with a focus on regulation means working from the bottom up, first working with functions related to the more primitive—and earliest to develop—parts of the brain, such as those functions related to the brain stem. Supporting capacity for regulation develops a strong foundation to build upon for further neurosequential development, a process that was likely absent in the client's early development.

One of the frequent comments by practitioners in relation to regulation work is that they feel as if they are "doing nothing" when attending to this subtle form of intervention. In the authors' opinion, this portion of the work is the most critical foundational work to be done with a client who has experienced developmental trauma—a very big something, which just happens to be quiet and incremental. It's the equivalent of the client's needing to learn the alphabet before she can begin to form words—it lies at the core of everything else that comes later in treatment.

The crucible within which developmental trauma unfolds is a lack of reliable access to safety and co-regulation. This deficiency compromises the ability to self-regulate, leading to various strategies, or defensive accommodations, that substitute for regulation. Depending on when the rupture occurred, some clients may have experienced zero sense of co-regulation. The lack of adequate parenting in their first few weeks after birth did not allow for connection or co-regulation with the caregiver.

In chapter 7, we discussed how the Faux Window of Tolerance may actually distance us from an experience of regulation that will help us find and expand our true Window of Tolerance. In this context, when we speak of regulation, we are referring to the ability to regulate arousal. In the Faux Window, we create a sense of stability and regulation of arousal by narrowing our range of responses, but that narrowing means we can't access the resilience that is affiliated with having flexibility and the full range in our response systems—what we would have with a healthy Window of Tolerance. The defensive accommodations that are necessary to keep our Faux Window stable require additional energy, reducing our flexibility and our ability to allow vulnerability, while also limiting resilience.

Before working more directly with the client's symptoms or defensive accommodations, which are often in place to maintain a false sense of regulation, a more balanced form of regulation needs to become the primary goal of therapy. Regulation is the key to restoring a healthy Window of Tolerance. Without regulation, the interventions employed by the therapist are not likely to fully integrate into the client's system overall. Without a foundational level of regulation available, high levels of activation can bring on intense dysregulation for the client. Such dysregulation has likely influenced many aspects of development for the client, including self-awareness and the ability to self-regulate. Therefore, it's important to turn our focus to the support of healthy regulation in all aspects of the self. This can establish a more resilient foundation for the therapist and client to build from during the recovery process. A client must be able to soothe herself without stress, at least to some degree, before adding too much demand for relational co-regulation.

Safety is a foreign concept for someone with severe early developmental and attachment ruptures. Safety includes our ability to discern whether our caretaker is safe, kind, and able to meet our developmental requirements while still being able to maintain his own self-regulation. Clinicians should consider their primary role, initially, to support the capacity for self-regulation in their clients. In later stages of therapy, the clinician can offer connection to the client and provide the experience of co-regulation. Co-regulation opens the door to a felt sense of safety.

Creating a safe haven in our offices and providing a secure base for our clients can help them find a path to greater resilience. We can assume that the need for what we term "regulation work" will carry on for many months, if not years, when working with clients with developmental trauma. The treatment plan for working with such clients could be summarized as follows: regulation, regulation, regulation . . . and then more regulation. The client needs a new map for experiencing the world with a sense of safety and openness, a map not based on trauma or the repetitive experiences of fear, but based on greater access to regulation and resilience.

As the client moves toward greater regulation, he typically becomes more clear about what he needs and possibly what he is missing in life. Meeting the client's earliest needs for connectedness and regulation helps him resolve the earliest memories of lack, or experiences of not having enough to meet his needs. In a sense, the clinician is reparenting and supporting the repairs of early attachment ruptures with the client. The idea of regulation work as a primary approach to treatment may seem unusual or foreign to some clinicians. Clients who are on the more severe end of the spectrum of developmental trauma can be some of the most challenging for clinicians due to the complexity of their symptoms, and such a simple intervention as regulation work might seem to be counterintuitive initially. But if clinicians have a clear sense of the landscape of developmental trauma, they can understand the types of interventions that are likely to be effective, helping them provide greater support for the client.

Earlier chapters of this book were designed to help the clinician understand the dynamics of developmental trauma and embrace different approaches for treatment. In the following sections, we outline several different ways to view the idea of regulation as it might inform our choices as clinicians—how we structure our work with clients, how we understand the indicators of lack of regulation, how we make meaning of our interactions with clients, and even how we consider trauma as a potential springboard for transformation.

Support for a client's capacity for regulation and resilience can take many forms. What follows are just a few examples of how a *regulation-informed* approach to treatment might provide a different perspective.

REGULATION: THE PRACTITIONER, THE CLINICAL ENVIRONMENT, AND PREDICTABILITY

One of the roles of the clinician when working with a client who endured early trauma is to provide the co-regulation that was not available to the client in early childhood, when she was dependent on care providers for soothing and for the regulatory functions of her physiology. We can expect that the client's neurosequential development, as an infant, did not result in the ability to self- and co-regulate.

Essentially, what did not happen in infancy for the client should begin to happen within the clinical setting. As noted above, clients who have consistently functioned outside of their Window of Tolerance will likely have developed a secondary system of managing arousal, bringing them into their Faux Window of Tolerance, which may make it seem, to both clinician and client, that their emotions and feelings are regulated (when, in fact, they are not). However, physiologically, the HPA (hypothalamic–pituitary–adrenal) axis, which controls reactions to stress and helps regulate many physiological processes, could be showing a high level of activation, which is affecting the heart and respiratory rate, and influencing other physiological reactions, which may be difficult to detect. This requires the clinician to train his observational skills to notice these sometimes subtle indicators of the client's underlying physiological state.

Infants come into the world with the ability to self-soothe: they turn away from loud noises and bright lights; they suck their fingers or thumbs. This signals to the world that their central nervous systems are functioning as designed. This is where "parentese" (or the sing-song voice of caregivers, with elongated consonants and vowels) becomes the "coo" language that Allan Schore has noted as bringing about co-regulation. Schore sees the transfer of regulation from external (dependence on others) to internal (ability to self-regulate) as the key task of early development (Schore 2001).

Co-regulation was defined in 2007 by Alan Fogel and Andrea Garvey as "a form of coordinated action between participants that involves a continuous mutual adjustment of actions and intentions" (Fogel and Garvey 2007, 1). Co-regulation, by its very definition, is never achieved alone. The back-and-forth exchange requires the ability to respond and adjust, based on how the other person is responding and adjusting. This "dance of co-regulation" becomes the parent-child regulation field wherein the parent and child are living in the moment and offering one another immediate feedback, which in turn determines the next interaction.

This dance of co-regulation continues and is utilized throughout our lifetimes. It is obvious here how difficult life can be for someone who never had the opportunity to learn this dance. This dance of regulation leads us into the development of higher-level thinking. We need the ability to recognize when someone or something triggers us, how to take a pause before we react, how to be responsive rather than reactive, and how to communicate and act in such a way that encourages a kind and empathic response. As Sbarra and Hazan state, "The ability to quickly use the resources of a close other may represent a so-called fast route to emotional regulation" (Sbarra and Hazan 2008, 157). This fast route is interpreted as faster than regulating on one's own. This act of regulation seems to bypass the thinking brain and makes a smoother, more efficient path to regulation, straight to the deeper-level physiological responses.

The clinician's own ability to self-regulate and co-regulate will be the most important piece of therapy in working with developmental trauma. The clinician takes on the caretaker's role during the treatment process. The clinician transforms into the "secure base" for the client, and together they develop new neural pathways for regulation.

It is possible that the client will not be able to "absorb" the offer of co-regulation initially. Her temperament, defensive accommodations, and Faux Window will likely work to protect her rather than aid her at first. It takes time and relationship to create the sense of a safe haven, so this ability to respond fully to the dance of co-regulation between client and clinician will most likely take a while—for some clients many, many months, and in severe cases of dysregulation a year or more. As clinicians, we need to understand that persistence in the offering of co-regulation is essential—being repetitive is the fastest way to bring about co-regulation.

In a healthy home environment, infants and small children persistently experience co-regulation with their care providers for many years. In healthy relationships that offer the child access to the experience of a safe haven and a secure base, the child will seek co-regulation experiences as a natural part of her desire for proximity maintenance, as well as the natural need for soothing when stressed or frightened. In adults, healthy relationships will also include the seeking of co-regulation opportunities.

Eventually, the focus on regulation—and the very persistence and reliability of the offer of co-regulation—will begin to change the client's ability to notice and respond to other offers of co-regulation. Something as simple as the client's unconsciously tuning her breathing rhythm to that of the clinician might be one of the earliest indicators that the client is beginning to feel access to the co-regulation "field" in the relationship. Another early indication is the subtle changes that begin to occur in the client's narrative.

As clinicians, we must attend to our own attachment styles and be aware of how they may affect our offers of co-regulation and mutuality to the client. For example, if we quickly lose interest when the client isn't obviously responding to us, this may be experienced by the client as a reenactment of her early attachment experiences. This topic will be discussed more fully in chapter 11.

We need to understand the significance of the client's behavior and responses, based on our understanding of how developmental trauma often undermines not only the capacity to regulate physiology and behaviors, but also the ability to be more consciously aware of the source of impulses that drive the physiology and related behaviors. Those who have experienced early trauma have often not experienced reliable access to a felt sense of safety, and therefore will not have a straightforward referencing system for noticing safety, particularly in relationship. For example, the clinician's behavior will likely be more closely scrutinized and greeted with skepticism; even facial expressions may be carefully parsed for hidden meaning. Those with early trauma often had to develop a very sensitive radar system for incongruence in behavior, communication, voice tone, facial expression, and posture. They are on the lookout for indicators that they will be disappointed, abandoned, or unheard.

Rather than using an internal, interoceptive-based sense of assessing safety, external factors are more likely to be used to determine safety or lack of safety. That, in turn, means clinicians must be aware that a client is not likely to have developed a proper vocabulary for assessing the clinician's intentions or meaning, which is why clinicians must be consistently reliable and congruent in their behavior and intentions. They need to provide predictability and transparency, and be very aware of, and clear about, boundaries.

A client's level of dysregulation and the degree of need for predictability are inversely linked. The more a client is dysregulated, chaotic, or "out of control," the greater the demand for a predictable external environment to provide a sense of safety and a new ability to settle. The client's own sense may be that everything is fine and normal. He may not fully understand why he is seeking therapy; he knows only that he is not getting the responses he desires from others, or parents may be seeking treatment for their children. Somewhat simple interventions can make a tremendous difference in developing a sense of safety for clients who are challenged by uncertainty and change. Being attentive to boundaries and predictability, such as starting and ending sessions on time, giving the client a ten-minute warning before a session ends, not canceling appointments routinely, giving clients plenty of notice when appointments need to be suspended for vacations—these can help clients settle and begin the process of identifying a more trustworthy sense of safety. For some clients, even ensuring that everything in the office is in the same place every time may be helpful.

Eventually, the need for such careful attention to these issues may lessen, but many clinicians who work regularly with developmental trauma clients make these types of behaviors a routine part of how they conduct themselves. Rather than dismissing the client's actions as attempts to control, defy, or resist, we should read them as indications of the still-underlying dysregulation. The need for external order is greater when there is not yet sufficient capacity for internal regulation or internal locus of control.

Those with early trauma can often thrive in highly structured environments, such as the military, police, clergy, or medicine. The clear hierarchy, rules for behavior, and regimented times for eating and sleeping can provide a sense of order and containment that can be very settling. Mimicking some of that predictability in the therapeutic setting can be helpful in putting the client at ease and allowing deeper work to begin.

THE PHYSIOLOGY OF REGULATION

Lack of regulation may permeate all levels of the self in the wake of developmental trauma. What's happening in the physiology is a very important part of that picture. Without regulation of the physiology, particularly in the ANS, it will be very challenging for the client to support deep change in other systems. As noted in chapter 4, which explored the polyvagal theory, there are some neural platforms that are important for supporting specific categories of behavior, and therefore we need to ensure that those important platforms are in place.

If, for example, a client has limited access to the ventral parasympathetic physiology, it will be more of a challenge for him to support healthy social engagement. That doesn't mean the client won't make his best attempts at social connection, but he may have to override his own physiology in order to do so. If his physiology is sympathetically dominant, for example, his self-communication is likely to be about danger and threat response. The client may assert his defensive accommodation efforts and ignore those voices in his head that are screaming *run!* But he will of course be at least somewhat less available for social connection than he would be if his physiology had better congruence with the social task at hand.

If the client is in the nonreciprocal range of the ANS, re-regulation of her physiology will be more challenging than it would otherwise be. It will be necessary to take the pressure off her response system so her Faux Window experiences aren't simply being reinforced, provoking further strategies of defensive accommodation. Clinicians will need to focus on helping the client stay within her Window of Tolerance, rather than provoking Faux Window management strategies.

A client's presenting symptoms need to be understood from this perspective, with the clinician looking a bit more deeply into a client's background to understand what might be helpful to bring more regulation on board, lessening the need for defensive accommodations that hold the client in the Faux Window.

Will is fourteen years old and seems to be angry at everyone in the world. Will's explanation for this is that no matter what he does, others will attack him verbally or physically. Will's narrative—both somatic and verbal—seems to show a teenager who is feeling hopeless about his life. Will lives with both of his parents but reports that they are frequently at work and he spends most of his time alone at home. When he does try to connect with other teenagers from school, he ends up in fights, and is no longer welcome in many of his classmates' activities. His parents have decided that Will needs more help than they can give him, and they've arranged for him to see a therapist who specializes in working with young people. As concerned as Will's parents seem about him, they both admit they are very busy people who have work commitments that cannot be broken, so there is no way for them to spend more time with Will to support his therapy.

It becomes obvious to the therapist very early in their work that Will's narrative works as his defensive accommodation. He reports several times that he feels trapped in his life. Will's therapist sees him, hears him, and believes him—he can hear that Will isn't happy being in trouble and being angry most of the time. As Will and his therapist work to find ways for Will to regulate his responses more effectively, Will is able to at least create a sense of being able to "pause" before he reacts. This pause allows him to think about his situation and to think of solutions, but he is still lashing out at people.

At first, Will felt there were no solutions: The world is bad and I'm bad and nothing will ever change. But then small changes began to happen for him. The pauses are allowing him to get a sense of how he would like to be different in his life, and to notice when he is reacting rather than settling. He realizes that he very often feels extremely lonely, but rarely lets himself feel that, moving quickly into anger instead. With his therapist's help, Will is able to identify his grandmother as the person who is always there for him, even though she lives in another state. He enjoys talking with her on video chat. Will and his therapist work out a plan, with Will's grandmother's full support, that she will help him stay within his Window of Tolerance by always being available if he is going to be home alone.

Will calls her, and together they decide that he will video chat with her whenever he is going to be alone for periods greater than one hour. She will even video chat during meals so he won't have to eat alone. These interventions help Will to stay within his Window of Tolerance. Up until this point, he never realized how much his loneliness functioned as the underlying root of his anger. Now that he knows he can chat with his grandmother, he can see how much that urge to connect with someone has been there the entire time. But his anger had not allowed him to notice how much he longed for contact in that way.

Will's new narrative is this: He may be alone physically, but his grandmother is there with him over video chat. Will begins to expand his capacity to pause his responses so that he rarely loses his temper. He has been able to repair his relationship with one of his classmates, and is beginning to have more social time outside of school. Will's mother had a frank talk with the parents of that classmate about how much time Will spends at home alone, and they agreed to invite Will over to their house for dinner at least once a week.

Sometimes these small and simple interventions are most important for the client to understand how much his Faux Window has been keeping him from finding regulation.

As clinicians, we may also need to help the client understand and reframe his experience of his own physiological responses, particularly those related to the sympathetic system, which prepares us for an active threat response. It is of course understandable that the client doesn't want to feel afraid, or feel unable to control his responses. It may be necessary to at least delve into some of those activation responses in order to move through them and toward better regulation. If the client is constantly moving away from experiences that contain an increased sense of threat, it sometimes makes it challenging to support better regulation.

For such clients, what has been coded as "dangerous" is mistakenly understood to be the danger itself. In other words, becoming activated and feeling afraid is the danger to be avoided. In reality, those responses are indicators of how hard the client has fought for her own survival. It's actually her own vitality she is feeling, locked in the struggle for survival. Unfortunately, that struggle has gone on for so long that it has increased the allostatic load, binding the vitality in ways that make it inaccessible for other uses.

By supporting regulation, we can unlock that vitality—gently, incrementally, and in the context of safety—so the client can gain access to it. This is one of the more delicate forms of regulation work: working gently to support the client in accessing her survival physiology in a controlled enough way to experience a successful survival effort. This work toward completions will be discussed more fully in chapter 11.

CONSIDERING BEHAVIOR IN THE CONTEXT OF REGULATION

There are different ways we can consider regulation as it relates to behavior. As stated earlier, one of those is to consider that survival physiology is meant to be compelling. It is meant to move us forcefully into a survival effort, to override more everyday concerns and push us toward survival behaviors. As discussed previously, our brains and sensory systems change dramatically under the influence of survival physiology. As long as survival physiology is "in the room," it will drive behaviors that might not be present under other circumstances and make those behaviors more difficult to inhibit.

Behavior is the number one reason parents seek therapy for their children. Someone—either the parent, a teacher, or another person outside the immediate family—has witnessed behavior or behaviors they find concerning. If a behavior is not temporary or short-lived, the parents may seek professional intervention. Some of the common diagnoses given to children and adults with dysregulation are attention-deficit/hyperactivity disorder, oppositional defiant disorder, spectrum disorders, anxiety disorders, and aggressive behaviors. Many of these disorders are treated with powerful prescription medications that may have serious side effects, particularly with long-term usage.

One example of a problematic behavior that might be driven by survival physiology is aggression. Even those of us who are mild-mannered and somewhat timid might become aggressive when we feel threatened. We might move quite strongly into the fight phase of survival effort if we are sufficiently provoked. This may be helpful when we are actually under threat, but not so helpful at the office when one of our coworkers critiques our work, or at school when a teacher asks us to follow directions, and we react as if our life is on the line. For clients whose physiology is chronically operating within the survival range, it is sometimes more difficult to regulate behaviors that arise from experiences of lack of safety.

Focusing on regulation of the physiology can often lighten the load that threat physiology adds to our responses, compelling us to react. Relieving the "push" of survival physiology is sometimes enough to give the client greater choice about his behaviors. This can also bring about a reduction in medication dosage, or the complete withdrawal of certain medications.

Beyond that, when the client is able to understand these behaviors as part of his threat response, or perhaps even as part of his defensive accommodation strategies, he can often bring more conscious awareness to choice points in his responses. Greater awareness of the choices available to him expands the Window of Tolerance and directly increases his capacity.

We can also consider that we learned behaviors related to our earliest experiences of co-regulation, or the absence of co-regulation, that now influence our current behavior. These learned behaviors played an important role in our development when they were necessary for survival, but these same behaviors later in life cause discord and separation.

Part of what the infant and toddler experience in the co-regulation process is the mutuality of the exchange. It is not only the infant/child who benefits from sharing mutuality; the care provider will also experience a positive impact from the connection and nurturing in the relationship, possibly even moving toward better individual regulation in the process of co-regulation. Through this process, the child gains a greater sense of agency and potency, which enhances her own ability to self-regulate. This is where there seems to be a mixed outcome in response. As the infant/toddler learns that the caretaker is also responding to her behavior, she has the capability of using it for defensive accommodation as well as intimate interaction. The infant can perceive the caretaker's potential weaknesses and take advantage of the "buttons" that, when pushed, cause the parent—or, later, partner—to move away or separate from the individual when intimacy seems overwhelming or threatening.

A potential defensive accommodation in children, and later in adult expressions of the same need, is acting out in attempts to get *any* response from caregivers, even those responses not actually related to co-regulation. The child's experience of agency and potency will come not from experiencing a co-regulation response with the caregiver, but by provoking some type of reaction in the caregiver—any response is better than no response.

Behavioral efforts that mimic co-regulation, or substitute for self-regulation, are another category of regulation work that is likely to be needed in the clinical setting. Part of regulation work is helping the client understand that his defensive accommodations and the development of his Faux Window were part of his survival strategy, which likely served him well to meet his early needs for self-care. It is worth noting here that it is not our intent to move the client immediately from the Faux Window, where he has experienced some sense of safety, into the Window of Tolerance. Rather, this is an incremental process that will be accomplished in small steps.

However, in an immediate sense, those early survival strategies limit the client's access to a sense of completion of a successful survival effort. It is helpful to support the client in understanding the function of his defensive accommodations, and help him identify the markers that appear when he is traversing the threshold of the Window of Tolerance and moving instead into his Faux Window.

ACCESS TO BETTER SOCIAL REGULATION

The events and conditions that contribute to developmental trauma are also often the same things that contribute to an inability to function comfortably and smoothly in social settings. Early trauma can mean that sensory systems are hyper- or hypo-sensitive. Light, sounds, smells, and tactile sensations may be exaggerated, making social situations unbearably stimulating. On the other end of the spectrum, there may be changes in perception, such as numbing to our own experiences and a sense of distance from the environment around us, again making social situations challenging.

Disrupted self-regulation and co-regulation can also drastically disrupt a child's learning abilities. We also know that social skills are learned through observation. At a very early age, we watch our caretakers and how they respond and interact in social settings. If our exposure to social settings has been limited, there is diminished opportunity to develop strong social engagement and social skills.

Isolation is a common side effect of trauma in general. With developmental trauma, it's often people (rather than environments or circumstances) who provide the source, or at least the perceived source, of threat. For those who experience a generalized and fundamental lack of safety, or a limited ability to differentiate between safe and unsafe people, social situations feel fraught with difficulty and littered with possible threats. Avoiding people can seem the most workable solution.

As the capacity for regulation increases, new experiences of the potential for social connection may become available, but the basic skills for navigating those social relationships may not be well developed. Particularly as physiological regulation increases and people seem more interesting than scary, there may be a need to help the client with basic regulation skills for social interactions. The clinician may need to help the client figure out how to titrate into social interactions in a way that feels safe.

REGULATION AND RESILIENCE

If regulation work is effective, the client will begin to spend more time within her Window of Tolerance, which will organically expand and lead to further regulation and resilience. However, that resilience and regulation often have a quality of quiet that some clients will find unnerving. It represents the unknown, and for those with developmental trauma, the unknown is inherently frightening. Moreover, for those who've endured developmental trauma, quiet—internal or external—is often affiliated with danger. Quiet can be the signal that something bad is about to happen, it can be perceived as the absence of needed information about where threat may be, it can cause us to notice things that aren't pleasant, or it may also be so unfamiliar that it can't be easily understood, which makes it stressful.

The very thing the client has been yearning for—access to safety, security, and regulation—feels wrong or dangerous on several different obvious and subtle levels. This is the new map for the previously unknown territory, the new territory of the self that is not organized around trauma but around resilience.

On medieval maps, unknown territories were sometimes marked "Here Be Dragons." Our clients are likely to have this same indicator written on their own maps, particularly as they begin to encounter new regulation states. They often have highly developed "danger maps," but limited experience of safety and regulation, so any novelty is often coded initially as potentially dangerous. In this case, it is necessary to titrate, or move incrementally, into what might be considered more positive states so that the client can gradually become familiar with them.

It is also critical that we help clients develop a new interoceptive vocabulary that supports perception of the indicators of regulation and nondanger states. After perhaps a lifetime of being acutely tuned toward danger, it may take time for the client to learn to notice the quieter forms of information that indicate safety, connection, and regulation. The slow building of resilience in turn promotes more predictability in the ANS responses that can support a wider range of behaviors.

One concise description for the overall pattern of development of regulation and resilience is this: challenge the system, and return to stability. The challenge may arise naturally when a client notices her own responses, or from accessing her trauma narrative, or from any form of stimulation that pushes the client outside of her Window of Tolerance. Initially, the client may need a good deal of support to return to stability. Eventually, however, the client will be able to return to stability with less and less effort. The repetition of this process itself builds resilience.

Resilience research indicates that the process of successfully meeting challenges can build resilience. But those challenges must fit within a workable range. It's a bit like the fairy tale of "Goldilocks and the Three Bears": not too much, not too little, but just right. We need enough challenge to stretch capacity, but not so much challenge that we are overwhelmed and feel ourselves failing to meet the challenge. In order to build resilience, we need to stretch enough beyond our comfort zone to know we're working at it. Regulation work must happen within a range that is workable for the client, but not so conservative that no change occurs.

As the work continues, the client will have greater access to her vitality, and she will experience a significant change in allostatic load. This increased capacity appears as an expression of increased vitality that may show in very physical ways: increased ability to fight off infection and inflammation, better regulation of sleep or menstrual cycles, and more energy, to name a few. Sometimes that expression of increased vitality will appear as an increased ability to engage with life, to connect socially, to feel safer, to be more empowered, or to find one's voice. The authors believe that at least some of the effects we see affiliated with high ACE scores can be offset, or perhaps even repaired, by access to better regulation, by lifting the allostatic load so the body can reallocate resources to healthy function.

Depending on the practitioner's scope of practice, he may provide greater support for the physical changes and restoration of physical or physiological resilience, and provide support for changing the somatic or illness narratives. Or the clinician may provide psychological, emotional, or spiritual support for the client's change process, when there may be a need for basic coaching on how to make friends, how to have conversations, and how to read social cues. When we can assess our own strengths as clinicians and understand gaps in our practice, we can begin to apply more tools and skills to help clients better regulate, which will impact all aspects of our clients' lives.

NARRATIVE: THE NEW REGULATION MAP

Those who have experienced developmental trauma have lived their lives under a continuous flow of challenging experiences. They now need to harness those challenges and transform them into a sense of greater resilience; they need access to the strength that allowed them to survive in the first place.

By focusing on the building of regulation and resilience, the client begins the process of remapping, of creating a new narrative that better describes the new territory now available to him. Experience of greater capacity increases our exploration of the world around us. That, in turn, will change our self-narratives. Our narratives begin when we try to create an internal understanding of why we are who we are, and why we behave to protect ourselves. As our capacity increases, our narratives are likely to change, to include the sense of success at meeting challenges, of developing curiosity, or of a willingness to explore. Eventually, our narratives may also include access to a sense of safety and connection. Rather than *I am constantly afraid and unhappy,* a client will begin to tell himself a different story: *I am stronger than I thought and able to meet challenges with greater balance and success.*

At the same time, our somatic narratives will begin to change. We may literally experience changes in our symptoms—decreased inflammation, less pain, fewer migraines. Our illness narratives may alter to include more positive beliefs about potential outcomes, and may now include the possibility of being free of pain, free of symptoms that have beleaguered us for most of our lives.

Greater access to regulation and resilience will likely have a profound impact on many aspects of our lives. And although it is a wonderful thing when clients experience positive changes, clinicians need to understand that, for someone whose life has centered around trauma, there can be tremendous disorientation when trauma is no longer the organizing principle, when regulation and resilience are now the more steady state of affairs. As will be discussed in the final chapter of this book, part of the treatment plan may need to include helping the client learn to manage greater access to his vitality. This is a wonderful "problem" to have, but for some clients, the implications of having the possibility of greater access to their hopes and dreams can raise even more fear than the familiar limitations they've lived with for years. As one client noted, "If I'm not spending all of my time focusing on my healing, what will I do with myself?"

10

The Role of Touch

THE ROLE OF TOUCH IN EARLY DEVELOPMENT

Touch is essential not only to healthy human development, but to survival. In 1971, Ashley Montagu published his landmark book, *Touching: The Human Significance of the Skin,* which proved to be one of the first detailed discussions of the importance of skin-to-skin contact for healthy development of infants.

Montagu points to earlier researchers who noted that some orphanages had infant mortality rates of 30–40 percent, even when infants' basic physical survival needs were satisfied. The researchers attributed the high mortality rate to insufficient physical nurturing (via touch), as well as insufficient relational nurturing with appropriate stimulation and responses by caregivers (Montagu 1971). More current research has confirmed the importance of skin-to-skin contact (sometimes referred to as "kangaroo care"), particularly in the first few days and weeks of life. Skin-to-skin contact can improve the connection required for breastfeeding, boost weight gain and growth rates, improve immune function, and increase the stability of hormone levels (Bigelow et al. 2014).

For babies born prematurely, this skin-to-skin contact can play a huge role in the infants' survival, partly because an infant's thermoregulation is better calibrated with skin-to-skin contact than it is in an incubator. This is because mothers who have recently given birth have a warmer skin temperature, up to two degrees higher than the rest of their body, on the area of their chest where the baby would naturally rest while being soothed or breastfed, which helps the baby maintain his body temperature more effectively.

We know from the research conducted with Romanian orphans that those who lived in orphanages for longer than eight months had higher levels of cortisol and lower levels of oxytocin and vasopressin (hormones affiliated with support for bonding and regulation of emotions)—even as long as twelve years later—than did babies who had been in the orphanages for less than four months (Nelson et al. 2011). Of course, it's not only touch that may have contributed to those differences. There are many factors that influence development and many different ways neglect can manifest in later development.

However, there is now sufficient research to show clearly that skin-to-skin contact does indeed make significant differences for the infant in long-term development and health outcomes. Particularly for newborns, touch helps calm the nervous system and improves sleep (Bigelow et al. 2014). Skin-to-skin contact also supports bonding and promotes physiological changes, in both the caregiver and the infant, that support better overall regulation. Tiffany Field's research at the Touch Research Institute has clearly shown that massage therapy, whether in newborns or senior citizens, provides the following benefits (Field 1998, 2017):

- Facilitates weight gain in pre-term infants
- Enhances attentiveness
- Alleviates depressive symptoms
- Reduces pain
- Reduces stress hormones
- Improves immune function

Skin-to-skin contact is our earliest experience of co-regulation outside the womb. It is fundamental to the essential process of learning mutuality. Babies thrive when caregivers are actively engaged with them, and this includes engagement through responsive touch. Some cultures are highly touch-oriented, whereas others have lower rates of social touch, but touching infants is universally common. Early, positive experiences of touch and physical connection with caregivers provide some of the critical architecture for self-regulation and resilience.

Touch also helps us develop our interoceptive abilities. As stated earlier, Porges (1993) refers to interoception as the "infant's sixth sense" and assigns it a critical role in survival. As discussed in chapter 2, accurate interoception helps regulate our physiological systems and helps us perceive safety and connectedness, the very underpinnings of resilience development. As was discussed in the previous chapter, infants learn during the co-regulation process that the caregiver not only affects them, but that they in turn have an impact on the caregiver; they learn that they have agency and active influence over their environments and the people who share those environments. Caregivers are responsive to babies; they are usually drawn to touch and enjoy cuddling infants. One of the most commonly repeated cycles between caregivers and babies—and even between strangers and babies, for that matter—is that of smiling. The baby smiles, and the caregiver smiles back. The baby begins to learn that she is the causal agent in this "smile cycle."

The same holds true with touch and co-regulation. The baby is not only learning how to regulate himself; he is learning he can influence the regulation of his caregiver. Much of the earliest experience of this comes from subtle somatic cues, including tactile responses, as well as experiencing the caregiver's somatic responses, such as heart rate and breathing changes, or changes in muscle tone. Touch research shows that healthy touch during our early development helps us develop empathy and deepens our ability to understand the social cues of those around us (Field 2014).

If we have reliable access to this early experience of co-regulation, we will more effectively develop our individual ability to notice cues regarding our own experience of regulation: settling, the pleasure of feeling well-fed, a sense of safety, and so on. As was discussed in previous chapters, the foundational development of the autonomic nervous system, which gives us full access to the ventral parasympathetic physiology, occurs during these early phases of our lives and requires the attentive responsiveness of our caregivers. Caregivers literally nurture our resilience.

As we also know from many different sources of research (Carter and Sanderson 1995), neglect, including lack of skin-to-skin contact, profoundly impacts our development, often throughout our lifetimes. Our stress chemistry is negatively impacted, our immune systems don't function as well, and we experience greater difficulty regulating both our physiological and emotional responses.

Research tells us that the long-term effects of neglect can be greater than those of physical or sexual abuse for the child. These changes are documented through MRIs and PET scans. The structure and chemical activity of the brain show a decrease in both size and structural connectivity. Such early neglect or abuse can also be blamed for hypersensitivity in stressful situations, as well as the inability to respond to nurturing and kindness (Shonkoff and Phillips 2000; Shonkoff, Boyce, Cameron, et al. 2004; Shonkoff et al. 2012).

Lack of healthy, appropriate, and nurturing touch is often one of the contributing elements of developmental trauma. There may have been abuse or neglect within the family environment, for example, which has made the experience of touch unsafe or given it a violent connotation. The ACE questionnaire provides an inventory for some of those categories of disruption to nurturing contact. But those are not the only potential sources for lack of access to nurturing touch, as discussed in chapter 6. Another example backed by research is the impact of extended stays in orphanages where sufficient care is unavailable. In some countries where there is limited understanding about the positive impact of regular skin-to-skin contact, or where caregiver/infant ratios don't allow time for individual babies to receive enough attention, children may be at risk in the ways noted in the Romanian orphan studies.

The Bucharest Project, a joint collaboration between researchers at Tulane University, the University of Maryland, and Boston Children's Hospital, began in Romania in 2000, led by Nathan A. Fox, Charles A. Nelson, and Charles H. Zeanah after the Romanian dictator Nicolae Ceausescu was removed from office. At the time, there were more than 170,000 children living in institutions. Due to extended periods of war, there were not enough adults to care for the nation's children, and children in institutions were segregated by age, which often meant they couldn't be near an older sibling who could function as a surrogate caretaker.

The Bucharest Project began the study with 136 Romanian children who had been living in impoverished orphanages since their birth. Approximately 68, or half, of the children were moved out of the orphanages into foster homes. The foster homes were recruited by the researchers and paid a stipend to care for the children. The other half of the children remained in the same living situations with no influence from the researchers. The children's ages ranged from six months to three years and averaged twenty-two months of age.

The researchers also included a control group of children who had never been placed in orphanages and were still living with at least one birth parent. The researchers returned frequently over the years to assess all the children in the study. Their research pointed to profound and disturbing results for children in the orphanages. Not uncommon among the children were delays in cognitive function, slowed motor development and language, psychiatric disorders, as well as deficits in socioemotional behaviors. The poor motor development was directly related to a lack of physical touch and stimulation by the caregivers. All the children were given EEG tests to measure their electrical brain activity. Obvious changes in patterns were noted, with many of the institutionalized children having disturbingly low levels of brain activity.

However, improvements were noted among the children who moved into foster care. These included higher-level language skills, higher IQs, and stronger socioemotional function. Some of these children formed secure attachments with their caregivers, and they found it easier to express their emotions. Although these results seemed far better than those for the institutionalized children, the foster care group still lagged significantly behind those in the control group. Results also indicated that the timing of a child's transition from the orphanage to a foster home influenced the level of improvement for that child. Those placed in foster homes before age two made the largest gains. Research also showed that by their eighth birthdays, the brain activity of those in foster care equaled the brain activity of those who had been placed out (Bos et al. 2009).

Structural MRI assessments were also used to determine differences among the children. Again, the results were staggering. Institutionalized children had smaller brains, with a lower volume of gray and white matter present. Gray matter is made up of the cells of bodies of neurons. White matter constitutes the part of the brain where nerve fibers transmit signals between the neurons. A history of institutionalization significantly affected brain function (Bos et al. 2011). However, children who moved into foster care regenerated portions of white matter over time, though there was no evidence of growth noted in the gray matter.

This research on neglect tells us a great deal about what happens when an infant grows up in the absence of loving touch and responsiveness from an attuned parent or caregiver. But it is also important to note that repair is possible. Current research shows that our brains remain plastic throughout our lives, which means it's possible that greater regulation and reparative touch in therapy can right some of the neurological and physiological wrongs caused by neglect.

Dr. Philip Fisher, a professor of psychology at the University of Oregon who researches early childhood interventions in socially and economically marginalized communities, began an adoption study around the same time the Bucharest Project began. Fisher's inquiry focused on children living in foster care systems in the United States. He theorized that the children's behaviors and problems were caused by early physical abuse. He realized later that his study's discoveries were very similar to those of the Bucharest Project.

But Fisher did uncover a specific finding about one particular underlying neurophysiological mechanism. He expected to find higher levels of the hormone cortisol in the children he studied in American orphanages. Instead, he discovered the opposite. Fisher wrote, "Their levels were low in the morning and stayed low throughout the day" (Weir 2014, 36). (Cortisol levels should be higher in the morning, and decline throughout the day, during a normal twenty-four-hour cycle.) Fisher later realized the correlation between dysregulated cortisol and early neglect: "This blunted daily pattern with low morning cortisol seemed to be a hallmark of neglect—that was a pretty powerful picture" (Weir 2014, 36). It is relatively common for those with any form of developmental trauma to show low levels of cortisol throughout the day. Disruption in cortisol levels is one of the symptoms of trauma generally; chronically low levels are considered a marker of longer-term traumatic stress physiology.

Fisher's research showed that foster children who lived with responsive caregivers were most likely to experience normal cortisol levels. When a child was placed with stressed parents, however, there was no change in cortisol levels for the child compared to cortisol levels for the children in the orphanages (Fisher et al. 2007). "We're more likely to see that blunted pattern when they don't get that support and there's a lot of stress in the family," says Fisher (Weir 2014, 36).

Neglect and abuse are more obvious sources of developmental trauma, but there can be other sources that are not so obvious. Extended illness and hospitalizations can also result in many of the same effects we often see in the aftermath of developmental trauma. There is now greater consensus within the medical community that nurturing touch is critical for the health of infants and small children, so many hospital settings are designed to facilitate skin-to-skin contact between caregivers and their children. However, this is a relatively new aspect of awareness in the medical field, so for some adults seeking help today, extended hospitalizations in their early childhood could explain lack of access to comforting touch and co-regulation. Even with modern awareness of the need for contact, a child's specific medical condition may impact how much touch is safely available.

The good news is that there is the possibility of repair, even after severe early neglect. As we discussed previously in this book, supporting healthier regulation will have an impact on health and well-being, even when that regulation comes later in life than it should have. Appropriate, healthy, and safe touch can be one of the ways repair and regulation can occur. Even with the Romanian orphans, researchers noted change over time for many of the children once they were adopted into stable households. Even some—but not all—of those with severe deficits from longer periods spent in the orphanages did eventually report better outcomes.

Dr. Ann Bigelow, a professor of psychology at St. Francis Xavier University in Nova Scotia, and part of a multidisciplinary team of researchers who conducted a study on skin-to-skin contact between mothers and infants, had the following response to an interviewer's question about what we can do for children who are coming out of an environment where they may not have received adequate physical touch or emotional engagement: "The main thing would be to give them what they didn't get" (Harmon 2010).

Bigelow nicely summarizes our reason for authoring this book. We feel strongly that working effectively with developmental trauma also requires effective work from a somatic perspective. That may not always include the use of touch, but touch can be one of the most powerful forms of healing for those whose early trauma included a disruption in their experience of safe, appropriate touch. This mode of treatment should at least be considered as one among several tools available for healing developmental trauma. Of course, as with any form of communication or intervention, touch can be counterproductive and must be used appropriately and cautiously.

SOMATIC AND TOUCH APPROACHES TO WORKING WITH DEVELOPMENTAL TRAUMA

Somatic approaches to working with trauma, by name and by nature, are body-oriented processes. Successful application of somatic approaches relies heavily on the practitioner's skill at understanding the client's somatic communication. Although we cannot directly experience our client's somatic states, we can rely on a kind of translation of those states into language we *can* understand. Sometimes that translation takes place at a verbal level, when clients verbally report what they are experiencing. We listen to their descriptions, noting what types of words are used and what is said, as well as what is not said. Sometimes our clients translate their internal experiences using nonverbal cues: gestures, postures, breathing cadence, trembling, weight shifts, or subtle circulation changes. All of these may be used as signals and can help us understand the client's process of renegotiating trauma. Because these somatic expressions are nuanced and subtle, somatic therapists must be highly skilled in their capacities to understand as many of the body's forms of communication as possible.

A keen awareness of subtle shifts within the client's somatic state can require all five of the practitioner's observational senses: hearing, vision, kinesthetic sense, smell, and touch. In this context, the use of touch is simply another tool therapists might use to enhance their observations of the client's renegotiation process. Sometimes the client's communication of her inner experience takes place through subtle tissue changes, which may not be observable by any other means than through contact with those tissues. This type of direct tissue observation may be understood by a skilled touch therapist in much the same way a client's verbal cues are widely understood by every therapeutic practitioner. The essential process remains the same; only the form of observation changes. The use of touch is not essential when using somatic approaches to developmental trauma; but when used appropriately, it adds another possible option to the list of tools available to the practitioner.

If touch is one of the tools utilized in the therapy mix, its impact must also be accounted for. The integration of touch into the psychotherapeutic and counseling environment continues to be a developing and sometimes controversial process, which is why care must be taken to ensure that all legal and ethical boundaries are respected if touch is used by a psychotherapist or counselor.

The amount and type of touch a clinician uses should be based on several different factors: licensure, practice setting, type of clients, practice style of the clinician, and so forth. If you will be using touch in more than an incidental way, it's recommended that you include material in your informed consent document specific to the use of touch. Clinical notes should include information on the purpose of the touch used in sessions, and how it supports the overall treatment plan. Most importantly, the client's informed consent and ongoing consent must be confirmed throughout the course of the work.

Even when touch is legally and ethically allowed, there are times when it should not be used, or when its use should be applied only with extreme caution and forethought. Likewise, there are times when touch is especially helpful in assisting the client's change process. (See the sidebar.) The two primary contraindications for the use of touch in any practice setting are:

1. The client is not comfortable with the use of touch, hasn't given consent, or doesn't understand the purpose of the touch.

2. The clinician is not comfortable touching the client.

Touch should be used only if both the client *and* the clinician are comfortable with integrating touch into the work with the client. In the context of working with developmental trauma, the intention of touch is related to the healing of early trauma; therefore, if the clinician is not certain that touch will be useful, or if the client or clinician is in any way uncomfortable, other methods of supporting the client's change process are likely to be more effective.

In chapter 11, we will discuss somatic transference and somatic countertransference more fully, because it is critical for clinicians to understand how their own histories may impact their work with their clients—including their experiences with, and understanding of, healthy touch.

In general, in the psychotherapeutic or counseling setting, touch should *not* be used under the following circumstances:

- To treat or repair physical injury; the exceptions to this are simple forms of touch used to work with the psychological or traumatic stress symptoms associated with the injury, but not specifically for treatment of the injury itself.

- For the purpose of sexual arousal, or any form of sexually oriented interaction with the client.

- For the purpose of causing harm to the client.

- If the practitioner is unclear about the purpose of the touch being used, and cannot articulate its purpose to the client.

- If the client has not explicitly agreed to the use of touch in the session and agreed to the specific purpose of the touch being used.

- If the practitioner feels confused or overwhelmed by the transference or countertransference dynamics occurring in the therapeutic relationship.

- If the client habitually uses touch work to avoid, rather than engage, the change process.

- If the practitioner uses touch work to avoid engaging the client's change process, particularly if that process is uncomfortable for the practitioner and if touch work is being used to set the practitioner at ease, rather than for the benefit of the client.

- If the practitioner is using touch simply because the practitioner can't think of anything else to do.

- If the practitioner's level of skill does not match the level of complexity of the client's needs related to touch. The more complex and subtle the client's symptoms, the more experience and training the practitioner needs.

Caution should be used when deciding whether to use touch under the following circumstances:

- When the client has a history of negative experiences with touch, especially from caregivers. This is particularly true if there is noticeable somatic shame associated with those early experiences.

- When the client has such limited experience of appropriate touch that she is at high risk of misunderstanding its purpose.

- When the client lacks enough developmental maturity to adequately manage the necessary contract related to touch. This may include otherwise-mature clients who are engaging developmental issues in the therapeutic relationship and are temporarily lacking in their usual resources.

- When the client is struggling to identify appropriate boundaries.

- If touch causes the client to be overwhelmed or overactivated by the sensations resulting from touch.

- When cultural difference may make it difficult to know how touch will be interpreted.

Appropriate touch can often be especially useful under the following circumstances:

- In working with developmental trauma that has a primarily physical origin, such as extended hospitalizations (particularly when this occurs in the child/infant's pre-verbal development phase). This is especially true when the client's symptoms are manifesting as primarily somatic complaints.

- When the client is beginning to learn how to differentiate between appropriate, caring touch and inappropriate, harmful touch they may have experienced in the past.

- When it is helpful to the client to promote a felt sense of safety and access to co-regulation.

- When touch helps the client integrate his change process more fully through all layers of self.

- When touch helps the client remain resourceful in managing his activation levels.

- When the use of verbal language is limited, due to either disability or language barriers. In this instance, consent must be clearly received by the practitioner and responses to touch clearly monitored throughout the process to ensure that the client is at ease with the contact.

As has been outlined in various chapters in this book, there are many different ways developmental trauma disrupts healthy development. Touch, when applied appropriately, safely, and ethically, can be useful to repair attachment ruptures, promoting healthier and more accurate interoception, creating a sense of safety and connectedness, supporting better access to co-regulation and self-regulation, and repairing chronic somatic shame. Touch can help clients to identify and more fully develop appropriate boundaries and to experience a sense of agency when determining how, when, and what type of touch occurs. Touch can, in part, provide what was not received during the early developmental phases, and provide a helpful option for those clients who are open to the use of touch and somatic forms of therapy.

Amria is thirty-five years old, married, and has three young children. She has a history of early medical trauma with frequent hospitalizations and separations from her primary caretakers. All the nurses knew when she would enter the hospital, because she would be screaming from the moment she entered. Many of the nurses who cared for her struggled with her because of her inconsolable screaming and crying.

Amria had been managing relatively well and, other than higher than normal susceptibility to colds and the flu, appeared to be doing okay. She knew how to manage her life and family and keep herself going with healthy meals and plenty of rest. This worked relatively well for her with a few minor glitches along the way—until the unexpected happened.

Amria's mother, Elena, who was living alone after Amria's father's death three years earlier, had a major fall and broke her hip. Elena had to undergo emergency surgery, followed by a six-week recovery in the hospital. Amria stayed by her mother's side as much as she could and took care of her mother, along with continuing to care for her three children.

Amria began to notice that her energy reserves were soon depleted. When Elena was discharged from the hospital, she came to live with Amria and her family. Elena continued to need support walking and taking care of daily needs. After Amria had spent six months as a constant caretaker, her health deteriorated rapidly. Her neighbor referred her to a somatic therapist for touch therapy to help her better regulate her physiological systems.

Before Amria began working with her therapist, she expressed that her body felt like it was shutting down and giving up. She was twenty minutes late for her first appointment, saying she had no energy and had trouble getting herself ready to get out of the house. She also reported that she had given up on her marriage, and no longer felt any sexual attraction for her husband. She was extremely irritable and frequently yelled at her children. Then her weight began to drop, and she showed even less interest in the world around her.

The clinician referred Amria to a physician for adrenal- and cortisol-level testing. Her results were shocking—she was in deep adrenal depletion. This reminded Amria of the bad old days when she had such severe fatigue that she could barely function, and it also took her back to her early hospitalizations. She was feeling hopeless again about her health.

Her clinician, however, was more positive about Amria being able to regain her energy. She had been doing so well for so many years that this was likely just a temporary setback, and proper support for regulation of her physiology could help to normalize her HPA axis chemistry. Amria was also working with a traditional Chinese medicine practitioner to help support her physical systems while she was recovering.

Amria's system began to respond almost immediately to her clinician's touch work. What felt most supportive and relaxing was when the clinician brought gentle contact and awareness to Amria's kidneys and adrenals. She felt clearly how that touch supported her system to find regulation. She began to feel such a deep sense of replenishment and rest that she realized that she may never have actually learned to let down her guard quite so fully before.

After six months of both touch support and working with the traditional Chinese medicine practitioner, Amria's adrenal and cortisol levels were checked again. She was still below the normal threshold, but was showing progress and was on the road to a more regulated system.

Touch can help magnify the interventions delivered by a clinician. Research on the use of touch in psychotherapy shows that clients perceive interventions to be more effective by therapists who integrate touch into their practices. Clients also report feeling a greater sense of caring on the part of the clinician and a greater sense of being better understood (Horton et al. 1995).

In the context of working with developmental trauma, there are very important effects that become available when touch is integrated appropriately into the work with clients. The clinician's touch also has practical and direct impacts on the client's building of capacity for somatic awareness: it helps the client focus his attention toward his own somatic "insides." Together with his therapist, the client strengthens his ability to identify internal sensations, identify their cause, and potentially regulate the associated feelings, providing him vastly improved interoceptive skills he will eventually use on his own.

However, some clinicians may never use physical touch with clients. Practice settings, client populations, limits on the use of touch with certain licensures or in certain geographic regions, or individual client-practitioner comfort with the use of touch may mean the use of touch simply isn't feasible. But there are still many options available to support the somatic changes that are essential for repairing developmental trauma.

Rather than using physical touch, the clinician and client can use what can be called "touch awareness," a form of somatic attention used by the clinician and client that helps the client focus her attention *as if* touch were helping to direct that attention. The client and clinician can work from the perspective of noticing *what is happening as if touch is occurring*. The nurturing presence of the clinician supports a sense of connectedness and access to co-regulation, even when physical touch cannot become part of the interaction. The use of guided imagery is another effective form of steering the client's attention somatically. When the clinician helps the client work within an image-based framework of noticing sensations and responses, the client can create imagery that expresses or describes her internal experiences. This can also increase interoceptive capacity and refine the client's ability to report her inner experiences.

Noticing co-regulation, with or without physical contact, should always be included in work with developmental trauma. Even sitting near the client and noticing her breathing can help develop the capacity for regulation. Or the clinician can bring gentle contact to the client's shoulder, for example, and notice how the breath moves or doesn't move.

SUPPORTING REGULATION

We know from research in developmental psychology that infants respond to attention, attunement, and responsiveness. Mirror neurons help us reflect facial expressions, gestures, and other indicators that we are seeing and that are being seen by others. Babies seem to notice when someone imitates their expressions and gestures, and some research indicates this may happen as early as the first few hours of life (Bigelow and Walden 2009; Meltzoff and Moore 1983). By four months of age, babies respond differently if mothers are not indicating that they are engaged and reflecting back what the baby does. The development of babies' responsiveness is contingent on how much interaction and responsiveness they receive from their caregivers. With mothers who are depressed, for example, and not responding to their babies, that lack of responsiveness has a clear impact on the infant.

> *If the mother was depressed and therefore not emotionally engaging with the baby, those babies are at risk because those babies are not learning about themselves. Babies get used to the one person that's most familiar, so if you're with a depressed mother who has low responsiveness, those babies will be most responsive to those who are least responsive, so they're perpetuating a risk factor for themselves. There's nothing wrong with the baby; they're just responding to what they're experiencing. (Harmon 2010)*

As infants, we are primed to receive soothing and stimulation through our tactile and somatic systems. If adequate stimulation or soothing doesn't occur in the right amount, early development is likely to suffer. As clinicians, we can look for opportunities to repair those missing elements, and restore—or perhaps even develop for the first time—regulation and resilience. Touch is just another form of human communication we can offer as a way to support a sense of co-regulation, soothing, calming, and connection.

As clinicians, if we are aware of using our own regulation as an intervention, this can open the door to understanding the more subtle types of somatic communication that must occur to facilitate repair of developmental trauma. Simply being present with the client and being in a regulated state ourselves allow the client to "ping"—to notice us in the co-regulation field: *Am I safe? Are we safe?* In this way, our physiology provides the primary intervention. This may not be how we usually consider interventions, but this is critical for supporting regulation and helping our clients build resilience.

11

Strategies and Pathways

WORKING WITH DEVELOPMENTAL trauma from a somatic perspective is of course only one possible approach. Awareness of the impact of all forms of trauma has changed many aspects of our culture through trauma-informed approaches: our social services and foster care systems, our criminal justice system, medical treatment, suicide prevention, and psychiatric and psychotherapeutic treatments, to name just a few.

The biophysiological models for working with trauma, such as Somatic Experiencing and Sensorimotor Psychotherapy, have expanded the range of available treatments that focus on the body. Bringing a somatic perspective to this developing field of trauma-informed care can expand the possible options for treatment, particularly for the underserved population of those who experience somatic symptoms affiliated with their trauma.

In this chapter, we present material that is not specifically somatic in nature, but that will likely also need to be addressed in the recovery process for someone who has experienced developmental trauma. Depending on their practice settings, different clinicians may utilize quite varied approaches for addressing each of these topics. Rather than offering a specific recipe for how to provide treatment, this chapter provides guidance for developing strategies to support the client's change process, a way of thinking about interventions and how to recognize opportunities when they present themselves. In addition, we will also provide information that's important for clinicians to keep in mind as they proceed in their work, such as assessing on an ongoing basis whether or not the client is within his Window of Tolerance.

Simply understanding more about how developmental trauma impacts clients is likely to change the interventions clinicians and other care providers choose to use with their clients and patients. Keeping a regulation-informed perspective will also likely bring a different focus for interpretation of symptoms.

TREATMENT STRATEGIES

Here we will discuss specific treatment strategies that are most effective when working with developmental trauma. As noted in the introduction, the chapters of this book are organized in the basic structure that is often used in the treatment of developmental trauma:

1. **Understand the impact early trauma has on our clients, so that we can assess their needs in the necessary context.** Symptoms related to all aspects of the self should be taken into account: psychological, emotional, physiological, social, and spiritual. Depending on the clinician's scope of practice, not all of these elements of potential disruption may be included directly in treatment, but each will inform the clinician of the possible underlying puzzle pieces that together form the full picture of the developmental trauma disruptions.

2. **Assess the client's capacity for regulation, perception of safety, and assessment of affiliated somatic symptoms.** The basic treatment plan for working with developmental trauma will almost invariably begin with a focus on regulation. It's important to assess where the client falls in his preexisting capacity for self-regulation. This will determine whether other work can proceed simultaneously with further bolstering of self-regulatory capacity, or whether the client is more at the beginning stages of developing self-regulation. The client's narrative, along with his treatment goals, will be extremely important in helping the clinician identify treatment priorities. Attending to the different aspects of narrative—verbal, somatic, physiological, behavioral, and social—will inform the clinician of areas of missing capacities that require support in their development.

   Of course the clients' treatment goals are also important sources of information about where attention should be placed during our work with them. Client education is also critical at these early stages of the process, because a regulation-informed approach may be an unfamiliar way of focusing on symptoms.

3. **Remember: regulation, regulation, regulation.** Attention to supporting the client's capacity for regulation will always be a part of any interventions when working with developmental trauma. For some clients, it will be the primary focus for extended periods of the early part of treatment. It would not be unusual to spend the first year or more of therapy focusing on regulation as the underpinning for all other interventions. For other clients— those who already have at least some capacity to stay within their true Window of Tolerance—the treatment process may move more quickly, and regulation will be supporting the process in the background more of the time.

4. **Pay attention to defensive accommodations and the Faux Window.** As the work with regulation proceeds, other elements of the client's management efforts will also need attention. Identifying the client's habitual defensive accommodations is often helpful for both the clinician and the client to become more conscious of how those strategies are provoked by movement outside the Window of Tolerance. In the process of identifying those defensive strategies, identification of the Faux Window versus the Window of Tolerance is often a side effect. As the client becomes more aware of how her defensive strategies are provoked, she will also become more attuned to how these strategies have kept her outside of her true Window of Tolerance.

This can be quite frustrating for clients who have a fairly narrow Window of Tolerance, but who have been successfully applying sufficient defensive accommodations to maintain a Faux Window that imitates regulation—meaning the client has been overriding herself enough that she believes her capacity is much greater than it is. Once she is attuned to her actual thresholds for overstimulation, it can be frustrating to stay within those limits as she works to expand her true Window of Tolerance. This is when client education is critical, so the client can understand the benefits of expanding her true Window of Tolerance, rather than simply strengthening her defensive strategies.

5. **Support more accurate interoception.** This is usually done simultaneously with both regulation work and working to lift defensive accommodation strategies. More accurate interoception is a critical element in the client's ability to notice his increasing capacity for regulation, to access a felt sense

of safety, to notice co-regulation, and to more accurately notice his internal experiences—and report those to the clinician.

6. **Change the narrative.** This often happens simultaneously with the previous two stages of work, although some clients will need coaching to perceive the differences in how they attend to their experiences, and the ways in which various aspects of their narrative are changing. Helping the client notice, for example, that her symptoms have changed is often necessary. It's good news that a client has normalized her progress and taken full ownership of it, but this can mean that she sometimes misses what great strides she has taken in her recovery, simply because she isn't noticing that she has changed.

7. **Remain focused on regulation.** As the work progresses, there is often a stage when it's time to return attention more fully to regulation. Because the client typically has expanded his true Window of Tolerance, has greater access to his ventral parasympathetic physiology, is more able to track his internal experiences, and has a more developed sense of safety, his capacity for regulation has often grown to the point that returning to this focus can help consolidate the gains he has made.

8. **Work with the more specific symptoms.** By the time the client has built the level of capacity we would expect at this stage of the process, she is likely ready to "clean out the back of the closet," so to speak. Her capacity to manage stressors and return to the Window of Tolerance is likely developed enough that working with specific content can occur without the client going over her threshold into defensive accommodations and the Faux Window. Likewise, the specific symptoms that may still be troubling her can be addressed without the client losing her capacity to stay connected to herself and those who provide co-regulation.

TOUCH AND REGULATION

A final note related to treatment strategies: the authors have a strong commitment to the incorporation of touch in the treatment of developmental trauma. Many of the strategies we use to support regulation in our practices are based on touch methods. The most common method we use—and teach to clinicians in our courses—is to support the kidney/adrenal system via touch. Making gentle contact at the lower midback, near the base of the ribcage, and then bringing attention to the structures of the kidney/adrenal area, which are just inside the ribcage, can provide a sense of connection to these structures, which are critical in the signaling system of the HPA axis. The "touch" is done primarily with a sense of attention and connection, not with physical pressure. Usually, the client is lying down when this is done, but it's equally effective when done with the client sitting comfortably. This simple contact provides a way for the clinician to notice the client's breath, to notice the muscles of the lower back and how tense or relaxed they are, to notice if the client seems braced around the kidney area (often affiliated with fear), and also to provide a sense of support and co-regulation for the client.

A full description of touch interventions for working with developmental trauma is beyond the scope of this book, but we invite the reader—if it feels appropriate for your practice setting—to try the simple exercise above and notice if it could be a useful addition to your "regulation" tools.

For those who do not incorporate touch into their practices, regulation work will primarily mean working with small, incremental changes to ensure the client stays within her true Window of Tolerance. For those who use a biophysiological model to work with trauma, a focus on regulation of the ANS would be included in this foundational level of work. For those who take a more traditional therapeutic approach, this means attending to the many ways that a regulation-informed method can alter interventions. An example would be to limit the demands for social engagement with a client who has limited access to his ventral parasympathetic physiology, or otherwise shows signs of having limited ability to manage social interactions without high levels of stress.

THE APGAR SCORE

As noted previously, it's important for the support of regulation that the client learns to notice when he is within his Window of Tolerance, rather than in the Faux Window. It is, of course, also important for the clinician to understand her methods for noticing that as well. One way to do this is to regularly monitor the client's physiological responses that indicate if he is experiencing hyper- or hypo-arousal. One tool for this is a variation on the Apgar assessment.

The Apgar score was first introduced by Virginia Apgar in 1952 to improve the survival rate of infants and to develop a universal measure of viability for the infant. The test is performed one minute after birth to determine how the baby tolerated the birth; it's performed again five minutes after birth to see how the baby is adjusting to life outside the womb. There is a simple scoring of zero to two points for each category assessed.

These indicators are bundled into an easy-to-remember mnemonic: Appearance, Pulse, Grimace, Activity, Respiration. For each of the five measures, a score of zero is given for the lowest function, a one for the next level of function, and a two for the highest level.

During the scoring, the medical team examines the baby's:

1. Skin tone: Blue, or indications of lack of oxygenation, on full body (0); body has good color, extremities blue (1); entire body has good color (2)

2. Heart rate: No heartbeat (0); heart rate too slow (1); heart rate normal (2)

3. Reflexes (grimace response or reflex irritability used as an indicator when there is a mild stimulation, such as mild pinching): No reaction (0); grimacing (1); grimacing and cough, sneeze, or vigorous cry (2)

4. Muscle tone: Loose and floppy (0); some muscle tone (1); active motion (2)

5. Breathing effort: No breathing (0); breathing slowly or irregularly (1); crying and breathing well (2)

The higher the score, the better the baby is functioning as she adjusts to her existence outside the womb. A total score of seven to nine indicates the newborn is healthy (a score of ten is unusual, because most babies have blue hands and feet initially, which is considered normal). A score of less than seven is usually a sign the baby needs medical attention to elevate her score (clearing of the airway, physical stimulation to raise the heart rate, or other interventions). The lower the Apgar score, the more help the baby needs to adjust outside the womb. A low Apgar score at one minute has, in most cases, changed by the five-minute mark.

A low Apgar score is also not an indicator of long-term health issues—it is a quick assessment of the newborn to indicate whether or not the baby needs immediate medical attention. This information tells the team whether or not the baby is in danger, so interventions can take place if needed.

As clinicians, we can use the Apgar score as a way to monitor our clients' responses during our work together. At the most basic level, we may see a reenactment of perinatal distress if the client's birth was challenging. We may see a regression, physiologically, back to lower Apgar indicators, with respiration and muscle tone reverting to the lower end of the Apgar scale, for example. If we know the client experienced a very challenging birth, or very early medical issues and interventions, we should keep an eye out for the Apgar indicators if we are working with anything distressing for the client, because his earliest stress events at the time of birth may have linked, or coupled, with that early stress physiology. We will discuss coupling dynamics later in this chapter, as they provide another important element that should be addressed in relation to any form of trauma.

Aside from specific birth-related trauma, we can use the Apgar assessment as a quick indicator of the physiological status of our clients, including adult clients, in relation to any developmental trauma work we may do with the client. Rather than taking each of the five Apgar categories as an assessment of a newborn, we can consider where on the Apgar scale our client is at any given time during a session. If we see her Apgar level reduce dramatically, we are likely seeing the manifestation of an elevated stress state, and we may need to reconsider whether our interventions are overstimulating the client beyond the point where she can adequately manage her physiological responses. As has been discussed previously—and as we will see again in the next section—many clients with developmental trauma have a physiological "habit" of overusing the dorsal physiology, so if we rely only on indicators related to sympathetic arousal to assess overstimulation in our clients, then we will incorrectly assess the clients who move into underresponsiveness as their indicator of stress.

At the time of birth, the stress-response networks are busy organizing. The stress-response system signals distress in the infant in relation to hunger, thirst, cold, or threat. The caregiver steps in to provide other patterned somatosensory and neural inputs for the developing stress-response system of the infant. Through interactions with the mother/caregiver, the infant receives responses to his distress—such as feeding and soothing—and the infant begins to move toward homeostasis, which promotes survival. Because of the dependence of the infant on the caretaker, the caretaker becomes the external stress regulator.

These early interactions with caretakers form a set of templates in the infant's response system about safety, threat, and soothing—including whether or not someone is safe and pleasurable, or unreliable and dangerous. These early experiences create the first neural platform for relationships, which may, without intervention, play out during the remainder of our lives. As clinicians, we will certainly witness these neural platforms and their patterning within our clients. By regularly considering the client's "Apgar" in our work, we develop a good habit that helps us become finely tuned to the client's stress responses, and keep interventions within the client's Window of Tolerance.

COUPLING DYNAMICS

The concept of "coupling dynamics" is one that has been used over many decades in various psychophysiological models. It provides a model for the ways in which fragments of behavior can integrate through complex psychophysiological mechanisms to result in what appears to be a coherent whole. Peter Levine integrated the concept of coupling dynamics into the Somatic Experiencing model of trauma recovery to help describe the dynamics that can occur with over- and under-coupling of the survival effort, and somatic or other responses that arise in the face of overwhelming experience. This is most commonly discussed in relation to shock trauma events. For example, someone involved in a car accident that resulted in serious injury will then feel anxiety at the thought of driving. The thought of driving is now "coupled" with the stress response related to his unresolved responses from the accident.

Those coupled responses (in this case, responses that are over-coupled, or tightly linked together) interfere with the ability to be in a relaxed and responsive relationship with the environment. The accident victim's over-coupled responses are now functioning as if driving and anxiety are a single thing—they are now inextricably linked as if they are one entity. What will likely help the client who had this car accident is support in separating the experience of driving from his feelings of anxiety. This would be a common part of the work involved in renegotiating a traumatic experience when using a biophysiological model of trauma recovery, such as Somatic Experiencing.

There are various ways coupling dynamics can manifest, with different levels of complexity. It is beyond the scope of this book to provide a comprehensive description of coupling dynamics as they can be used in the healing of trauma. Here we provide an overview to introduce the clinician to the basics of this model in relation to developmental trauma in order to provide additional tools to work with some of its common side effects.

There are two basic variations of coupling:

- **Over-coupling:** Elements of experience that do not inherently belong together are now linked in some way. A specific response inevitably leads to another, and then another, without interruption (such as would happen when a panic attack is triggered). Two elements are now inextricably linked, as if they are one thing, when they should be considered independent of one another (like anxiety and driving, as noted above).

- **Under-coupling:** Elements that *do* belong together are no longer clearly connected. Two ideas or experiences have been made separate when they are actually connected. If we use the same basic example as the one mentioned above—the client involved in a car accident—he might come to therapy for anxiety but not remember that it developed immediately after he had a car accident. He might avoid driving, but not notice he's doing so because of anxiety. His responses related to the car accident are under-coupled; the links that should be present are not. Dissociation can be a form of under-coupling.

Sometimes these coupling dynamics occur almost as a natural side effect of a highly stressful experience. We may link things together simply because they coincidentally happened at the same time during a stressful experience. For example, smells that were present when something terrible happened to us will later make us feel disturbed when no actual threat is present. The linking occurs spontaneously, as a kind of somatic and psychological misunderstanding of cause and effect, or as a misunderstanding of interrelationships between different elements of the experience. Or we may have been in a dissociated state during the experience, and so various elements of the experience have a sense of disconnection or independence from each other, or from our sense of self.

These are all common concepts within the psychotherapy field, and many clinicians commonly work with these types of dissociative states or links in experience. Dissociation is viewed in the psychology field as a mental process.

The main thing to understand about coupling dynamics in relation to trauma is that the coupling dynamics themselves "hold" the experiences of the overwhelming trauma, a secondary form of stabilization that (with varying degrees of success) prevents underlying experiences from overwhelming us again and again. The two basic rules when working with coupling dynamics are:

1. Whenever under-coupled elements are rejoined—brought back into relationship—anything that was held at a distance by the under-coupling will be mobilized, will become accessible to the client, and will flow back

into memory. In short, the survival energy that was bound by the under-coupling will now come into the room.

2. Whenever over-coupled elements are separated—broken down into their components—the bound survival responses will be mobilized, the memories will become available, and the responses will flow.

We can think of coupling dynamics as a survival energy management process, a way for us to keep ourselves stable and away from memories, or bodily memories, of events that were too distressing for us to cope with directly. Over- and under-coupling are two variations of that same process; they have the same purpose but take different forms.

There are many variations in the way these two forms of coupling dynamics manifest, including utilizing both forms of coupling in the wake of a single experience. We can be over-coupled in relation to some parts of the experience, and under-coupled in relation to others. This is one of the reasons why coupling dynamics can be a complex process to untangle with a client.

There are two slightly different manifestations of coupling dynamics that are particularly helpful to understand when working with developmental trauma. Learning to work effectively with these basic forms of coupling dynamics will provide clinicians with effective tools for helping clients move toward completion (as discussed later in this chapter), which in turn helps them achieve greater regulation and resilience.

The first form is relatively simple and shows up in what we call *response cycles,* or *response sequences.* In this manifestation of coupling dynamics, there is a specific, repeated cycle of interconnection (in over-coupling), or of disconnection (in under-coupling), that has been formed as a result of the trauma experience. Over time, these response patterns can become quite complex, masking the original source. The original response pattern may have been adaptive at the time of the trauma, but, over time, will become maladaptive.

In over-coupling, a trigger of some kind precipitates a particular response, and will reliably do so again and again, eventually strengthening the response until there is little possibility of responding differently. Triggers can take many forms: environmental, physiological, flashbacks, smells, or thoughts. Likewise, the responses can fall into many categories: physical or physiological responses, memories, somatic patterns, or behaviors.

A common example of over-coupling of this type would be of certain smells triggering memories and flashbacks of sexual abuse, perhaps in turn precipitating a panic attack, a migraine, frantic efforts at escape, and, quite commonly, overwhelming feelings of shame. In under-coupling, a connection that would normally be made is not. Taking the example above, the smell triggers a racing heart and a migraine, but we decide it has to do with the fact that the room is stuffy and the lights are too bright. In the first case, the response system is overly linked, and in the second, the links that should be there are not. In either case, the habituated responses are interrupting the ability to complete the unresolved survival response in relation to the experience, integrate those survival responses into the here and now, and dissolve the coupling dynamics.

With developmental trauma, the original stress triggers for the response cycles are often unknown. Sometimes the responses are so clear that an educated guess can be made, but very often the responses have built and morphed over time to the point that they now bear very little resemblance to the original trigger response. Or perhaps the response cycle is related more to dysregulation than behavior, so there may be physical coupling dynamics, such as migraines or other chronic physical symptoms, that seem to occur randomly. In this case, the triggering experience has been lost in time, and the response sequences have developed a life of their own, almost completely separate from any specific narrative.

The second form of coupling dynamics is something we can think of as a "packaging" of experience, a way the client has organized overwhelming experiences into manageable structures in order to limit the "overwhelmingness" of those experiences. What begins as an adaptive response to challenging experiences becomes maladaptive over time, just like the evolution of defensive accommodations. In fact, coupling dynamics can be considered a form of defensive accommodation.

As a metaphor for the overwhelming experience, let's substitute a household full of dirty, smelly laundry. The laundry is everywhere, covering the furniture, getting in the way when we want to prepare a meal, preventing us from moving from room to room easily. The smell of it bothers us, makes us feel like our house isn't ours anymore. In short, it has intruded in and taken over our lives to the point that we are constantly faced with overwhelming feelings about it. In this circumstance, over-coupling would be the equivalent of finding a big suitcase, stuffing all the dirty laundry into it, shoving it into the back of the closet, and slamming the door. Now all that mess and clutter can be forgotten. We only have one suitcase to deal with, and that's manageable—as long as we never open it.

Under-coupling, in this circumstance, would be the equivalent of flinging some of the laundry over the neighbor's fence, tossing some into the basement, stuffing some under the bed, and loading some into the trunk of our car. Perhaps now there is only a stray sock or two left, and that's not so bothersome—as long as we never look under the bed or into the trunk of our car.

Of course, what we manage with coupling dynamics is not as simple or mild as dirty laundry. In the context of trauma, we use coupling dynamics to manage experiences so overwhelming that we could not integrate them into our sense of self, and so we had to find a way to "hide" them from ourselves in order to carry on with the task of living.

In this form of over-coupling, we collapse and compress overwhelming experiences down into manageable chunks. We so strongly overlink things that we can no longer access any of the specific elements within those experiences. In relation to those experiences, we have little or no ability to differentiate one aspect of the event from another. We simplify multiple elements of an overwhelming experience into one or two that we *can* manage. "School was a scary place for me" might be the way a client describes the experience of having to walk through dangerous neighborhoods to get to school, being bullied at school, being beaten at home for poor grades, and being sexually abused by a teacher. The client may not have conscious memories of the individual events that contributed to the "scary" quality of school, and so may not be consciously or actively avoiding those elements of her narrative. The over-coupling may be so effective that "scary" is just a general feeling of fear in relation to school, a way of blurring details into an indistinguishable mixture of fear and pain.

In under-coupling, we discard parts of our experience that are too overwhelming to include. Experiences are highly differentiated, and connections aren't available to us for understanding how one thing relates to another. For example, a woman has a relationship-ending argument with her spouse and rushes out of the house, overcome with anguish and anger, and then she has a car accident. Later, the argument is dropped from the narrative, and she is instead angry with herself for having an accident at an intersection she passes through every day. She may literally no longer remember the argument, or she remembers it happening on a different day—she has disconnected an element of the experience that was too much to bear. She has broken apart the experience to the point that some important aspects of it are unrecognizable.

Each of these strategies has the same basic purpose: to keep us away from events that are disturbing or overwhelming for us. We simply use a different method when we under-couple than we do when we over-couple, but the underlying need for managing the experience is identical. We will use over- and under-coupling to sequester ourselves from memories, bodily sensations, portions of our narrative, information about another person that is too much to take in, physiological responses—anything that contains the experience of overwhelming helplessness that lies at the basis of trauma. The term "dynamics" is apt, because this is often a system that must respond daily to the challenge of managing unresolved survival states that are continually pushing for expression.

One by-product of coupling is the difficulty of learning from our experiences. If one thing is the same as another, it may be impossible for us to learn about differences and nuances—in our responses, in our sensations, in our understanding of past experiences and their impact on us. Conversely, if everything is unique and unconnected, we cannot learn to identify themes, to transfer our knowledge about one situation to another similar situation, to understand how one thing is actually connected to another.

The point of this type of coupling is to hold us away from our own experience, and people unconsciously utilize this defensive accommodation because it works, to some extent. When those coupling dynamics are successful, then elements of the experience are invisible to us, as was the case with Valeria, who did not remember her father's shaming behaviors. Part of the role of the clinician is to support the client in gaining access to the under- and over-coupled elements, to help those elements integrate and move to completion. One critical thing we must remember in our role as clinicians is that the coupling dynamics act to bind the survival energies, to provide the best attempt at making those high-energy states inert. That metaphorical suitcase at the back of the closet isn't empty. It contains all the unresolved elements of the survival responses, memories, sensations, and physiological states of activation that are affiliated with the traumatic experiences held within.

As might be imagined, if we were to work with the client's narrative of school being scary and we tried to identify the individual elements of "scary" all at one time, we would likely provoke a perhaps overwhelming response. The work should instead proceed slowly, with attention to the client's capacity to stay within her Window of Tolerance. Likewise, the implications of the argument that precipitated the car accident could be overwhelming, and the clinician would need to attend to the same issues of titration and staying within the client's capacity in order to bring the under-coupled elements together without over-whelming the client again.

The examples we've used above are of events that happened to adults, beyond the usual age range of early trauma. By contrast, with developmental trauma, the survival-challenging experiences occur when we are very young, when we are not differentiated fully from our caregivers, when we are not fully developed physically, emotionally, psychologically, or spiritually. In those circumstances, the coupling dynamics tend to be so strongly embedded in essential qualities of our self-narrative, in our somatic sense of self and our responses, that it is a challenge to tease them out. The clinician must develop refined skills for detecting the subtle cues that indicate the presence of coupling dynamics. Coupling dynamics can be the hidden elements in a client's response. They can drive behaviors, physiological responses, and ways of thinking.

With practice, we can learn to notice when a client is missing the necessary differentiation between particular aspects of an experience (over-coupling), and support them to achieve better differentiation. It is usually more difficult to work with under-coupled elements than it is to work with over-coupled elements, because the clinician is trying to find what should be there but isn't. As discussed previously, the narrative of developmental trauma is often deeply somatic, so the work with coupling dynamics in relation to early trauma often includes working with subtle somatic states that express those coupling dynamics.

Typically, the most basic interventions are the only way to begin, because the coupling process has occurred so early that it is foundational to the way the client organizes his experience. Something as simple as having the client notice what's different, or what is the same—in terms of sensations, their symptoms, their responses to different experiences—can support this change in the coupling dynamics. When over-coupling is at play, we can ask the client to notice subtle differences between one thing and another; this can build capacity for the differentiation needed to identify over-coupled elements. We can also help the client notice how things are linked when they should be separate. The clinician can do the same by feeding back what she notices, and helping the client differentiate one type of experience from another: "I notice that the way you sit when remembering how well you did in your speech at work is very different from when you're remembering your times in school."

By contrast, having the client notice similarities, what belongs in the same category, can help her make connections between things she has disconnected, building the skills for working with under-coupled elements, and building the capacity to notice how things that belong together are currently disconnected. The clinician can again support this with her own observations: "I notice that the way you talk about your helplessness after the accident is similar to the language you use when talking about your former wife." Categorizing experiences, feelings, sensations, and thoughts into the boxes of same and different can bring attention to the ways in which the client habitually uses over- and under-coupling to manage her experiences.

This is not an easy skill to master as a clinician. Not only do coupling dynamics prevent the *client* from identifying underlying experiences, these dynamics can keep the *clinician* away as well. It takes practice to become familiar with these dynamics. This is just an introductory foray into the topic, but even these simple interventions can support the client in her change process.

One of the most common elements that will couple with early trauma is shame. As discussed in chapter 8, shame plays a strong role in our sense of survival, and in that role it can become intertwined with our early experiences in a way that continues to inhibit our development of resilience.

As with any form of work with coupling dynamics, work with somatic shame or identity trauma should proceed slowly and carefully. Shame can be maladaptive and can drive strong responses. The goal of working with coupled elements in relation to shame is to support the client to uncouple shame from healthy impulses and behaviors, and to restore a sense of connection and belonging. This uncoupling also helps clients gain access to differentiation between somatic survival states and somatic shame.

As with all other work with developmental trauma, the first step is to focus on regulation and restoration of the Window of Tolerance. As the client gains more access to self-regulation, and greater capacity in his Window of Tolerance, shame in its physiological role of inhibition will be less necessary. That often allows easier access to the uncoupling of shame and survival effort—although, of course, working with deep levels of shame will likely take time.

WORK WITH COMPLETIONS

Using biophysiological methods for working with shock trauma renegotiation, such as Somatic Experiencing, we would focus on completion of threat responses to integrate a sense of successful survival effort. We would do that by supporting healthy orientation to the environment, by developing a felt sense of completion of effective self-protection (such as fight or flight), and by then helping the client move into deactivation of his threat physiology, integrating those responses back into normal resting physiology. The concept of completing incomplete self-protective responses as one of the critical elements for healing trauma is one of the great contributions that Peter Levine has made to the field of trauma recovery (Levine and Frederick 1997). Influenced by Gellhorn's material on the inter-relationship between autonomic and somatic systems (Gellhorn 1967), Levine recognized the need for the physiology of survival responses to be resolved in order to return to nonthreat physiological states. This type of work is sometimes referred to as "working with completions," because part of the benefit of this type of work is that the client experiences success at completion of survival effort and, in theory, would naturally return to his Window of Tolerance.

This is an effective method for resolving shock trauma, and can be readily adapted for work with developmental trauma, as long as the clinician understands the difference between completions related to shock trauma and those appropriate to developmental trauma.

With developmental trauma, completion of a specific threat response is not readily available, simply because the trauma occurred at a time when we would have had little capacity for active self-protection. Even at age three, we have an extremely limited ability to fight or flee—our primary survival mechanism is our caregiver. When clinicians consider "working with completions" in relation to developmental trauma, we must consider this concept in a developmentally appropriate context. Most fundamentally, when considering completion around developmental trauma, we must think of the primary completion as gaining access to a felt sense of safety. We are completing the interrupted or distorted impulses for connection, bonding, or movement away from pain and toward safety. Successful completion of self-protection, therefore, will be affiliated with gaining a sense of safety.

In addition, we need to consider completions as also being deeply somatic. Under the stress of developmental trauma, we may have co-opted and honed somatic strategies for managing our arousal—overuse of the dorsal physiology being one of the most common, as noted above. "Completions" will also necessarily include the lifting of Faux Window defensive accommodations, including those in the physiological and somatic systems, allowing the underlying regulation impulses to complete.

Completion can also include gaining access to states related to pleasure and safety. Developmental trauma can create a "filtering" process, whereby only states related to perception of threat and response to threat merit attention. Through that filtering process, we limit our access to perception of pleasure, connectedness, safety, creativity, and adaptability. These are some of the markers of resilience. Therefore, limited access to the felt sense of these qualities can also limit our perception of our own capacity for resilience.

Taking the time to notice and bring the client's attention specifically to successes, to experiences that are pleasurable (or at least *less bad* and *less scary*), and to the somatic and interoceptive details of those experiences is a powerful tool for supporting a sense of completion of survival effort in relation to developmental trauma. "How would you know it if you felt it?" can be an important question for almost any quality the client is identifying as a marker for success: "How would you know safety if you felt it?" "How would you know someone wishes you well?" "How would you recognize that a difficult experience is in the past?" Until the client can identify the somatic and interoceptive markers that help him notice these states of success, the experience is likely to remain too cognitive, too much rooted in the higher functions of the brain that weren't online at the time of the traumatic experiences.

MOVING TOWARD SECURE ATTACHMENT

It's important to remember here that all attachment styles, even those that seem most insecure, are the result of positive attempts to cope with less than ideal access to healthy parenting in childhood. The reason for the less than ideal parenting is not as significant as understanding that these attachment styles, which seemed to work so well as defensive accommodations in our families of origin (birth, foster, or institutionalized), are less effective at helping us maneuver through relationships in the adult world.

Attachment styles and relational patterns are not created overnight. They take many years to develop, beginning in utero and continuing with innumerable interactions with and reactions to our caregivers and family systems. Through the repetition of these experiences, we gain extensive practice using our defensive accommodations, which form our attachment styles. Transforming insecure attachment styles to "earned secure" attachment takes time, patience, and the right setting for this goal to be accomplished.

That setting is one in which the therapist creates a milieu in the treatment space that allows the client to reexperience her earlier developmental experiences. The difference this time is that the milieu is safe for the client's exploration of these basic needs. The milieu would be seen through the therapist's eyes as a type of therapeutic reparenting for the client and should contain the four components of attachment proposed by Bowlby, as outlined in chapter 1: creating a safe place, processing separation distress, exploring proximity maintenance, and forming a secure base.

The safe place is where the client is able to develop trust in the therapist. As a result of this trusting relationship, the client can express or demonstrate a threat response and rely on the therapist to provide empathy and compassion in return. By creating this milieu, the therapist and client develop a deeper level of interconnectedness than is seen in most therapies that are not attachment based. This interconnectedness and trust allow the client a safe environment in which to tell her story, discover behavioral patterns and their links to defensive accommodations, and so on.

Leaving the therapy office at the end of an appointment, and separating from the therapist, can bring on a sense of reenactment of earlier experiences of abandonment. The therapist holds the safe space in the office, but also eases the transition of leaving the office until the next appointment by staying available (within reason) for the client. Through proximity maintenance, the therapist supports the client as he tries new things and explores the world, and makes herself available to hear about the experiences without passing judgment. Becoming the second-chance secure base is necessary to repair the early, disrupted co-regulation experience if the original secure base was not reliable enough to provide a sense of safety and security. This foundation as a secure base encourages the client to continue to sort out and learn things about himself. It takes all of these components of attachment to adequately transform the insecure to secure.

In 2009, Daniel Hughes established the Dyadic Developmental Psychotherapy Institute (DDPI) to train professionals to work with children and families who had experienced developmental trauma. In DDP, Hughes acknowledges the need for the parent-child relationship in recovery. Hughes reinforces the concept of the parent being present and aware with the child and adapting to an attitude of Playfulness, Love, Acceptance, Curiosity, and Empathy (PLACE). Moving attachment from insecure to secure takes significant repetitive practice. PLACE is an attitude a therapist can adapt in his office and repeat again and again to help the client move toward secure attachment.

In working with developmental trauma from an attachment perspective, the primary focus is to create safety and continuity. Once the client has a greater felt sense of access to safety—and belonging—greater resilience is the natural side effect.

SOMATIC TRANSFERENCE AND SOMATIC COUNTERTRANSFERENCE

When considering any somatic approach to working with developmental trauma, we must also consider transference and countertransference—not because they are more problematic than in nonsomatic approaches, but because there are certain elements of somatic dynamics that clinicians should include in their awareness. Transference and countertransference are of course a common factor when working with developmental trauma, no matter what modality is used. Working with clients on such a deeply somatic level, and integrating the components of attachment, quite naturally produces a sense of deeper connection between the client and the therapist, which in turn invites a deeper expression of transferential dynamics.

There is a very large body of knowledge related to traditional transference and countertransference dynamics within the therapeutic environment, and this section is not intended to duplicate that comprehensive set of information. Although nonsomatic therapists sometimes express concerns that working somatically, whether with touch or without, can produce impossibly complex transferential dynamics, research does not bear this out. As noted in the previous chapter, research about the inclusion of touch in the psychotherapeutic environment indicates that clients experience their therapists as being skillful in their interventions and feel better understood by their therapists. A somatic approach does not inherently bring more complexity to transference and countertransference, but it does bring the need for particular awareness and attention on the part of the clinician.

We focus here on one of the important elements of transferential dynamics that clinicians should keep in mind as they approach their work with clients who have experienced developmental trauma—somatic transference and somatic countertransference (also referred to as body-centered countertransference). The classic concept of transference in psychotherapy focuses on the redirection of the client's feelings, beliefs, or behaviors onto the therapist. Treating the therapist with disdain as a reenactment of the disdain felt for an alcoholic parent would be an example of a simple form of transference. Countertransference would consider the therapist's feelings, beliefs, or behaviors in response to her clients. Reacting strongly to a hint of criticism from the client, which triggered the therapist's "not-good-enough" feelings, would be a simple example of countertransference. In somatic transference and somatic countertransference, we also need to consider the physical, somatic responses as part of what might occur within relational dynamics.

In its most simple form, this might mean the client, when experiencing new and possibly uncomfortable interoceptive qualities, might decide the therapist is causing those sensations by the way the therapist is directing her attention. Here, the client expresses an external-locus-of-control perspective that may relate directly back to early relational experiences; this is a common form of this type of somatic transference.

In more complex manifestations, it might mean the client has difficulty differentiating between qualities that he is experiencing within his own body, versus the somatic responses of the therapist. When working with co-regulation, for example, it's natural for the client to use the therapist's somatic expressions—such as changes in breathing patterns or greater settling and relaxation as revealed by facial muscles—to help indicate what the transitions will look like when moving from more anxious states to more relaxed states. For some clients, it might actually be difficult to notice that the clinician is having her own unique experience. It may seem as though the clinician's responses arise from *within* the client. *Is that you, or me?* is a relatively common question clients raise when beginning to notice how connectedness produces mutual responses. This is actually the very nature of co-regulation. But, for a client who has had little or no experience with co-regulation, it can at first be challenging to understand how mutuality will manifest in a healthier form. If past relational/attachment experiences have allocated control of regulation to the "omnipotent other," then it's likely the client will need support in order to gain a sense of agency regarding his own regulatory capacity.

On the other side of the proposition, somatic countertransference will include the clinician's physical, somatic responses related to his work with his clients.

Using the Egan and Carr Body-Centred Countertransference Scale developed in 2005, a study at the National University of Ireland and the University College Dublin measured the experience of countertransference of female trauma therapists (Booth, Trimble, and Egan 2010).

The study showed that many therapists had strong physical responses related to their work with clients. Many therapists also felt embarrassed by those responses. The most common responses, in descending order, were yawning, tearfulness, unexpected shifts in the therapist's body, and headaches. The least reported symptoms were numbness, sexual arousal, genital pain, and stomach or throat issues. One of the weaknesses of the study is that it did not gather the same information about male therapists' responses, but it is likely that male therapists would have similar types of experiences.

Many somatic therapists consider their somatic responses to be potentially useful sources of information that might inform their interventions with clients. However, as with any tool, practice and experience will help to hone the accuracy and reliability of these somatic indicators. When a clinician includes her own physical/somatic responses as part of what she will attend to during a session, she will need to refine her ability to identify what types of responses might be related to what's happening with the client, versus what might simply be occurring within herself.

When the therapist learns to track the client's Apgar level, notice gut feelings and reactions in the room—in the "resonant field" between client and clinician—and follow other somatic indicators, a rich, somatic dialogue will develop that can inform therapeutic interventions. Therapists can also learn to follow their own interoceptive responses, and use their own somatic systems to help interpret changes in their clients' systems.

Many somatic indicators are subtle and would normally remain below conscious awareness. It takes practice and perseverance to develop finely honed capacities to attend to somatic information, whether within the client or within the therapist.

NURTURING RESILIENCE

As is true for many clinicians who work with trauma, we—the authors—hold an optimistic perspective toward recovery from early challenges. We have experienced firsthand the humbling experience of accompanying someone who makes the commitment to the path toward better health—and ultimately transformation—in spite of sometimes unimaginable early challenges. All of us who work with developmental trauma know it has deep, lasting effects, and can manifest in a myriad of ways. However, there are identifiable patterns to the ways in which developmental trauma shows itself; and armed with the right knowledge we can refine our skills at detecting those patterns and clues, and further develop our ability to help clients recover from the effects of their early challenges.

Supporting our clients in recovering from those challenges is time-consuming and often requires a tremendous amount of patience. Resilience is often hard won for those who have faced severe early trauma; and nurturing the development of resilience is a long game, taking commitment on the part of all involved. What we are ultimately trying to do for our clients is to help them shift from survival mode to greater confidence, ease, and health, and to help them feel less helpless, be more empowered, and have more direct access to resilience.

With better understanding of trauma, we can help our clients renegotiate their orientation toward life and themselves. The tools and strategies for this are many, but a compassionate, knowledgeable approach that honors the client's history, challenges—and strengths—can facilitate gradual change.

If we return to the beginning of this book, when we articulated the most common factors that have been identified that support the development of resilience, we can adapt that information in the clinical setting to inform us not so much about the specific interventions we might use, but about the framework within which every intervention can be delivered:

1. Stable and supportive adult-child relationships

2. A sense of self-efficacy and perceived control (specifically, an internal locus of control)

3. Adaptive skills and self-regulatory capacity

4. Sources of faith, hope, and cultural traditions (Shonkoff et al. 2015)

In addition to the factors noted above, learning to cope with manageable stress is another critical element in the development of resilience (Shonkoff et al. 2015). In this case, the key term is "manageable." Stress that stays within an appropriate threshold, which does not trigger our defensive accommodations, can actually have a strengthening effect on resilience. Especially in relation to early trauma, it's important that we understand that there is a range of stress—what's termed "positive stress"—that is helpful to clients, but that stress outside of that range is not. If we are attentive to the client's Window of Tolerance, and provide positive challenges that expand capacity without provoking defensive accommodations, that will tend to expand resilience rather than restrict it.

Of the above factors, we know that the single greatest factor that supports resilience is stable and supportive adult-child relationships. As we have discussed, the clinician is likely to—at least initially—be a surrogate for the stability and connectedness that her clients missed as children. Even for adult clients, the experience of a caring, persistent, and attuned relationship will have a positive impact on many of the factors related to resilience. "The capabilities that underlie resilience can be strengthened at any age . . . it is never too late to build resilience . . . Adults who strengthen these skills in themselves can better model healthy behaviors for their children, thereby improving the resilience of the next generation" (Shonkoff et al. 2015, 7).

As clinicians, if we are attentive to the idea that the consistent, supportive relationship we have with our clients is itself the most critical intervention in helping clients recover from early trauma, then we are less likely to miss the important opportunities that may arise for showing that support, for offering co-regulation, and for providing stability. It can also perhaps take the pressure off always having to be "active" in the way we offer support. "I see you, I hear you, and I believe you" is often the most potent way we will express to clients that they are finally being understood.

Supporting the development of self-regulatory skills, of a stronger sense of an internal locus of control, and helping clients develop an expanded Window of Tolerance that supports greater adaptability are all elements that will inherently support greater resilience. The development of these capacities takes time, and as clinicians we need to deeply understand how critical these elements are so that we attend to them at every possible moment in our work with clients. These are not typically interventions that are done as somewhat freestanding techniques; but, rather, they inform our choices as we move forward in our work with clients.

Most typically, as clients have a greater sense of health, self-efficacy, and confidence, they will quite naturally become interested in more social connection, and a more expanded sense of community—and have the capacity to support those types of connections. If a client has been struggling with severe health issues, it's often quite difficult to maintain even basic social connections. Once energy has been freed up from the survival effort, it becomes available to support other endeavors—creative pursuits, spiritual and cultural connectedness within her community, and self-expression.

It is not an exaggeration to say that helping a client recover from developmental trauma is life-changing—not only in this generation, but for future generations as well. Those of us who work with developmental trauma are investing in healthier futures not only for our clients, but also for those whose lives are touched by our clients. Our hope is that this book will contribute to the support of those more positive futures.

BIBLIOGRAPHY

ACES Too High. 2017. "ACEs Science FAQs." *ACEs Science 101.* ACES Too High news. Accessed October 21. https://acestoohigh.com/aces-101.

Adolphs, R. 2008. "Fear, Faces, and Human Amygdala." *Current Opinion in Neurobiology* 18 (2): 166–72.

Ainsworth, M. D. S. 1967. *Infancy in Uganda: Infant Care and the Growth of Love.* Baltimore: Johns Hopkins Press.

Ainsworth, M. D. S. 1973. "The Development of Infant-Mother Attachment." In *Review of Child Development Research,* edited by B. Cardwell and H. Ricciuti, 1–94. Chicago: University of Chicago Press.

Ainsworth, M. D., M. Blehar, E. Waters, and S. Wall. 1978. *Patterns of Attachment: A Psychological Study of the Strange Situation.* Hillsdale, NJ: Lawrence Erlbaum.

Ainsworth, M. D. S., and B. A. Wittig. 1969. "Attachment and Exploratory Behavior of 1-Year-Olds in a Strange Situation." In *Determinants of Infant Behaviour IV,* edited by B. M. Foss, 111–36. London: Methuen.

Andreassen, C., P. Fletcher, and J. Park. 2007. "Toddler's Security of Attachment Status." *Early Childhood Longitudinal Study, Birth Cohort (ECLS-B): Psychometric Report for the 2-Year Data Collection: Methlology Report.* Washington, DC: National Center for Education Statistics. https://nces.ed.gov/pubs2007/2007084_C8.pdf.

Bazhenova, O. V., O. Plonskaia, and S. W. Porges. 2001. "Vagal Reactivity and Affective Adjustment in Infants during Interaction Challenges." *Child Development Journal* 72 (5) (September/October): 1314–26.

Bazhenova, O. V., T. A. Stroganova, J. A. Doussard-Roosevelt, I. A. Posikera, and S. W. Porges. 2007. "Physiological Responses of 5-Month-Old Infants to

Smiling and Blank Faces." *International Journal of Psychophysiology* 63 (1) (January): 64–76.

Bechara, A., H. Damasio, and A. R. Damasio. 2000. "Emotion, Decision Making and the Orbitofrontal Cortex." *Cerebral Cortex* 10 (3): 295–307. doi:10.1093 /cercor/10.3.295.

Beck, J. C., and B. van der Kolk. 1987. "Reports of Childhood Incest and Current Behavior of Chronically Hospitalized Psychotic Women." *American Journal of Psychiatry* 144 (11): 1474–6.

Beck-Weidman, A., and D. Hughes. 2008. "Dyadic Developmental Psychotherapy: An Evidence-Based Treatment for Children with Complex Trauma and Disorders of Attachment." *Journal of Child and Family Social Work* 13 (3) (August): 329–37.

Benassi, V. A., P. D. Sweeney, and C. L. Dufour. 1988. "Is There a Relation between Locus of Control Orientation and Depression?" *Journal of Abnormal Psychology* 97 (3): 357–67.

Bermúdez, J. L., A. J. Marcel, and N. Eilan, eds. 1995. *The Body and the Self.* Cambridge, MA: MIT Press.

Berntson, G. G., J. T. Cacioppo, K. S. Quigley, and V. T. Fabro. 1994. "Autonomic Space and Psychophysiological Response." *Psychophysiology* 31: 44–61. doi:10.1111/j.1469-8986.1994.tb01024.x.

Bigelow, A. E., M. Power, D. E. Gillis, J. MacLellan-Peters, M. Alex, and C. McDonald. 2014. "Breastfeeding, Skin-to-Skin Contact, and Mother-Infant Interactions over Infants' First Three Months." *Infant Mental Health Journal* 35: 51–62.

Bigelow, A. E., and L. M. Walden. 2009. "Infants' Response to Maternal Mirroring in the Still Face and Replay Tasks." *Infancy* 14 (5): 526–49. doi:10.1080 /15250000903144181.

Booth, A., T. Trimble, and J. Egan. 2010. "Body-Centred Counter-Transference in a Sample of Irish Clinical Psychologists." *Irish Psychologist* 36 (12): 284–89.

Bos, K. J., N. Fox, C. H. Zeanah, and C. A. Nelson. 2009. "Effects of Early Psychosocial Deprivation on the Development of Memory and Executive Function." *Frontiers in Behavioral Neuroscience* 3: 1–7. PMID: 19750200; PMCID: PMC2741295.

Bos, K., C. H. Zeanah, N. A. Fox, S. S. Drury, K. A. McLaughlin, and C. A. Nelson. 2011. "Psychiatric Outcomes in Young Children with a History of

Institutionalization." *Harvard Review of Psychiatry* 19 (1): 15–24. doi:10.31 09/10673229.2011.549773.

Bowlby, J. 1944. "Forty-Four Juvenile Thieves: Their Characters and Home-Life." *International Journal of Psycho-Analysis* XXV: 19–52.

Bowlby, J. 1947. *Forty-Four Juvenile Thieves: Their Characters and Home-Life.* London: Baillière, Tindall & Cox.

Bowlby, J. 1949. "The Study and Reduction of Group Tensions in the Family." *Human Relations* 2: 123–28.

Bowlby, J. 1969. *Attachment.* Vol. 1 of *Attachment and Loss.* New York: Basic Books.

Bowlby, J. 1973. *Separation: Anxiety and Anger.* Vol. 2 of *Attachment and Loss.* New York: Basic Books.

Bowlby, J. (1988) 1998. *A Secure Base: Clinical Applications of Attachment Theory.* London: Routledge.

Brandchaft, B. 2007. "Systems of Pathological Accommodation and Change in Analysis." *Psychoanalytic Psychology* 24 (4) (October): 667–87. http://dx.doi .org/10.1037/0736-9735.24.4.667.

Broussard, E. 1995. "Infant Attachment in a Sample of Adolescent Mothers." *Child Psychiatry and Human Development* 25 (4): 211–19.

Browning, K. N., and R. A. Travagli. 2014. "Central Nervous System Control of Gastrointestinal Motility and Secretion and Modulation of Gastrointestinal Functions." *Comprehensive Physiology* 4 (4) (October): 1339–68. doi:10.1002/cphy.c130055.

Bucharest Early Intervention Project. 2017. Multiple publications. Accessed July. www.bucharestearlyinterventionproject.org/BEIP-Publications.html.

Burgo, J. 2012. "The Origins of Shame: Its Roots in Early Trauma and Failures of Attachment during Infancy." *Psychology Today.* November 8. www .psychologytoday.com/blog/shame/201211/the-origins-shame.

Cameron, O. G. 2001. "Interoception: The Inside Story—A Model for Psychosomatic Processes." *Psychosomatic Medicine* 63 (5): 697–710.

Carlson, V., D. Cicchetti, D. Barnett, and K. Braunwald. 1989. "Disorganized/ Disoriented Attachment Relationships in Maltreated Infants." *Developmental Psychology* 25 (4): 525–31.

Carter, A., and H. Sanderson. 1995. "The Use of Touch in Nursing Practice." *Nursing Standard* 9 (16). http://journals.rcni.com/doi/abs/10.7748/ns.9.16.31.s37.

Carter, L. E., D. W. McNeil, K. E. Vowles, J. T. Sorrell, C. L. Turk, B. J. Ries, and D. R. Hopko. 2002. "Effects of Emotion on Pain Reports, Tolerance and Physiology." *Pain Research & Management* 7: 21–30. doi:10.1155/2002/426193.

Carter, S. 2014. "Oxytocin Pathways and the Evolution of Human Behavior." *Annual Review of Psychology* 65: 17–39. doi:10.1146/annurev-psych -010213-115110.

Center on the Developing Child. 2017. "Resilience." Center on the Developing Child, Harvard University. http://developingchild.harvard.edu/science/key-concepts /resilience/.

Ceunen, E., J. W. S. Vlaeyen, and I. Van Diest. 2016. "On the Origin of Interoception." *Frontiers in Psychology.* May 23. https://doi.org/10.3389 /fpsyg.2016.00743.

Charon, R. 2001. "Narrative Medicine: A Model for Empathy, Reflection, Profession, and Trust." *JAMA* 286 (15): 1897–1902. doi:10.1001/jama.286.15.1897.

Cornier, M. A., S. S. Von Kaenel, D. H. Bessesen, and J. R. Tregellas. 2007. "Effects of Overfeeding on the Neuronal Response to Visual Food Cues." *American Journal of Clinical Nutrition* 86 (4) (October): 965–71.

Craig, A. D. 2015. *How Do You Feel? An Interoceptive Moment with Your Neurobiological Self.* Princeton, NJ: Princeton University Press.

Critchley, H. D., and N. A. Harrison. 2013. "Visceral Influences on Brain and Behavior." *Neuron* 77 (4) (February): 624–38.

D'Andrea, W., J. Ford, B. Stolbach, J. Spinazzola, and B. A. van der Kolk. 2012. "Understanding Interpersonal Trauma in Children: Why We Need a Developmentally Appropriate Trauma Diagnosis." *American Journal of Orthopsychiatry* 82 (2): 187–200.

de Rosenroll, D. 2017. Personal correspondence.

DiPietro, J. 2004. "The Role of Prenatal Maternal Stress in Child Development." *Current Directions in Psychological Science* 13 (2): 71–74.

Dollard, J., and N. E. Miller. 1950. *Personality and Psychotherapy.* New York: McGraw-Hill.

Duncan, B., H. Mansour, and D. I. Rees. 2015. "Prenatal Stress and Low Birth Weight: Evidence from the Super Bowl." *IZA Discussion Paper No. 9053. Bonn, Germany: Institute for the Study of Labor.* http://ftp.iza.org/dp9053.pdf.

Ehlers, A., and P. Breuer. 1992. "Increased Cardiac Awareness in Panic Disorder." *Journal of Abnormal Psychology* 101 (3): 371–82.

Eley, T., T. McAdams, F. Rijsdijk, P. Lichtenstein, J. Narusyte, D. Reiss, E. L. Spotts, J. M. Ganiban, and J. M. Neiderhiser. 2015. "*The Intergenerational Transmission of Anxiety: A Children-of-Twins Study.*" *American Journal of Psychiatry* 172 (7): 630–37.

Ellason, J. W., C. A. Ross, and D. L. Fuchs. 1996. "Lifetime Axis I and II Comorbidity and Childhood Trauma History in Dissociative Identity Disorder." *Psychiatry* 59 (3): 255–66.

Elsevier. 2016. "Trauma's Epigenetic Fingerprint Observed in Children of Holocaust Survivors." *ScienceDaily.* September 1. www.sciencedaily.com/releases /2016/09/160901102207.htm.

El-Sheikh, M., and S. A. Erath. 2011. "Family Conflict, Autonomic Nervous System Functioning, and Child Adaptation: State of the Science and Future Directions." *Development and Psychopathology* 23 (2): 703–21. http://doi .org/10.1017/S0954579411000034.

Erath, S. A., M. El-Sheikh, and E. M. Cummings. 2009. "Harsh Parenting and Child Externalizing Behavior: Skin Conductance Level as a Moderator." *Child Development* 80 (2): 578–92. doi:10.1111/j.1467-8624.2009.01280.x.

Felitti, V. J., R. F. Anda, D. Nordenberg, D. F. Williamson, A. M. Spitz, V. Edwards, M. P. Koss, and J. S. Marks. 1998. "Relationship of Childhood Abuse and Household Dysfunction to Many of the Leading Causes of Death in Adults: The Adverse Childhood Experiences (ACE) Study." *American Journal of Preventive Medicine 14 (4) (May): 245–58.*

Field, T. 1998. "Massage Therapy Effects." *American Psychologist 53 (12) (December): 1270–81.*

Field, T. 2014. Touch, 2nd ed. Cambridge, MA: MIT Press.

Field, T. 2017. Touch Research Institute website. Accessed July. www.miami.edu /touch-research/.

Fisher, P. A., M. Stoolmiller, M. R. Gunnar, and B. O. Burraston. 2007. "Effects of a Therapeutic Intervention for Foster Preschoolers on Diurnal Cortisol Activity." Psychoneuroendocrinology 32 (8–10): 892–905.

Fogel, A., and A. Garvey. 2007. "Alive Communication." Infant Behavioral Development 30 (2): 251–57.

Garfinkel, S. N., and H. D. Critchley. 2013. "Interoception, Emotion and Brain: New Insights Link Internal Physiology to Social Behaviour. *Commentary on:* 'Anterior Insular Cortex Mediates Bodily Sensibility and Social Anxiety' by

Terasawa et al. 2012." *Social Cognitive and Affective Neuroscience* 8 (3): 231–34. http://doi.org/10.1093/scan/nss140.

Gellhorn, E. 1967. *Principles of Autonomic-Somatic Integrations: Physiological Basis and Psychological and Clinical Implications.* Minneapolis: University of Minnesota Press.

Gold, E. 2007. "From Narrative Wreckage to Islands of Clarity: Stories of Recovery from Psychosis." *Canadian Family Physician* 53 (8): 1271–75.

Greenberg, M. T., D. Cicchetti, and E. M. Cummings, eds. 1990. *Attachment in the Preschool Years: Theory, Research, and Intervention.* Chicago: University of Chicago Press.

Gruber, H. E., and J. J. Vonèche, eds. 1977. *The Essential Piaget.* New York: Basic Books.

Harmon, K. 2010. "How Important Is Physical Contact with Your Infant?" *Scientific American.* May 6.

Hinnant, J. B., S. Erath, and M. El-Sheikh. 2015. "Harsh Parenting, Parasympathetic Activity, and Development of Delinquency and Substance Use." *Journal of Abnormal Psychology* 124 (1): 137–51. doi:10.1037/abn0000026.

Hirsh, J. B., and J. B. Peterson. 2009. "Personality and Language Use in Self-Narratives." *Journal of Research in Personality* 43 (3): 524–27.

Horton, J. A., P. R. Clance, C. Sterk-Elifson, and J. Emshoff. 1995. "Touch in Psychotherapy: A Survey of Patients' Experiences." *Psychotherapy* 32 (3) (September): 443–57. doi:10.1037/0033-3204.32.3.443.

Huttenlocher, P. R. 1979. "Synaptic Density in Human Frontal Cortex—Developmental Changes of Aging." *Brain Research* 163 (2): 195–205.

Huttenlocher, P. R., and A. S. Dabholkar. 1997. "Regional Differences in Synaptogenesis in Human Cerebral Cortex." *Journal of Comparative Neurology* 387 (2): 167–78.

Huttenlocher, P. R., and C. de Courten. 1987. "The Development of Synapses in Striate Cortex of Man." *Human Neurobiology* 6 (1): 1–9.

Huttenlocher, P. R., C. de Courten, L. J. Garey, and H. Van der Loos. 1982. "Synaptogenesis in Human Visual Cortex—Evidence for Synapse Elimination during Normal Development." *Neuro-science Letters* 33 (3): 247–52.

Janak, P. H., and K. M. Tye. 2015. "From Circuits to Behaviour in the Amygdala." *Nature* 517 (7534): 284–92. doi:10.1038/nature14188.

Kellermann, N. P. F. 2013. "Epigenetic Transmission of Holocaust Trauma: Can Nightmares Be Inherited?" *Israel Journal of Psychiatry and Related Sciences* 50 (1): 33–39.

Kolb, L. C. 1989. "Chronic Post-Traumatic Stress Disorder: Implications of Recent Epidemiological and Neuropsychological Studies." *Psychological Medicine* 19 (4): 821–24.

Kozlowska, K., P. Walker, L. McLean, and P. Carrive. 2015. "Fear and the Defense Cascade: Clinical Implications and Management." *Harvard Review of Psychiatry* 23 (4) (July/August): 263–87.

Krishnakumar, A., and C. Buehler. 2000. "Interparental Conflict and Parenting Behaviors: A Meta-Analytic Review." *Family Relations* 49 (1): 25–44.

LeDoux, J. E. 2015. "The Amygdala Is NOT the Brain's Fear Center: Separating Findings from Conclusions." *Psychology Today.* August 10. www.psychologytoday.com/blog/i-got-mind-tell-you/201508/the-amygdala-is-not-the-brains-fear-center.

Levine, P. 2010. *In an Unspoken Voice: How the Body Releases Trauma and Restores Goodness.* Berkeley, CA: North Atlantic Books.

Levine, P. 2015. *Trauma and Memory: Brain and Body in a Search for the Living Past.* Berkeley, CA: North Atlantic Books.

Levine, P., with A. Frederick. 1997. *Waking the Tiger: Healing Trauma.* Berkeley, CA: North Atlantic Books.

Levinson, L. 2011. "Can the Simple Act of Storytelling Help Them Heal?" *Huff Post.* November 9. www.huffingtonpost.com/leila-levinson/ptsd-veterans-writing_b_1078971.html.

Ludy-Dobson, C. R., and B. Perry. 2010. "The Role of Healthy Relational Interactions in Buffering the Impact of Childhood Trauma." In *Working with Children to Heal Interpersonal Trauma: The Power of Play,* edited by E. Gil, 26–43. New York: Guilford Press.

Lyons-Ruth, K., and E. Spielman. 2004. "Disorganized Infant Attachment Strategies and Helpless-Fearful Profiles of Parenting: Integrating Attachment Research with Clinical Intervention." *Infant Mental Health Journal* 25 (4): 318–35.

Main, M., and E. Hesse. 1990. "Parents' Unresolved Traumatic Experiences Are Related to Infant Disorganized Attachment Status." In *Attachment in the Preschool Years: Theory, Research, and Intervention,* edited by M. T. Greenberg, D. Cicchetti, and E. M. Cummings, 161–81. Chicago: University of Chicago Press.

Main, M., and J. Solomon. 1986. "Discovery of a New, Insecure-Disorganized/ Disoriented Attachment Pattern." In *Affective Development in Infancy*, edited by M. Yogman and T. B. Brazelton, 95–124. Norwood, NJ: Ablex.

Main, M., and J. Solomon. 1990. "Procedures for Identifying Infants as Disorganized/Disoriented during the Ainsworth Strange Situation." In *Attachment in the Preschool Years: Theory, Research, and Intervention*, edited by M. T. Greenberg, D. Cicchetti, and E. M. Cummings, 121–60. Chicago: University of Chicago Press.

McEwen, B., T. Seeman, and Allostatic Load Working Group. 2009. "Research: Allostatic Load Notebook." Research Network on SES & Health, UCSF. www.macses.ucsf.edu/research/allostatic/allostatic.php.

McEwen, B., and E. Stellar. 1993. "Stress and the Individual: Mechanisms Leading to Disease." *Archives of Internal Medicine* 153 (18) (September): 2093–101.

Mearns, J. 2017. "The Social Learning Theory of Julian B. Rotter." *California State University, Fullerton, Psychology Department*. http://psych.fullerton.edu /jmearns/rotter.htm.

Meltzoff, A. N., and M. K. Moore. 1983. "Newborn Infants Imitate Adult Facial Gestures." *Child Development* 54 (3): 702–9.

Montagu, A. 1971. *Touching: The Human Significance of the Skin*. New York: Columbia University Press.

Nelson, C. A., K. Bos, M. R. Gunnar, and E. J. S. Sonuga-Barke. 2011. "The Neurobiological Toll of Early Human Deprivation." *Monographs of the Society for Research in Child Development* 76 (4): 127–46. doi:10.1111/j.1540 -5834.2011.00630.x.

Ong, A. D., C. S. Bergeman, and S. M. Boker. 2009. "Resilience Comes of Age: Defining Features in Later Adulthood." *Journal of Personality* 77 (6): 1777– 1804. doi:10.1111/j.1467-6494.2009.00600.x.

Paulus, M. P., and M. B. Stein. 2010. "Interoception in Anxiety and Depression." *Brain Structure and Function* 214 (5–6): 451–63. doi:10.1007/s00429 -010-0258-9.

Payne, P., and M. A. Crane-Godreau. 2015. "The Preparatory Set: A Novel Approach to Understanding Stress, Trauma, and the Bodymind Therapies." *Frontiers in Human Neuroscience* 9: 178. http://doi.org/10.3389/fnhum .2015.00178.

Peckham, H. 2013. "Epigenetics: The Dogma-Defying Discovery That Genes Learn from Experience." *International Journal of Neuropsychotherapy* 1: 9–20.

Perry, B. D. 2002. "Lesson 2: The Psychology and Physiology of Trauma: How We Respond to Threat." *Surviving Childhood: An Introduction to the Impact of Trauma. ChildTrauma Academy.* www.childtraumaacademy.com/surviving _childhood/lesson02/printing.html.

Perry, B. D. 2004a. *Maltreated Children: Experience, Brain Development, and the Next Generation.* New York: W. W. Norton.

Perry, B. D. 2004b. "Maltreatment and the Developing Child: How Early Childhood Experience Shapes Child and Culture." Margaret McCain Lecture Series. London, Ontario: Centre for Children and Families in the Justice System. https:// childtrauma.org/wp-content/uploads/2013/11/McCainLecture_Perry.pdf.

Perry, B. D. 2006. "*The Neurosequential Model of Therapeutics: Applying Principles of Neuroscience to Clinical Work with Traumatized and Maltreated Children.*" In *Working with Traumatized Youth in Child Welfare,* edited by Nancy Boyd Webb, 27–52. New York: Guilford Press.

Perry, B. D. 2009. "Examining Child Maltreatment through a Neurodevelopmental Lens: Clinical Application of the Neurosequential Model of Therapeutics." *Journal of Loss and Trauma* 14: 240–55.

Perry, B. D., and R. Pollard. 1998. "Homeostasis, Stress, Trauma, and Adaptation: A Neurodevelopmental View of Childhood Trauma." *Child and Adolescent Psychiatric Clinics of North America* 7 (1) (January): 33–51, viii.

Perry, B., R. Pollard, T. Blakley, W. Baker, and D. Vigilante. 1995. "Childhood Trauma, the Neurobiology of Adaptation, and 'Use-Dependent' Development of the Brain: How 'States' Become 'Traits.'" *Infant Mental Health Journal* 16 (4): 271–91. doi:10.1002/1097- 0355(199524)16:4<271::AID- IMH-J2280160404>3.0.CO;2-B.

Pollatos, O., E. Matthias, and J. Keller. 2015. "When Interoception Helps to Overcome Negative Feelings Caused by Social Exclusion." *Frontiers in Psychology* 6: 786. doi:10.3389/fpsyg.2015.00786.

Porges, S. W. 1993. "The Infant's Sixth Sense: Awareness and Regulation of Bodily Processes." *Zero to Three: Bulletin of the National Center for Clinical Infant Programs* 14 (2) (October/November): 12–16.

Porges, S. W. 1995. "Orienting in a Defensive World: Mammalian Modifications of Our Evolutionary Heritage: A Polyvagal Theory." *Psychophysiology* 32 (4): 301–18.

Porges, S. W. 2004. "Neuroception: A Subconscious System for Detecting Threat and Safety." *Zero to Three: Bulletin of the National Center for Clinical Infant Programs* 24 (5): 19–24.

Porges, S. W. 2007. "The Polyvagal Perspective." *Biological Psychology* 74 (2) (February): 116–43.

Porges, S. W. 2009. "The Polyvagal Theory: New Insights into Adaptive Reactions of the Autonomic Nervous System." *Cleveland Clinic Journal of Medicine* 76 (Suppl. 2): S86–S90.

Porges, S. W. 2011a. *The Polyvagal Theory: Neurophysiological Foundations of Emotions, Attachment, Communication, and Self-Regulation.* New York: W. W. Norton.

Porges, S. W. 2011b. "Somatic Perspectives on Psychotherapy." November. Transcribed audio interview with Serge Prengel.

Rains, M., and K. McClinn. 2006. "The Resilience Questionnaire." Developed at Southern Kennebec Healthy Start, Augusta, Maine. Updated 2013.

Roazzi, A., G. Attili, L. Di Pentima, and A. Toni. 2016. "Locus of Control in Maltreated Children: The Impact of Attachment and Cumulative Trauma." *Psicologia: Reflexão e Critica* 29 (1) (April 14): 1–11.

Rotter, J. B. 1975. "Some Problems and Misconceptions Related to the Construct of Internal versus External Control of Reinforcement." *Journal of Consulting and Clinical Psychology* 43 (1) (February): 56–67.

Salter, M. 1940. *An Evaluation of Adjustment Based upon the Concept of Security.* University of Toronto Studies, Child Development Series, No. 18. Toronto: University of Toronto Press.

Sbarra, D. A., and C. Hazan. 2008. "Coregulation, Dysregulation, Self-Regulation: An Integrative Analysis and Empirical Agenda for Understanding Adult Attachment, Separation, Loss, and Recovery." *Personality and Social Psychology Review* 12: 141–67.

Schore, A. N. 1991. "Early Superego Development: The Emergence of Shame and Narcissistic Affect Regulation in the Practicing Period." *Psychoanalysis & Contemporary Thought* 14 (2): 187–250.

Schore, A. N. 1994. *Affect Regulation and the Origin of the Self: The Neurobiology of Emotional Development.* Hillsdale, NJ: Lawrence Erlbaum.

Schore, A. N. 2001. "The Effects of Early Relational Trauma on Right Brain Development, Affect Regulation, and Infant Mental Health." *Infant Mental Health Journal* 22 (1–2): 201–69.

Schore, A. 2013. "Allan Schore Neurobiology of Secure Attachment.f4v." YouTube. January 12. www.youtube.com/watch?v=WVuJ5KhpL34 www.youtube.com/watch?v=LpHpm_b0vRY.

Shapiro, J. 2011. "Illness Narratives: Reliability, Authenticity and the Empathic Witness." *Medical Humanities, BMJ Journals* 37 (2) (December): 68–72.

Shonkoff, J. P., W. T. Boyce, J. Cameron, et al. 2004. "Young Children Develop in an Environment of Relationships." Working Paper 1. National Scientific Council on the Developing Child, Harvard University.

Shonkoff, J. P., and S. J. Eisels. 2000. *Handbook of Early Childhood Intervention.* Cambridge: Cambridge University Press.

Shonkoff, J. P., P. Levitt, W. T. Boyce, et al. 2004. "Children's Emotional Development Is Built into the Architecture of Their Brains." Working Paper 2. National Scientific Council on the Developing Child, Harvard University.

Shonkoff, J. P., P. Levitt, W. T. Boyce, et al. 2012. "The Science of Neglect: The Persistent Absence of Responsive Care Disrupts the Developing Brain." Working Paper 12. National Scientific Council on the Developing Child, Harvard University. http://developingchild.harvard.edu/index.php/resources /reports_and_working_papers/working_papers/wp12/.

Shonkoff, J. P., P. Levitt, S. Bunge, et al. 2015. "Supportive Relationships and Active Skill-Building Strengthen the Foundations of Resilience." Working Paper 13. National Scientific Council on the Developing Child, Harvard University. www.developingchild.harvard.edu/resources/supportive-relationships-and -active-skill-building-strengthen-the-foundations-of-resilience/.

Shonkoff, J. P., and D. A. Phillips. 2000. *From Neurons to Neighborhoods: The Science of Early Childhood Development.* Washington, DC: National Academy Press.

Siegel, D. J. 1999. *The Developing Mind: Toward a Neurobiology of Interpersonal Experience.* New York: Guilford Press.

Siegel, D. J. 2014. "The Self Is Not Defined by the Boundaries of Our Skin." *Psychology Today.* February 28. www.psychologytoday.com/blog/inspire-rewire/201402 /the-self-is-not-defined-the-boundaries-our-skin.

Stakenborg, N., M. Di Giovangiulio, G. E. Boeckxstaens, and G. Matteoli. 2013. "The Versatile Role of the Vagus Nerve in the Gastrointestinal Tract." *European Medical Journal* 1 (December): 106–14.

Stroufe, L. A. 1995. *Emotional Development.* New York: Cambridge University Press.

van der Kolk, B. A. 1998. "Trauma and Memory." *Psychiatry and Clinical Neurosciences* 52 (Suppl. 1): S52–S64. doi:10.1046/j.1440-1819.1998.0520s5S97.x.

van IJzendoorn, M. H., and P. M. Kroonenberg. 1988. "Cross-Cultural Patterns of Attachment: A Meta-Analysis of the Strange Situation." *Child Development* 59 (1): 147–56. www.jstor.org/stable/1130396.

Wadhwa, P. D., S. Entringer, C. Buss, and M. C. Lu. 2011. "The Contribution of Maternal Stress to Preterm Birth: Issues and Considerations." *Clinics in Perinatology* 38 (3) (September): 351–84.

Walsh, B. 2015. "The Science of Resilience: Why Some Children Can Thrive despite Adversity." Harvard Graduate School of Education. March 23. www.gse.harvard.edu/news/uk/15/03/science-resilience.

Weaver, I. C. G., N. Cervoni, F. A. Champagne, A. C. D'Alessio, S. Sharma, J. R. Seckl, S. Dymov, M. Szyf, and M. J. Meaney. 2004. "Epigenetic Programming by Maternal Behavior." *Nature Neuroscience* 7 (8) (August): 847–54.

Weir, K. 2014. "The Lasting Impact of Neglect." *American Psychological Association* 45 (6): 36.

Wright, R. J., and M. Bosquet Enlow. 2008. "Maternal Stress and Perinatal Programming in the Expression of Atopy." *Expert Review of Clinical Immunology* 4 (5): 535–38.

Yehuda, R., and L. M. Bierer. 2007. "Transgenerational Transmission of Cortisol and PTSD Risk." *Progress in Brain Research* 167: 121–35.

Yehuda, R., N. P. Daskalakis, L. M. Bierer, H. N. Bader, T. Klengel, F. Holsboer, and E. B. Binder. 2016. "Holocaust Exposure Induced Intergenerational Effects on FKBP5 Methylation." *Biological Psychiatry* 80 (5) (September 1): 372–80.

Yehuda, R., J. Schmeidler, M. Wainberg, K. Binder-Brynes, and T. Duvdevani. 1998. "Vulnerability to Posttraumatic Stress Disorder in Adult Offspring of Holocaust Survivors." *American Journal of Psychiatry* 155 (9) (September): 1163–71.

Zerach, G. 2016. "The Role of Fathers' Psychopathology in the Intergenerational Transmission of Captivity Trauma: A Twenty Three-Year Longitudinal Study." *Journal of Affective Disorders* 190: 84–92.

Zweyer, K., B. Velker, and W. Ruch. 2004. "Do Cheerfulness, Exhilaration, and Humor Production Moderate Pain Tolerance? A FACS Study." *Humor: International Journal of Humor Research* 17: 85–120.

INDEX

ABOUT THE AUTHORS

KATHY L. KAIN, MA, has been practicing and teaching bodywork and trauma recovery for thirty-seven years. A senior trainer in the Somatic Experiencing® trauma resolution model, she is an expert in integrating touch into the practice of psychotherapy and trauma recovery, as well as in somatic approaches to working with developmental and complex trauma. She teaches therapists about the physiology of traumatic stress through her popular program "Touch Skills Training for Trauma Therapists" and is the principal author of *Ortho-Bionomy: A Practical Manual*. She lives in Portland, Oregon.

STEPHEN J. TERRELL, PsyD, SEP, is a leading expert in the field of developmental trauma and adoption. The founder of the Austin Attachment and Counseling Center, Dr. Terrell works directly with individuals and families affected by trauma and teaches throughout the United States, Japan, and Europe. A licensed professional counselor (Texas) with a background in Somatic Experiencing® and EMDR, he has also been a featured keynote speaker at international adoption conferences and a presenter at attachment and play therapy conferences. Dr. Terrell is a single adoptive parent of two sons and lives in Pflugerville, Texas.

About North Atlantic Books

North Atlantic Books (NAB) is an independent, nonprofit publisher committed to a bold exploration of the relationships between mind, body, spirit, and nature. Founded in 1974, NAB aims to nurture a holistic view of the arts, sciences, humanities, and healing. To make a donation or to learn more about our books, authors, events, and newsletter, please visit www.northatlanticbooks.com.

North Atlantic Books is the publishing arm of the Society for the Study of Native Arts and Sciences, a 501(c)(3) nonprofit educational organization that promotes cross-cultural perspectives linking scientific, social, and artistic fields. To learn how you can support us, please visit our website.